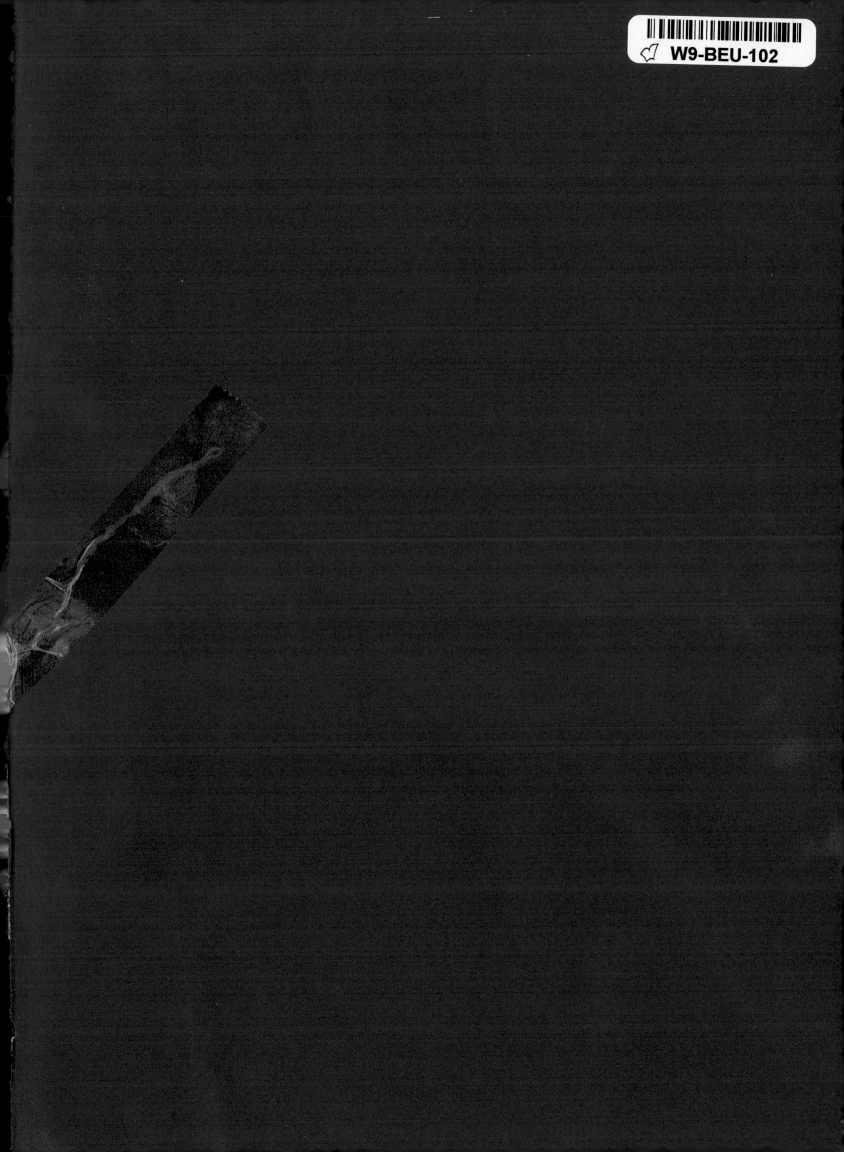

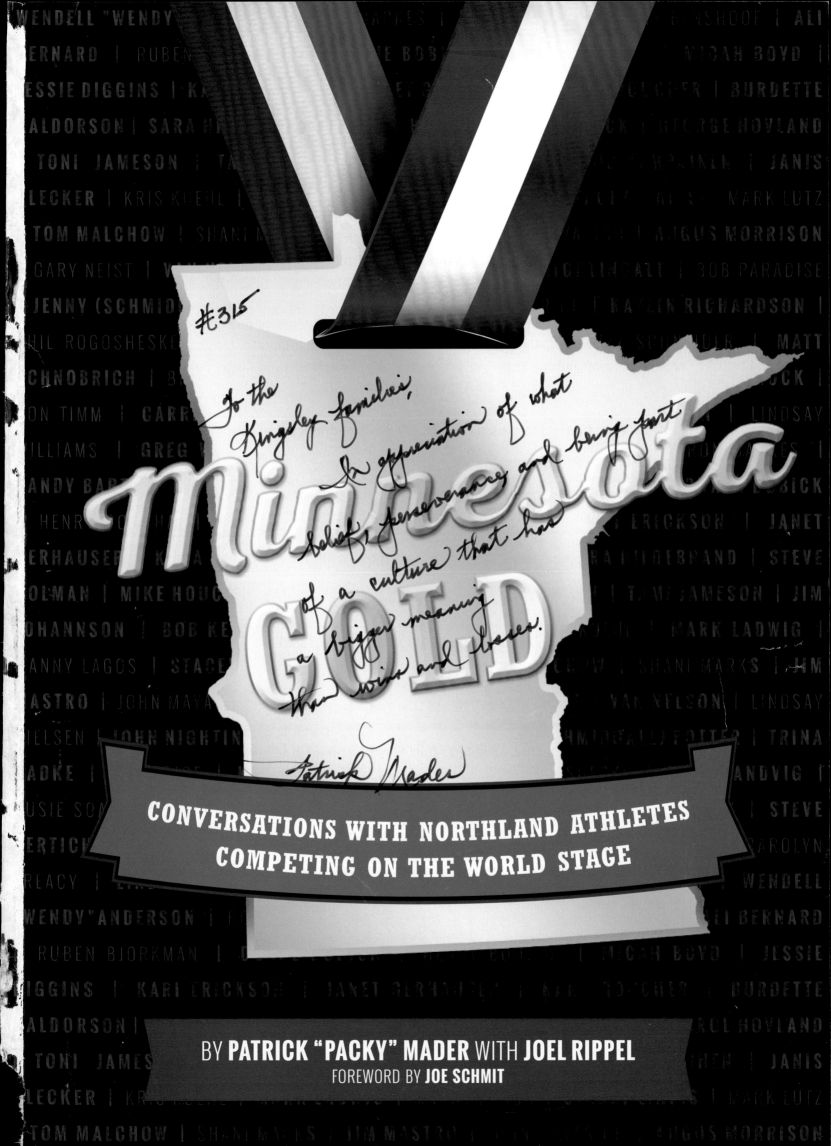

#315

To the Kingsley families,
In appreciation of what
belief, perseverance and being part
of a culture that has
a bigger meaning
than wins and losses.

Patrick Mader

minnesota GOLD

CONVERSATIONS WITH NORTHLAND ATHLETES COMPETING ON THE WORLD STAGE

BY PATRICK "PACKY" MADER WITH JOEL RIPPEL
FOREWORD BY JOE SCHMIT

Photo credits for back cover and front jacket flap: David Carmichael Photography (Mark Ladwig); University of Minnesota Athletics (Wendell "Wendy" Anderson, Lindsay Whalen, and John Mayasich); Kirby Lee, Image of Sport (Shani Marks and Carrie Tollefson); and St Paul Pioneer Press (Mark Lutz).

"Canoeists and Carrot" illustration on page 207 Art ©Sandra Boynton. Used by permission. All rights reserved.

We are proud to report that everyone involved with the publication of this book lives in Minnesota. The publisher and printer are Minnesota-based businesses.

Uncredited photographs are those of the author.

ISBN 13: 978-1-63489-007-6

Library of Congress Catalog Number: 2015950348
Printed in the United States of America
First Printing: 2015
19 18 17 16 15   5 4 3 2 1

Cover and interior design by Emily Shaffer Rodvold at Lift Creative.

Wise Ink Creative Publishing
837 Glenwood Avenue
Minneapolis, MN 55405
wiseinkpub.com

To order, visit itascabooks.com or call 1-800-901-3480. Reseller discounts available.

DEDICATION

To the 2012 NCAA Division III Track & Field All-Americans and their coaches from Wheaton College in Norton, Massachusetts (left to right): Coach Kathrine Bright, Ben Miklovich, Miles Ketchum, Mark Williamson, Karl Mader, Didi Jusme, Coach Dave Cusano, Ashley Dell'Aira, Lauren Cardarelli, Amanda Claflin, Meredith Scannell, Ashante Little, and Coach Kim Spence. Also to cross country coach Paul Carr.

Running with the Lyons

and to Karen, Karl, and Ellen
family Olympians

ENDORSEMENTS

"Minneapolis Washburn's Van Nelson goes stride for stride with the iconic Billy Mills. Austin's Burdette Haldorson teams with Bill Russell and K.C. Jones as American basketball dominates the world in the 1950s. Patrick Mader tracks down and interviews more than fifty living Minnesotans who made it to the absolute highest level in their respective sports."

—Dave Mona, WCCO's *Sunday Sports Huddle*

"I didn't believe it possible for me to feel any more proud of Minnesota, but Patrick Mader's Minnesota Gold *has done it. A perfect ten."*

—Don Shelby, broadcast journalist, author, and explorer

"A wonderful book capturing incredible stories and events of our many outstanding and talented Minnesota athletes. [Minnesota Gold's] stories of courage, passion, and dedication will capture your heart."

—Jody Eder-Zdechlik, six-time All-American in cross country
and track & field, University of Minnesota Athletics
Hall of Fame member, and Big 10 Medal of Honor recipient

"I thoroughly enjoyed reading the stories about impressive athletes from the Twin Cities and small towns around Minnesota. Patrick Mader's research provided new and entertaining information on some of Minnesota's finest. For Minnesotans and sports fans alike."

—Joel Maturi, University of Minnesota
Director of Athletics, 2002 – 2012

"Having been involved in hockey for a lifetime, I've had the privilege of being exposed to the Olympic movement at an early age. Our author, Patrick Mader, in his research has found some 300 Minnesota athletes that have participated in the Olympic games, either summer or winter. The biographies of a number of them are recorded in this book for fascinating reading and great memories of sports in our Minnesota heritage. The Olympic movement has deep roots in Minnesota . . . an amazing and important part of our great state's history."

—Walter L. Bush, Jr. Chairman, USA Hockey, Inc.

"Inspiring to all who aspire, impressive for those who know what it takes to be an elite athlete. This book shows that there is opportunity for anyone willing to dream and do."

—John Albrecht, US national speedskating
team member 1982 – '85 and '87

"Each athlete's story in Minnesota Gold *gives insight into how a champion is born. The fact they are from Minnesota makes me proud to be associated with sports in this state."*

—Bob Hauck, St. Olaf College swimming and diving head coach,
1988 US Olympic swimming trials competitor

HOMETOWNS OF PROFILED ATHLETES

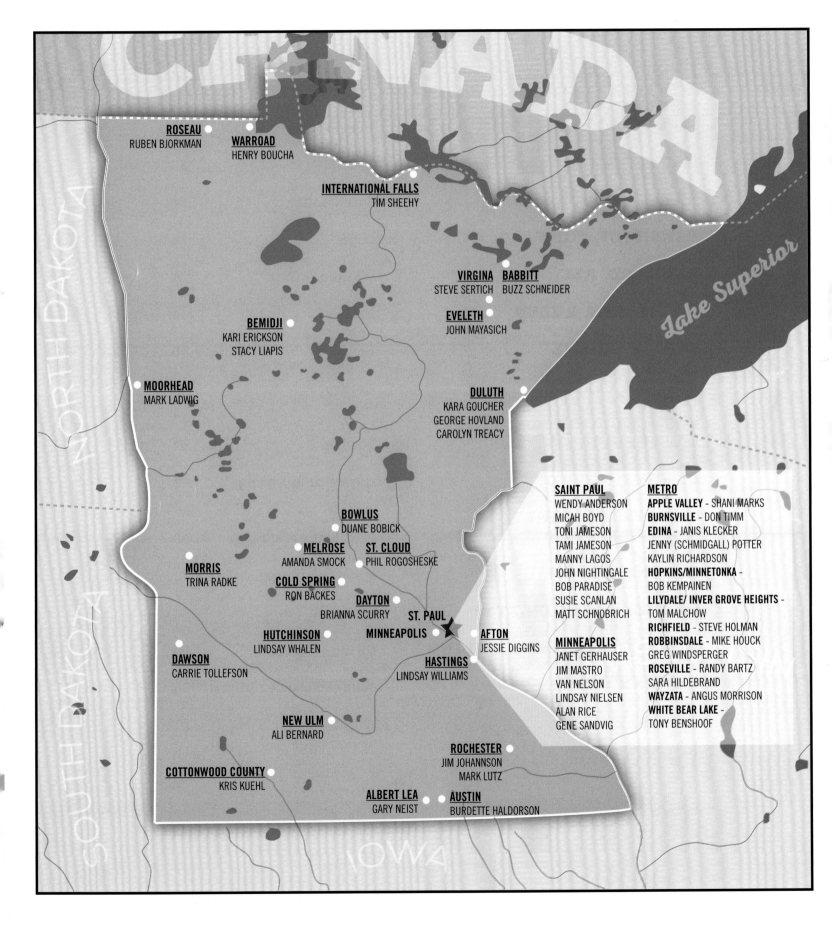

CANADA

NORTH DAKOTA

SOUTH DAKOTA

IOWA

Lake Superior

ROSEAU
RUBEN BJORKMAN

WARROAD
HENRY BOUCHA

INTERNATIONAL FALLS
TIM SHEEHY

VIRGINA
STEVE SERTICH

BABBITT
BUZZ SCHNEIDER

EVELETH
JOHN MAYASICH

BEMIDJI
KARI ERICKSON
STACY LIAPIS

MOORHEAD
MARK LADWIG

DULUTH
KARA GOUCHER
GEORGE HOVLAND
CAROLYN TREACY

BOWLUS
DUANE BOBICK

MELROSE
AMANDA SMOCK

ST. CLOUD
PHIL ROGOSHESKE

MORRIS
TRINA RADKE

COLD SPRING
RON BACKES

DAYTON
BRIANNA SCURRY

ST. PAUL
MINNEAPOLIS

AFTON
JESSIE DIGGINS

HUTCHINSON
LINDSAY WHALEN

DAWSON
CARRIE TOLLEFSON

HASTINGS
LINDSAY WILLIAMS

NEW ULM
ALI BERNARD

ROCHESTER
JIM JOHANNSON
MARK LUTZ

COTTONWOOD COUNTY
KRIS KUEHL

ALBERT LEA
GARY NEIST

AUSTIN
BURDETTE HALDORSON

SAINT PAUL
WENDY ANDERSON
MICAH BOYD
TONI JAMESON
TAMI JAMESON
MANNY LAGOS
JOHN NIGHTINGALE
BOB PARADISE
SUSIE SCANLAN
MATT SCHNOBRICH

MINNEAPOLIS
JANET GERHAUSER
JIM MASTRO
VAN NELSON
LINDSAY NIELSEN
ALAN RICE
GENE SANDVIG

METRO
APPLE VALLEY - SHANI MARKS
BURNSVILLE - DON TIMM
EDINA - JANIS KLECKER
JENNY (SCHMIDGALL) POTTER
KAYLIN RICHARDSON
HOPKINS/MINNETONKA -
BOB KEMPAINEN
LILYDALE/ INVER GROVE HEIGHTS -
TOM MALCHOW
RICHFIELD - STEVE HOLMAN
ROBBINSDALE - MIKE HOUCK
GREG WINDSPERGER
ROSEVILLE - RANDY BARTZ
SARA HILDEBRAND
WAYZATA - ANGUS MORRISON
WHITE BEAR LAKE -
TONY BENSHOOF

TABLE OF CONTENTS

MANNY LAGOS AT UW MILWAUKEE (1990, 1991)
Photo credit: UW Milwaukee Athletic Communications

AMANDA SMOCK BY TRIPLE JUMP, 2012
Photo courtesy of Amanda Smock

**GREG WINDSPERGER WITH
JIM DENNEY, JERRY MARTIN AT
BISCHOPSHOFEN, AUSTRIA**
Photo courtesy of Greg Windsperger

FOREWORD

IN MY YEARS AS A SPORTS REPORTER, I'VE HAD THE opportunity to interview over 10,000 athletes. Although I can't claim to remember every single one of them, some have stuck with me for decades.

One of these memorable stories is of a wrestler who was determined to make the United States Olympic team. He spent six years working towards that goal, training for hours a day in hopes of qualifying to compete on the world stage. When the time came, he won a gold medal at the Olympic Trials and made it onto the team, but it came at a cost. Although he had reached his dream, his finances were a nightmare. After all, training for the Olympics is a full-time job without a salary. He and his wife had maxed out all their credit cards and did not have enough money for those who meant the most to him to travel to the games. Fortunately, a white knight stepped up and made it happen, but there is no question that Olympic dreams are not free. Not only does the athletic honor take tremendous work and dedication, but also tremendous personal sacrifice. Ask any athlete who has reached the pinnacle of the Olympics and given up much to get there: Was it worth it? They will answer you with a big, wide smile and say, "Absolutely." It's hard to put a price tag on pride.

In this important and influential collection, Packy Mader and Joel Rippel tell the personal stories of men and women who paid the price to compete in the greatest sporting event in the world. These are stories of triumph, sacrifice, and 100 percent pure Minnesota Gold. Each of these athletes cares so deeply for their sport that it's impossible to read this book without being inspired.

It's incredible that a state the size and population of Minnesota has had so many magical Olympic moments over the years. The pride these gifted and hardworking athletes have in wearing USA on their uniform while representing the state of Minnesota will give you goose bumps the size of gold medals. These Olympians deserve this book as a testimony to their greatest achievements and their contributions to our state's history. As Minnesotans, we need this book as a reminder that, with determination and perseverance, we can be the best in world.

—Joe Schmit, sixteen-time Emmy Award-winning broadcaster, speaker, and author of *Silent Impact: Stories of Influence through Purpose, Persistence, and Passion*

Wendell Anderson
Defense

Photo courtesy of University of Minnesota Athletics

WENDELL "WENDY" ANDERSON

Happy in Hockey, Happy in Politics

STILL TRIM AT THE AGE OF EIGHTY, FORMER STATE legislator, governor of Minnesota, and United States Senator Wendell Anderson puts a guest immediately at ease by saying, "I prefer 'Wendy.' I really do." A proclamation signed by Governor Mark Dayton cited February 1, 2013, Wendy's eightieth birthday, as Wendell R. Anderson Day, honoring the 1956 Olympian and political officeholder. The following day, a surprise tribute attended by many of Minnesota's politically powerful and elite was held at the Wayzata Country Club. It was appreciated by the man once pictured as a youthful state governor smiling broadly while hoisting a large northern pike pictured on the cover of Time magazine on August 13, 1973, alongside the title "The Good Life in Minnesota." It was a heady time for then–Governor Wendell Anderson. And so were the 1956 Winter Olympics.

One of three athletic boys growing up on St. Paul's East Side, Wendy was born in 1933 and grew up near Phalen Park. His father was a meatpacker, and the family was proud of their Swedish heritage. As a youngster, Wendy believes he had an advantage in ice hockey because he was able to play with older boys since he tagged along with his older brother, Orv, to the Phalen ice rink. Younger brother, Rod, later a Dartmouth player and longtime Blake High School hockey coach, discloses, "Hockey was big on the East Side. It was a big part of our lives. We'd shovel and flood the skating area—high school kids would help maintain the rink." Wendy was encouraged to work at a young age and earned thirty-five cents per hour at age twelve when he worked at a truck farm. He attributes work for some of his success in hockey. "Later I did heavy labor as a construction worker. It gave me strength and endurance for hockey. We had no weight-training program."

Dedication and passion for the sport were clearly part of the Anderson success in hockey too. Wendy's second daughter, Elizabeth, has memories of her father telling the kids this story: "Dad told the kids that he shot pucks across Wheelock Parkway at a snowfence by a home until the residents would complain."

Orv—generally acknowledged as the best Anderson family hockey player and a final cut on the 1952 Olympic team—and Rod played on state championship ice hockey teams for St. Paul Johnson High School (named after Governor John A. Johnson, the first Minnesota-born governor, who later died in office during his third term). The aptly named Governors appeared in every Minnesota State High School League tournament from 1946–57, except for three years, 1948–50, the years Wendy was on the varsity squad. "I'm still mad about that," he says without a trace of a smile. He remembers staying at a motel for the first time in his life in 1950 when the hockey team lost to Eveleth in northern Minnesota. Willard Ikola—a future Olympian—was the opponent's goalie who showed flashes of greatness then. Wendy considers graduating later that year at the age of seventeen a bit of a disadvantage for a hockey player since others had gained more game experience.

The University of Minnesota (U of M) was an attractive place to continue his education. "Tuition was twenty-seven dollars per quarter, I could play hockey, and it was close by," Wendy says, ticking off the reasons to enroll there. There were no athletic scholarships for hockey at the time, but a strong team was assembled by coach Doc Romnes. Freshmen were not eligible to play varsity hockey, so Gene Campbell, Dick Dougherty, Wendy, and others joined a team called Downtown Ford. "We sometimes played the Rochester Mustangs. We rarely—if ever—won because they had some good Canadian hockey players, but they offered us tough competition," he recalls.

During the 1952–54 seasons, Wendy played defense on the first line with either Tom Wegleitner or Ken "Jim" Yackel, a three-sport star for the U of M Gophers. John Mariucci became coach of the team in 1953. Wendy calls him "a great coach and perfect gentleman" who was very influential in his life. The team made the National Collegiate Athletic Association (NCAA) finals in Colorado Springs, Colorado, in each of Wendy's final two years of eligibility. He credits much of the team's success to John Mayasich, the acclaimed, prolific scorer from Eveleth. "Mayasich was the best player I ever played with or against," Wendy states flatly. "I was not a great skater, but I was quick to the corners and strong enough to pass it out of a crowd to Mayasich, who would take it from there." The size of players was commonly exaggerated, and Wendy claims he was listed at 175 pounds even though he actually weighed 167 pounds. In 1953, his high school nemesis, Willard Ikola, who by now was a standout goalie at the University of Michigan, stymied the Gopher attack. The following year, the team was denied the championship by Rensselaer Polytechnic Institute (RPI) in a 5–4 sudden-death defeat in overtime, a loss that still haunts Wendy.

With a bachelor of arts degree in history, Wendy continued coursework for a master's degree in the subject he found enthralling. Enrolled in the Reserve Officers Training Corps program during his undergraduate years, he became an infantry second lieutenant. Wendy was also able to continue playing hockey for the national team as a defenseman. Wendy relates a favorite story about a game in Germany during the World Championships in 1955. "I was in the penalty box during a game against the Soviet Union. The Soviet's star player was getting the best of a teammate in a fight, so I jumped out of the penalty box and pulled the Soviet off. I was then ejected from the game. When I arrived back at the University, a professor said to me, 'Anderson, if you ever run for office, the Republicans will never be able to accuse you of being weak on communism!'" jokes Wendy.

WENDY PLAYED DEFENSE FOR THE GOPHERS HOCKEY TEAM
Photo courtesy of University of Minnesota Athletics

Mariucci had been named the 1956 Olympic ice hockey coach, and Wendy was confident that he would make the team since the coach knew his caliber of play. After the trials in Duluth and several exhibition games, the next stop would be Cortina d' Ampezzo, Italy, later a setting for the ski chase scene in the 1981 James Bond movie *For Your Eyes Only*. The venue would be a three-deck, horseshoe-shaped bowl outdoors. The 1956 United States hockey team lost their first game in pool play to Czechoslovakia but rallied and went on a winning streak that included triumphs over a powerful Canadian team. They later avenged their loss to Czechoslovakia in the final round by trouncing the Eastern European rival 9–4. The young American squad lost only to the dominant Soviet Union team by a 4–0 score, earning a silver medal. Wendy's only scoring was a single assist in a 7–2 victory over Germany. Mayasich led the American team in scoring with ten points. "It was a tremendous experience," Wendy relates. "All of my hockey experiences have been one hundred percent enjoyable."

Returning to Minnesota, Wendy completed the coursework for his master's degree in the spring quarter of 1956, but he never finished his thesis. "I'm still working on it," the octogenarian smiles. Another year of military obligations and participating on the national hockey team followed. In the fall of 1957, Wendy entered law school.

As a first-year law student, Wendy decided to run for the Minnesota House of Representatives in 1958. The gutsy decision paid off for the twenty-five-year-old. Representative Wendell Anderson represented St. Paul during his final two years in law school. After a second term, Wendy ran for the state senate in 1962. Again he was victorious, and he became a political figure worth watching. He married Mary McKee from Bemidji, one of only two women enrolled in architecture classes at the U of M. Eventually Mary graduated with a specialty of interior design from the School of Home Economics in 1963. Warren Spannaus, who would later win three terms as state attorney general and was a close friend of Wendy's (Wendy would be best man at the Spannaus's wedding), knew his friend's ambitions were for higher office. That time came in 1970, when Wendy sought the Democratic-Farmer-Labor (DFL) party endorsement for governor. "Wendy was an attractive candidate. He was a good speaker, [an] honest, handsome guy who knew legislative issues," reports Spannaus.

> ## "Wendy was an attractive candidate. He was a good speaker, [an] honest, handsome guy who knew legislative issues . . ."

Wendy thought the key to securing the endorsement was to visit outstate Minnesota. "I worked very hard for the endorsement. I drove all over the state—often alone—talking to groups and trying to line up delegates. I won most of the outstate delegates, and the metro area was split among many of the candidates. I didn't do well in Minneapolis, but St. Paul was fairly even between Nick Coleman and me." Five candidates vied for the endorsement at the DFL convention in Duluth. On the sixth ballot, Coleman, a colleague of Wendy's in the state senate from St. Paul, asked his delegates to support Wendell Anderson for governor of Minnesota. Wendy was only thirty-seven years old and only a November election away from being the nation's youngest governor.

Incumbent Governor Harold LeVander had surprised his Republican party by deciding not to seek a second term. Doug Head, the Minnesota attorney general, had captured the party's endorsement and squared off against Wendy in the general election. Polls indicated that it would be a tight race. On November 3, 1970, Wendell Anderson was elected governor of the state of Minnesota with 54 percent of the vote. Wendy and Mary, looking and acting like energetic young parents, now had three children under the age of five years old. In a separate election, endorsed DFL lieutenant governor candidate Rudy Perpich of Hibbing won a narrow victory over Duluth mayor Ben Boo.

WENDY AND MARY ANDERSON WITH CHILDREN AMY, ELIZABETH, AND BRETT, AND DOGS NIBS AND FREIDA, 1970
Photo courtesy of Elizabeth (Anderson) Crow

Campaign manager and prominent Twin Cities lawyer David Lebedoff laughingly says that he wrote hockey jokes for Wendy when he was first enlisted to work on the campaign. Lebedoff lists Wendy's positive political attributes, saying, "He was a charismatic television speaker. Wendy had a strong will to win and was very self-disciplined. People could tell that he really believed in issues. The same qualities that made him good in hockey made him good in politics. He was born to be governor."

The youthful, vigorous governor quickly achieved legislative success in 1971 with the passage of a bill dubbed the "Minnesota Miracle"—legislation that reformed the financing of Minnesota public schools. In 1972 the local World Hockey Association team, the St. Paul Fighting Saints, drafted the governor as a publicity stunt. With his popularity rising and the successful passage of bills at a breathtaking pace, Wendy and the state of Minnesota received national attention with the *Time* magazine story. He was reelected in a landslide in 1974, winning all eighty-seven Minnesota counties, doubling the votes his Republican opponent John W. Johnson received. Wendy was enjoying his life in the statehouse. "Being governor was absolutely fascinating!"

GOVERNOR WENDY ANDERSON WITH COLLEGE
HOCKEY TEAMMATE JOHN MAYASICH (RIGHT)
Photo credit: Minnesota Historical Society

he says enthusiastically.

Family life included playful times on the ice that were also embraced by the relatives. Beth and Amy wore figure skates and used their father's tall left-handed hockey sticks as they scrounged around to find skates and sticks. "We played 'shinny hockey,'" relates daughter Elizabeth. "We played outdoors at Klapprich Park in Wayzata without protective gear. Family members ranging from ten to fifty years old would be on the ice. The whole Anderson family likes high-standard amateur hockey." Later in life, Wendy would be interviewed for the documentary *Pond Hockey* and advocate for the playing of more outdoor hockey with friends and neighbors.

The election of Jimmy Carter and Walter Mondale as president and vice president of the United States in 1976 offered another opportunity to the celebrated governor. Mondale, a United States senator from Minnesota, would be vacating his office to accept the vice presidency. Wendy now had national aspirations and decided to resign as governor and become appointed US senator by his successor, Rudy Perpich. It proved to be a fateful political decision. The public intensely disliked the decision, and Wendy struggled to win back the public's favor before he had to face the electorate in 1978. His Republican opponent was business owner Rudy Boschwitz, who hit hard on the issue of Wendy arranging to have himself appointed US senator. The public's peeved attitude remained unforgiving, and Boschwitz trounced Wendy by over 250,000 votes. It was a blow to Wendy's string of electoral successes.

"When I returned to Minnesota after the 1978 defeat, I found it hard to find a good job. The DFL is supported by labor. There weren't opportunities for a huge salary for me as a business lobbyist." Wendy landed a job with the law firm Larkin Hoffman from 1979–91, but practicing law was not what he really enjoyed, and he often didn't feel that he was providing clients to the firm. Another effort to seek the DFL US Senate endorsement in 1984 fell short. He found solace playing the game he loved. "Hockey has been a lifetime sport for me," he comments. Another source of enjoyment was being elected to the University of Minnesota Board of Regents, a position he held from 1985–97. "I thought that I could really contribute. I had two degrees—almost a third—from the University, was an athlete there, worked as a summer laborer at the golf course, and had been very involved with legislative issues affecting it."

Wendy has also been a director on various boards, including Fingerhut and National City Bancorp; a political commentator on Minnesota elections; and Minnesota's honorary Swedish consulate.

Daughter Amy is a businesswoman. The middle child, Elizabeth, is an obstetrics and gynecologist physician in Alaska, and her daughters are continuing the Anderson family tradition as they play hockey. The youngest child, Brett, is a restaurant critic for the *Times-Picayune* newspaper in New Orleans. Mary and Wendy divorced in 1990.

ON DISPLAY AT MARIUCCI ARENA ON THE UNIVERSITY OF MINNESOTA CAMPUS

The hockey player and politician is critical of today's toxic politics on the national level. "Howard Baker, the Republican leader of the US Senate, came to Minnesota to campaign for Boschwitz and said, 'Wendy Anderson is my friend, but I am here to support a Republican.'" He still has fond memories of his time in politics and considers people he met in those years among his best friends.

Wendy acquired his other close friends by sharing his passion for hockey. "I skated until I was seventy-eight years old. I had scored a goal and was just standing on the ice having a conversation when I lost my balance, fell, and broke my left arm. I think God was sending me a signal that it was time to quit."

Photo courtesy of University of Minnesota Athletics

RON BACKES

One Small Centimeter, One Giant Life Change

FOR A TOWN OF 4,000 PEOPLE, COLD SPRING, MINNE-sota, has gained state and national attention with its commercial enterprises and athletic successes.

Located less than twenty miles southwest of St. Cloud, a regional center, it is the headquarters of two large well-known employers, Cold Spring Brewery Company (240 employees) and Coldspring, a natural stone manufacturer formerly known as Cold Spring Granite (more than 700 employees).

The town's athletic successes are highlighted by its amateur baseball team, the Cold Spring Springers, a team that has made more than fifty appearances in state tournaments and achieved eight tournament titles. An individual athlete, Eric Decker, starred in football and baseball at the University of Minnesota and has achieved fame as a receiver in the NFL. His sister, Sarah, was a Division I All-Academic track athlete at Columbia University in New York.

Less known to the public is that Cold Spring is also the hometown of an Olympic athlete, Ron Backes. Born in 1963, Ron is the youngest of six children of Pierre, an employee at Cold Spring Granite, and Lorraine, a homemaker. His childhood was heavily influenced by his environment and older brothers. While Ron enjoyed camping, hunting, and being involved in Boy Scouts, it is evident that his participation in sports dominated his thoughts and actions. "I followed my brothers into sports—three played at the collegiate level. My brother Doug was in track at the Naval Academy; John participated in track and football at Bemidji State University; and Patrick played football and basketball at St. Cloud State University. In middle school I was in five sports: football, basketball, wrestling, baseball, and track and field. All five boys became Eagle Scouts too. By age twelve, I had the goal to compete in the Olympics."

In high school Ron (standing 6 feet 3 inches) limited his sports choices to football, basketball, and track and field (shot put and discus). As a senior, he won the state class AA discus competition in 1981 with a throw of 175 feet 8 inches but was never a threat to win a championship in the shot put. In the next decade, that would change dramatically.

Ron signed a letter of intent to attend school and play football at the University of North Dakota, but decided at the last minute to instead enroll at Hamline University in St. Paul. The abrupt change of heart, Ron explains, was due to his childhood dream of becoming an Olympian; he did not see football as a vehicle to achieving that goal. Another attraction was Dick Mulkern, the esteemed track and field coach at Hamline, who suggested that he use his strengths from throwing the discus and incorporate them into the shot put. Ron changed from a glide style to using a spin and began to challenge other Division III shot putters at the national level, eventually earning All-American status.

Due to financial considerations and wanting to pursue his Olympic dream at a higher collegiate level, Ron walked on at the University of Minnesota (U of M) in 1982 and redshirted that season. The throwing coach, Steve Forseth, helped him modify the spin to fit his strengths. "Steve was always willing to listen to other people's ideas and opinions," Ron discloses. "He was very open-minded, and we developed a warm and close relationship." Despite the significant increase in weight of the shot from 12 pounds at the high school level to 16 pounds at the collegiate level, Ron was throwing farther. "The growth was due to weight training while maintaining technique," Ron explains. More big gains were ahead for the 255-pound Ron Backes.

Longtime throws coach Forseth says, "I've worked with many athletes who have become champions, but Ron was very, very driven with his goal of becoming an Olympian. After his redshirt year, he showed me a list of places he wanted to compete. They were all top relays that required sixty-foot throws to qualify. And he did it! He'd try to keep the shot and his shoulders as far back as possible, rotate his hips, and generate a tremendous amount of torque. It took a lot of athleticism to do that. Ron could even do a 360-degree basketball dunk off of two feet!"

A relative unknown, Ron surprised the national throwing scene by placing fourth in the NCAA Division I outdoors championship in 1984. "That was so much fun. Just being in Eugene, Oregon, and renting dune buggies—I even rolled mine— the night before finals!" exclaims Ron. From that point forward, Ron became a force in national competitions and would soon be prominent at international competitions. Ron proceeded to win six Big Ten championships, five in shot put (three outdoor, two indoor) and one in the discus event. Now throwing consistently in the mid-sixty-foot range with a personal best of 68 feet 7¾ inches (20.64 meters), he placed eighth in the shot put at the NCAA outdoor championships in 1985 and felt primed to win the title in 1986. "I was throwing seventy-two feet in warm-ups, but then I pressed in the finals," Ron recalls ruefully of his third-place finish. He took some consolation from having won the 1986 NCAA indoor championship earlier in the season in Oklahoma City. "I felt so calm, comfortable, and confident in the circle. Everything felt right. My mom and dad were there too. Afterward, I got to jog around the track and hug my parents."

Gary Kostrubala, a Big 10 track and field foe from the University of Iowa who was also the Rose Bowl football team's punter, competed against Ron in many meets and remembers their collegiality. "Ron was a big guy with a full, bushy mustache. When we got into that ring, we were very competitive, but once we were outside it, we could goof off because the results were in. Ron always made sure everyone was included; he was very polite and genuine. He was a good student of the sport who had a smooth technique and got stronger. In 1986 Ron had won the shot put, but I had the lead in the discus until the very last throw. Ron beat me." In fact, Ron also set a U of M school record in 1986 with a personal best of 196 feet 6¼ inches (59.90 meters) in the discus throw. Ron echoes the bonding: "My favorite memories of throwing are at college. I loved practice and training. The throwers would talk and coach each other afterwards. There was no big pressure to win in track at the time. Being part of the track team was a good deal. I got to travel and compete around the country."

> "*My favorite memories of throwing are at college. I loved practice and training. The throwers would talk and coach each other afterwards. There was no big pressure to win in track at the time . . .*"

Obtaining a degree in marketing education, Ron decided to concentrate on fulfilling his dream and attempting to become a member of the 1988 United States Olympic team. Training with Coach Forseth, Ron worked hard to improve his strength. While bench pressing 395 pounds and squatting 680 pounds was very impressive, it paled in comparison to the premier shot put athletes, who surpassed those statistics by 100 pounds or more. Nevertheless, Ron's commitment to mastering technique

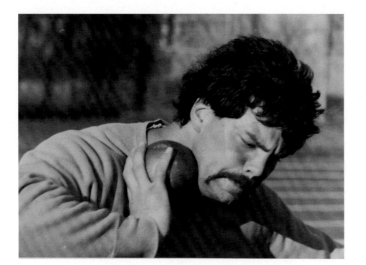

RON BACKES AT PRACTICE ON APRIL 23, 1986
Photo credit: St. Paul Pioneer Press

and diverse training dedicated to improve his overall athleticism enabled him to be ranked in the top ten of the world in shot put. He was primed to make the team by placing in the top three of the Olympic Trials in Indianapolis. "I was throwing the shot over seventy feet in practice," relives Ron, and then disaster struck. "I pulled a muscle in my right leg, which prevented me from practicing the two weeks before the trials." Still, Ron succeeded in the qualifying rounds and advanced to the preliminaries and then the finals. He was in third place with a throw of 20.62 meters (67 feet 8 inches) until a final throw by Jim Doehring eclipsed Ron's best by 1 centimeter (¼ inch). Although shattered and numb, Ron now states with conviction that the failure to make the Olympic team in 1988 was "the best day of my life."

Ron admits it took time to recover from the devastating experience and regain the motivation to try to make the 1992 Olympic team. He pledged to make better lifestyle decisions and train hard. Ron had great success in the shot put ring, capturing three indoor national championships (1988, 1991, and 1992); a bronze medal in the World Indoor Track and Field championships in Seville, Spain; and an outdoor national crown (1991). There continued to be some personal struggles, but an invitation to attend church by a friend two weeks before the Olympic Trials helped Ron find the solace he was seeking. "God helped me use the failure in 1988 to start a journey that led me to a right and personal relationship with Jesus Christ." Ron describes 1992 as a "transformational year."

In the 1992 Olympic Trials in New Orleans, it was a peace-filled Ron Backes who was the third and final shot put qualifier for the Olympic Games. In an article that Ron authored, he writes, "that was a pretty good day too." At the Olympics in Barcelona, Spain, Ron observes, "I was not nervous, but I was experiencing low energy that day. Generally I am an adrenaline thrower and perform better at meets than at practice." This did not hold true in Barcelona, however. While Ron did have the eleventh-best throw in the qualifying round, his Olympic run ended in the preliminaries where he placed tenth with a throw of 19.75 meters (64 feet 9½ inches). His best throw was not marked because the toe of his shoe rubbed atop the curb, disqualifying the throw.

Returning to Minnesota, Ron became engaged in the Fellowship of Christian Athletes (FCA) and held a series of jobs in financial services and teaching and coaching at Rosemount and Eastview high schools. He earned a master's degree at Minnesota State University–Mankato and through FCA met Michelle Peterson, a St. Olaf graduate who played basketball and softball at the Northfield, Minnesota, college. Michelle and Ron married in 1995 and moved to Columbus, Ohio, in 1997, where Ron accepted a position as the throwing coach for the Ohio State University men's and women's track and field teams. Another try for the 1996 Olympic team fell short with a respectable sixth-place finish.

Since 1999 Ron has been employed by the FCA and is currently the FCA coaches ministry director for the state of Minnesota. While on staff, he has also served as the chaplain for the Minnesota Vikings and the U of M men's basketball team. "I coach coaches to live out their faith in coaching the rest of their lives," notes Ron. The FCA office is located in a unique structure in the heart of the U of M athletic complex above Buffalo Wild Wings on the second floor of Station 19, an original Minneapolis firehouse, on University Avenue SE, directly across from TCF Bank Stadium. The historic building is often cited as the birthplace of "kittenball," a forerunner to the sport of softball. He remains active in his Olympic sport as the throws coach at Forest Lake High School.

Michelle taught and coached at the high school level for many years at Eagan, Minnesota, and Worthington, Ohio. She currently serves as chaplain for the U of M women's basketball team and the professional Minnesota Lynx basketball team (since 1999) and is also an assistant coach on the Chisago Lakes High School girls' basketball team. Ron and Michelle are the proud parents of a daughter, Carmen, and a son, Beau.

Ron is most thankful and appreciative of his Christian faith and opportunity to serve people of sports. It began in earnest due to one small centimeter.

MINNEAPOLIS FIRE STATION NUMBER 19 ACROSS FROM TCF BANK STADIUM HOUSES FELLOWSHIP OF CHRISTIAN ATHLETES OFFICES

Photo courtesy of Randy Bartz

RANDY BARTZ

Silver Record

TO HAVE A SMALL ROLE INTRODUCING AN ACtion-packed sport referred to as "rush-hour traffic unleashed" to the general American populace was thrilling to short track speedskater Randy Bartz. A member of the 5,000-meter relay team in the 1994 Olympics in Lillehammer, Norway, Randy firmly believes that their success served as a breakthrough for the increasing popularity of the sport. A demonstration sport in the 1988 Olympics in Calgary, Alberta, Canada, short track speedskating became a full-fledged medal sport in the 1992 Olympic Games in Albertville, France.

Born in 1968, Randy is the middle of three children of Ron, a pharmacist, and Fran, a surgical nurse. While living in Roseville, Minnesota—an inner-ring suburb located north of St. Paul in Ramsey county—he enjoyed playing and racing with sisters Becki and Gretchen, his cousins, and friends on Como Lake using old Viking speed skates. Como Lake had a 440-yard speedskating oval that served as host for many national speedskating meets while the Pavilion functioned as a warming house.

While his sisters eventually switched to figure skating, Randy forged ahead with speedskating, besides playing football and baseball in various leagues and at Mounds View High School. He was a 5-foot-9 starting free safety for the Mustangs' football team and also in the starting lineup of the 1987 state tournament baseball team as a centerfielder. Randy appreciates his parents' attitude toward his athletic career.

Randy cites watching Eric Heiden, winner of five gold medals in speedskating at the 1980 Winter Olympics at Lake Placid, New York, as making an impression on his speedskating career. He saw the speedskating events at the home of Bill Cushman, the president of the Midway Speedskating Club (founded in 1945) and team manager of the Olympic speedskating team, and he decided to devote more time to the sport. Cushman, also the team manager for the United States Olympic speedskating teams in 1984 and 2002, was very influential in the family-oriented club and served as its president for decades. The purpose of the club was to provide support for speedskaters, but youth development was an integral part of the club's mission as well. Cushman's son, Tom, raced in the 1,000-meter long track event in Calgary as a member of the 1998 US Olympic speedskating team.

Many racers at the Midway Speedskating Club showed promise at the novice level, but Randy observed, "Many quit, choosing to play hockey because the sports overlapped. They had learned good technique and were fast. Some former members went on to play at the collegiate level."

Randy advanced steadily, dedicating more time to training in speedskating when he was a high school sophomore. The next year he was rewarded with a slot on a 1986 Olympic Sports Festival team that competed in Houston, Texas, having placed among the top sixteen in the trials. Qualifying again in 1987, the same year he graduated from high school, Randy had the opportunity to compete again at the junior national level in Greensboro, North Carolina. Tom Cushman returned to the Twin Cities periodically from training and competing and assessed Randy's progress this way: "He began to differentiate himself with his dedication. He was willing to do the sacrifices necessary to improve, and that was impressive. He had excellent body control, and after you suggested something, he could go do it. So when he put the work in, you could see the result."

Randy enrolled at the University of Minnesota and tried to balance a challenging curriculum in the mechanical engineering department, being a member of the fraternity, working on polymers as a technician aide at 3M, and continuing to train as a speedskater.

" In the early day of short track, some guys would actually have a wrench in their hand at the starting line."

Short track speedskating had evolved from pack-style racing on ice hockey rinks. Competitions are now in ice hockey rinks with international-sized dimensions. The oval track is 111 meters (121 yards) in length, with four or more contestants racing simultaneously. Randy comments, "I now preferred short track. I liked the strategy and competitiveness." Radical changes have altered the speed of the sport. In short track's pioneering days, part of being a good skater was being able to configure a properly curved blade. The curve was crafted by wedging the blade in a door jamb

OLYMPIC SPEEDSKATERS FROM MINNESOTA: AMY PETERSON, RANDY BARTZ, PEGGY CLAUSEN, AND MICHELLE KLINE,
AT A RECEPTION HOSTED AT THE GOVERNOR'S MANSION, 1994
Photo credit: Frances Bartz

and striking it with a mallet! Randy claims, "In the early day of short track, some guys would actually have a wrench in their hand at the starting line."

Deciding to try out for the 1992 US Olympic speedskating team was a normal progression after qualifying for the World Championships from 1990–92 (and continuing to qualify through 1994), but Randy missed making the team by one place. He took a calculated risk to devote the next two years to full-time training in an attempt to make the 1994 winter Olympic team since the Olympic Committee offset the years for the summer and winter Olympic Games by two years instead of having them within the same calendar year. Thus the winter Olympic Games had a one-time interval of only two years.

The summer training, spearheaded by Susan Sandvig, consisted of three workouts per day of high-volume but low-intensity sessions with other Midway Speedskating Club members, including Amy Peterson, who had short track speedskating Olympic experience in both 1988 and 1992. In the fall, Randy often skated at Aldrich Arena, where the two daily workouts were more intense. The goal of the athletes was to peak at the time of the trials for the speedskating World Championships. Randy had shown marked improvement during the two years he had committed to training for the forthcoming Olympic Trials at Lake Placid over two weekends in 1994.

Consistently finishing among the top three spots in American speedskating races, Randy was confident about making the 1994 Olympic team. He made the mistake of lacing his skates too tightly for the first time trial, though, causing his feet to numb; he had to battle his way back to twelfth to earn a spot among the sixteen finalists. Randy steadily climbed in rank through the succeeding heats and then knew he had secured a place on the Olympic roster through the point system before the final heat. It was fortunate, because Randy admits to losing focus and being disqualified on the final race due to a sloppy pass that resulted in zero points for the last heat. He tied for third place in the overall trials, which meant he would be a member of the 5,000-meter relay team, but he did not qualify for an individual event. Still, Randy Bartz was going to Lillehammer, a picturesque Norwegian city of 25,000 inhabitants on the shores of Lake Mjosa and surrounded by mountains.

Canada, South Korea, and Japan were dominating the World Championships in the early 1990s and were considered the favorites in the Olympics, along with Italy and Australia. The United States squads had limited success in competition as teams and individuals. The sole qualifying event for the Olympics was the World Championship that determined which eight teams would qualify for the Olympics. The results shook up the predicted favorites as South Korea failed to qualify, and possible contender Great Britain was also eliminated while the upstart American team qualified.

After attending the opening ceremonies in Lillehammer, the US Olympic speedskating team relocated to Oslo to train and maintain concentration away from the crowds and celebrations in the host city. Randy thought it was a wise decision by Coach Jeroen Otter, a native of the Netherlands. "It kept the squad focused. We were peaking at the right time." Racing in the Olympic finals of short track speedskating requires not only single-mindedness, but a strong set of nerves. "I am totally fried after skating the intervals in a 5,000-meter relay event. It takes intense concentration. The ice gets chewed up, you tire, and yet you have to stay focused," Randy reports.

Away from distractions, the American relay quartet of Andy Gabel, John Coyle, Eric Flaim, and Randy practiced making seamless exchanges, propelling each other as part of the relay, providing coverage in the event of a fall, and finding the optimal distance to skate before the exchange. Tony Goskowicz, just sixteen years old, was also a member of the team, but would not participate in either of the two relay races. In the forty-five-lap relay, each relay team member would receive seven exchanges and sprint for one and a half laps before launching a teammate with a push.

"Andy Gabel was a great sprinter, a good starter who would get the lead. He would try to get us out of the scrap," explains Randy as he describes the order of the relay. "John Coyle was second. He wasn't only a very good racer, but he was also very smart—a Stanford graduate. I was third and would push Eric Flaim. Eric brought credibility to short track speedskating because he was a silver medalist in the 1,500-meter long track race in 1988. And he was just a fabulous skater."

Since the eight qualifying teams had already been established, there were only two relay heats of four teams each in the 5,000-meter men's short track speedskating relay. At the Hamar Olympic Amphitheatre, fifty-four kilometers (thirty-four miles) south of Lille-

SHORT TRACK RELAY TEAM CELEBRATES THEIR SECOND-PLACE FINISH
Photo credit: Frances Bartz

hammer, the American team finished second to Italy in its first race after the latter had ousted China and Norway. That paved the way to the finals, where Italy and the United States would be joined by Canada, the winner of the other semifinal, and Australia.

Gabel dashed to the front in the finals, and the team maintained a slim lead for about fifteen laps of the forty-five-lap race until Australia overtook the Americans. One of the teams favored for the gold medal, Canada, literally fell out of contention when a skater slipped. Randy remembers thinking about a place on the podium, "If we can only stay on our feet, we'll medal!" The American team actually briefly regained the lead after about twenty-five laps, but quickly fell to third as they became fatigued and Italy and Australia came on strong. Eric Flaim recaptured second with a burst of speed on the final exchange to claim silver medals for the relay team members in a time of 7 minutes 13.37 seconds, nudging ahead of Australia by 0.3 seconds. Italy won by the comfortable margin of 2 seconds.

While Randy has fond memories of the hijinks and card playing that team members did at the Olympics, he affirms, "The exhilaration of winning some hard-

NOLAN, KIM (BORROWMAN), STELLA, AIDAN, AND RANDY BARTZ ON THE STONE ARCH BRIDGE
Photo credit: Kjersti Mortenson, Mortenson Photography

ware, winning the silver medal at the Olympics . . . I don't think anything can trump that."

Randy retired from competitive speedskating after the Olympics, but the other members of the relay team and Tony Goskowicz continued and experienced more success on the national level. In 1998, Randy was selected as the commentator for the short track speedskating events at Nagano, Japan, while Ted Robinson voiced the play-by-play. He had only a phone interview and modestly confessed, "I fell into the position. I had a medal, and all the other racers were still competing. The producers probably had few options." It proved to be a very challenging and exhausting time since he was recruited for his expertise on the sport for some behind-the-scenes decisions on camera angles and coverage, as well as tasked with learning the backgrounds of the competitors. Chuckling, Randy recalls stumbling over the names of one short track race that included two South Korean and two Chinese skaters. "The names of the South Koreans were Ko Gi-Hyun and Choi Eun-Kyung and Yang-Yang was the translated name of both Chinese skaters. Now trying to describe that race was tough!"

"The exhilaration of winning some hardware, winning the silver medal at the Olympics . . . I don't think anything can trump that."

Randy returned to lend his expertise for the 2002 Olympics in Salt Lake City, Utah, and served as a consultant in the video truck. He is now the sole principal of Coating Resources Inc., a small business that provides high-performance protective coating solutions to places and structures that experience heavy traffic or harsh weather elements.

In 1999 Randy and Kim Borrowman, a construction sales representative, were married. They have three young children: Aidan, Nolan, and Stella. While still proud of his records and the silver medal, Randy is now a proud parent, and his thinking on many subjects has evolved. He would like to emulate his father, Ron, who had the perspective Randy would like to achieve, not just about sports, but also about life.

RANDY WITH HIS FATHER, RON BARTZ
Photo credit: Frances Bartz

**TONY BENSHOOF FOLLOWING HIS FINAL
RUN AT THE 2006 OLYMPICS IN TORINO, ITALY**
Photo credit: ©John Mebango/Corbis Images

TONY BENSHOOF

Slider Search Success

THE SPORT OF LUGE (A FRENCH WORD MEANING "sled") billing itself as "the fastest sport on ice" may have a history dating back many centuries to sled races in various countries. But the first recorded international competition was hosted by winter resorts near Davos, Switzerland, in 1883.

Luge debuted in the 1964 Winter Olympics in Innsbruck, Austria. Now, in the twenty-first century, luge racers hurtle down the course at astounding speeds nearing one hundred miles per hour, and the sport is one of the rare events timed to the thousandth of a second. It appears to be the kind of sport that leaves an observer breathless at the fearlessness of the athletes. They participate in a sport where the exposed rider is in a supine position while rocketing down a course that drops thirty stories with a centrifugal pull of five Gs, all on a fragile-looking sled raised two inches above the ice surface.

Tony Benshoof, a 1993 graduate of White Bear Lake High School, longtime resident of the St. Paul suburb, and three-time Olympian, explains, "The perception is that luge is a kamikaze sport, but we race on a sharp edge and you do have control. In fact, the best lugers are patient and methodical in finding a hundredth of a second to shave off their time."

A casual observer wonders where such a thing as a luge course even exists. There are not many around; there are only fifteen worldwide, and just four of them are situated in North America. So how did a White Bear Lake thirteen-year-old start luge racing when the nearest track (and only course in the United States at the time) was in Lake Placid, New York?

Tony considers it a "stroke of luck." Previously, he had shown ability in boxing. Then in 1989 he read an article about a luge recruitment opportunity called "USA Luge Slider Search." Tony received his parents' permission to go to the event and was one of twelve hundred invitees nationwide who participated in some skill tests, including a run down a summer version of a short luge track. Of the invitees, one hundred were selected to go to New York for additional training. The product of two St. Paul East Side teachers was hooked. "I loved it and still do," he says with a light in his eyes affirming the words are spoken with conviction.

"I loved it and still do . . ."

Leaving the comfortable quarters of his home and family in White Bear Lake for the months of October through March as a ninth-grade student, Tony embarked on a new and exciting lifestyle, although he admits to having bouts of homesickness. His parents and two brothers, Geno and Vince (also a luger for a time), were supportive because they recognized the opportunity Tony had to travel and compete in luge at the national and international levels.

Tony continued and later completed his studies at White Bear Lake High School through correspondence with his teachers and mailing assignments through the US Postal Service—sometimes from Europe. He looked forward to returning to Minnesota in the spring, reentering school, and enjoying the rich resources of Minnesota as he went camping, waterskiing, hunting, and fishing. In his senior year, he joined the track team and earned a varsity athletic letter while competing in the triple jump.

Young sliders at the junior level (age nineteen or younger) spend years training at the Lake Placid facility. They focus on learning to improve technique and taking three to six training runs per day on the luge track; the runs are increased incrementally in distance and difficulty. This work is supplemented with a regimen of resistance training, plyometric movements (repeated rapid stretching and contracting of muscles, sometimes referred to as jump training), and physioball exercises—all geared to improve strength, explosiveness, and technique. The hard work paid dividends when Tony collected two medals in the 1995 Luge World Junior Championships.

Progressing quickly in what teammate, flag bearer of the 2010 Winter Olympics, two-time men's luge doubles medalist, and five-time Olympian Mark Grimmette solemnly refers to as "a long development sport," Tony barely missed making the 1998 Winter Olympic team and was listed as first alternate. Tony remembers, "It was the most grueling process I've been through."

Being so close to winning a spot on the Olympic team only served to stoke the competitive fire for Tony. Teammate Grimmette observed, "He is a persistent, de-

Photo courtesy of USA Luge; photo by Nancie Battaglia

termined, and very coachable athlete. His sliding form is very aerodynamic, his start is very explosive, and he is a well-rounded driver. It's a tribute to him to reach the level of success he experienced. He never gave up."

Strides of progress continued in 2001 under the direction of head coach Wolfgang Schädler, a native of Liechtenstein, viewed by Tony as "the best coach existing in luge. He built all the American sleds and served as my eyes." Tony participated in a series of races as part of the World Cup and won a bronze medal at Winterberg, Germany. In 2002 Tony felt redeemed and made the Olympic luge team, finishing seventeenth overall (based on the combined time of four runs) in the men's luge single event hosted near Park City, about thirty miles southeast of downtown Salt Lake City. Tony calls it his favorite luge track.

The succeeding years were very successful for Tony. He became a force to be reckoned with on the international circuit. He was now stepping onto the podium among the many competitors in pursuit of excellence, and he loved the sport which drew big crowds in Europe. Luge tracks vary from 1,000 to 1,500 meters, and each course has its own personality. In 2005, he set a track record at the feared course in Altenberg, Germany. The pinnacle of his career was reached when he was crowned as the overall bronze medalist in the 2005 World Cup. "It was a pretty special moment," Tony recalls. "I was locked in for the 2006 Olympics."

"It was a pretty special moment," Tony recalls. "I was locked in for the 2006 Olympics."

TONY BENSHOOF PREPARES FOR A LUGE RUN AT PARK CITY, UTAH, 2009
Photo courtesy of USA Luge

It was almost a foregone conclusion that Tony would be on the 2006 Winter Olympic team that would be participating in Cesana Pariol, Italy, near Turin (Torino). And the Olympic Trials were not a struggle as he easily qualified for the team. The course in Italy was 1,435 meters in length and had 19 turns. After two runs, Tony was in third place. The third run was a bit off, and Tony dropped to fourth. In what he called a "fly or die situation," Tony felt confident that he would be a medalist because he had performed tight and steady, the best he could on his final run, and was back in third place. A Latvian luge racer then dashed down and edged Tony by 0.153 of a second. Naturally, Tony felt a rush of emotions: disappointment at finishing fourth, pride in knowing that he had done his best, and, he laughs, beating his nemeses, the Germans.

Tony continued to collect medals on the national and international levels, and he prepared for a third Olympics. Making the 2010 men's luge single team was a similar scenario to that of 2006, as it was not a struggle. The luge venue was at Whistler Sliding Center, about eighty miles north of Vancouver, British Columbia. Tragically, a Georgian luger crashed and died during a training run. A decision was made to shorten the course, and Tony believes that the shortened course and competing with injuries diminished his chances to place. He had solid runs despite receiving injections for a ruptured disc and again placed the highest of any American athlete in the men's single luge competition with an eighth-place finish. He retired from competitive luge racing shortly after the Olympics with seven national titles and thirty-seven medals in international competition. He cited the back injury, "an occupational hazard," and two surgeries for ending his career.

Throughout his years of luge racing, Tony continued his education, first attending Century College in White Bear Lake for two years, later attending the University of Minnesota, and finally graduating with a business management and economics degree from the State University of New York (SUNY)–Empire State College. He completed graduate school through a US Olympic Committee scholarship, obtaining a master's degree in business administration with a hospitality concentration. Putting this knowledge to use, Tony has been employed as a general manager in the hospitality industry. He also juggles a photography business, speaking engagements, and coaching along with his studies.

Tony still has goals, though, in the world of luge. He hopes to see a short luge track erected in his home state—perhaps around Afton, Minnesota, on the St. Croix River just east of St. Paul. He also serves as a national junior coach and maintains, "It has been a super fun experience. It has been rewarding to mentor astoundingly innocent youths and see marked improvement. I believe that I have an advantage as a coach since I have been through the entire program."

It could lead to another Slider Search success story.

ALI BERNARD AFTER VICTORY OVER NIGER OPPONENT IN 2008 OLYMPICS
Photo courtesy of Larry Slater

ALI BERNARD

New Ulm Has Lots of Ali Cats

A FORTY-FIVE-FOOT-TALL GLOCKENSPIEL, THE AUgust Schell Brewing Company, and the Hermann Heights Monument (affectionately known as Hermann the German) all reflect the German heritage of New Ulm, Minnesota. Located ninety miles southwest of Minneapolis, the city of 13,500 people situated at the confluence of the Minnesota and Cottonwood rivers is probably most known for baseball in the Minnesota sporting world. Johnson Park, a municipal athletic facility with separate baseball and football fields, is located on German Street—one block from Minnesota Street. Combined, the Steinbach brothers, Tim, Tom, and Terry (a catcher who played thirteen full seasons in the major leagues), played hundreds of games at Johnson Park. New Ulm is also the home of the Ali Cats, a loyal support group for two-time Olympic women's wrestler Ali Bernard.

Ali, born in 1986, is the fourth of Rocky and Sue Bernard's five children. She was a bit jealous of her only brother winning at wrestling tournaments that she watched with her family. Of her first experience in what has traditionally been a male sport, Ali reports, "I wanted some medals too. I went with Andy to practice one day and liked it. It would have been a whole different story if all the coaches in New Ulm hadn't been inclusive. They treated me the same as any other wrestler."

Starting with the New Ulm Rolling Thunder Wrestling Club as a sixth grader, Ali continued to advance in the sport while also playing volleyball and softball as a youth. Eventually Ali dedicated her time to wrestling because the travel to distant wrestling tournaments for girls interfered with her participation in the other sports. Primarily wrestling on the school's varsity team

ALI BERNARD WITH NEW ULM HIGH SCHOOL WRESTLING TEAM
Photo courtesy of Sue and Rocky Bernard

(composed only of boys other than Ali) starting her sophomore year, her coaches believe that she had a record of as many wins as losses, although some were forfeits because the opponents did not want to wrestle a girl. "She wrestled some strong farm boys," smiles Rocky, a former heavyweight wrestler for New Ulm High School.

Brandon Reichel, one of her coaches, was impressed with Ali. "She had a really good work ethic and a desire to win. She is extremely flexible. The boys didn't treat her any differently. The hardest part was to find other females to wrestle."

ALI BERNARD FACING OFF WITH MALE OPPONENT WHILE WRESTLING FOR NEW ULM HIGH SCHOOL
Photo courtesy of Sue and Rocky Bernard

The year 2004 proved to be an eventful year for Ali. Women's wrestling would be debuting at the Olympic Games in Athens, Greece, that summer. Ali won both the 2004 Junior National Wrestling Championships and rolled to victory with dominating matches at the 2004 US National Championship at 67 kilograms (147.7 pounds), qualifying for an invitation to the Olympic Trials. These championships led to Ali being named 2004 Girls High School Wrestler of the Year, a national award. While she lost decisively to Katie Downing in the Olympic Trials final, the Olympic wrestling coaches requested that Ali do some goal setting. Her goal: to become a 2008 Olympian. Graduating from New Ulm High School, she was recruited by Northern Michigan University (one of just a handful of American colleges that had a women's wrestling program) and the University of Regina in Saskatchewan, Canada. In a quirk of timing, the University of Minnesota–Morris, the first US college to offer women's wrestling as a varsity sport in 1993, cut its entire wrestling program a year before Ali's commencement. After visiting both colleges, Ali decided to go to Regina, where one of the benefits would be to wrestle with members of the men's team. "Women's wrestling was more developed in Canada. There were direct flights to the Twin Cities too," she explains.

Canadian universities permit five years of athletic eligibility, and Ali had unprecedented success as a woman wrestler in the country. She won the Canadian Interuniversity Sport (CIS) Rookie of the Year Award in 2005, winning the 80 kg (176.4 pounds) division. She later proceeded to capture CIS titles in 2006 and 2007 in the lower 72 kg (158.5 pounds) class and 2008 back at the 80 kg division. The fourth championship coincided with Ali's stated 2004 goal of becoming an Olympian. Her training consisted of a thirty-minute run and working on technique in the morning, then relaxing or taking a nap before two hours of live wrestling in the afternoon and working on position. Ali estimates that she worked out about twenty-four hours per week, besides learning about nutrition and studying videos of wrestling. Although seeded fourth, Ali won the US National Championships in Las Vegas, Nevada, and then returned to that tourist mecca two months later for the Olympic Trials to realize her goal.

Wrestling in the 72 kg class, one of only four women's weight divisions, Ali reversed the results of 2004 by defeating Downing in two matches and won the 2008 Olympic Trials. Ali, twenty-two years old, would be going to Beijing, China, with her parents, her four siblings, and a staunch band of Ali Cats from New Ulm.

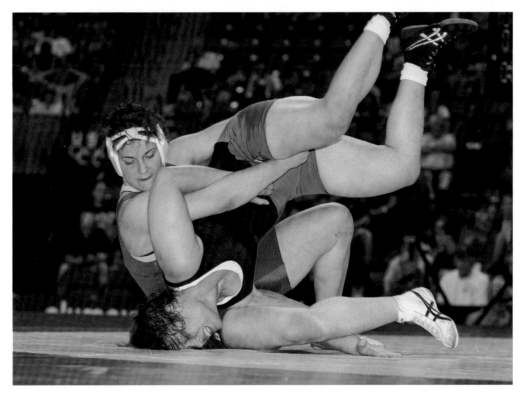

ALI WINNING THE FINAL MATCH TO MAKE THE USA OLYMPIC TEAM IN 2008
Photo courtesy of Larry Slater

In Beijing, Ali scored a resounding victory with a pin in forty-four seconds over her Nigerian opponent in the opening round. In the second round, Jiao Wang of China, the eventual gold medalist, beat Ali, but the New Ulm native bounced back with a victory over Jenny Fransson, a Swedish wrestler. Ali's final match would be against Kyoko Hamaguchi for the bronze medal. While the Japanese wrestler defeated Ali, the US Olympic women's wrestling head coach, Terry Steiner, voices this opinion: "She has the unique combination of flexibility and strength and an innate awareness and ability of the sport. I think that Ali just fell in love with the sport. She found she could do something in wrestling if she focused on it. She's a great role model, got involved in a sport that not many were willing to get involved in. She's just a winner."

> "She has the unique combination of flexibility and strength and an innate awareness and ability of the sport . . . She found she could do something in wrestling if she focused on it. She's a great role model . . ."

Ali decided not to return to the University of Regina for the 2008–09 academic year and opted to transfer to another college in Canada, the University of Alberta in Edmonton, in 2009–10, for her fifth year of eligibility and to continue her schooling. Ali won the 72 kg division for her new team, becoming the first woman wrestler to sweep five CIS championships, a highlight in personal achievements. Ali remained at the University of Alberta to continue to train, coach the women's wrestling team, and obtain her degree in recreation sports and tourism.

In 2010, Ali won gold medals at the University World Championships and Pan Am Games. The next year, Ali won a bronze medal at the prestigious World Championships in Istanbul, Turkey. "It was one of my better tournaments," admits Ali. "It was uplifting because I did well." Well indeed. The win included a pin of 2008 gold medalist Wang and another pin of the 2004 silver medalist from Kazakhstan, earning the American team a berth at the 72 kg weight class for the 2012 Olympic Games in London, England. Sue Bernard, who had attended many national and international matches, had never seen her daughter so expressive after winning a match. "It was the happiest I'd ever seen her after a wrestling match. She gave a hand clap!" exclaims Sue. As a result of her triumphs on the mat, Ali was named 2011 Women's Wrestler of the Year by USA Wrestling.

With such successful years leading to the 2012 Olympic Trials in Iowa City, Iowa, Ali seemed a prime candidate for the American team going to London, England. However, Ali was upset by Stephany Lee in two matches in the finals. Weeks later it was revealed that Lee had tested positive for marijuana metabolic, and she accepted a one-year suspension from wrestling and forfeited her spot on the Olympic wrestling team. As runner-up, Ali was nominated to replace Lee to be the US representative at the 72 kg weight class. Again, her family and a steadfast group of Ali Cats from New Ulm would be joining the two-time Olympian—this time in London.

Disaster struck during training in Japan, though. Ali broke her fibula and was off the mat for about six weeks, which limited her training in the brief period between the trials and the Olympic Games. At London, Ali had just a single appearance on the mat—a close loss to Fransson of Sweden, an opponent she had defeated at Beijing. Fransson then lost her next match, and that defeat also ended any chance for Ali to continue wrestling at the Olympic Games, but she is still grateful for her experiences. "Being able to travel the world with my teammates created deep friendship bonds," Ali acknowledges. She points to Olympic coach Steiner as the person she has the highest regard for in wrestling. "He was an encyclopedia on wrestling. I probably respect him the most."

ALI BERNARD WITH NEPHEWS IN ALI CAT SHIRTS AT WELCOME HOME RETURN, 2012
Photo courtesy of Sue and Rocky Bernard

After a hiatus from wrestling, Ali returned to the sport, sharing her passion by coaching the Minnesota Storm girls' team. "Hopefully it's something that will grow. They are starting earlier and are more advanced than I was," Ali observes about her monthly practices. She works in the Twin Cities metropolitan area and is completing requirements to acquire her personal trainer certification.

Ali Bernard still visits her hometown regularly. "New Ulm is the best! It's a tight-knit community that gave me a lot of support. My family, the community, coaches, and, of course, the Ali Cats—their support made it possible to compete at the Olympic level."

BOB HARRIS, ARCHIE LEE, RUBE BJORKMAN, CA. 1945
Photo courtesy of Roseau County Historical Society

RUBEN BJORKMAN

Masked Marvel Was in St. Moritz in 1948

IN ROSEAU, MINNESOTA, ICE HOCKEY REIGNED SU-preme in the 1940s," Ruben Bjorkman says matter-of-factly of his youth. "You skated on any ice you could find: ditches, ponds, packed roadways."

Roseau, the birthplace of Polaris Industries (a snowmobile and all-terrain vehicle manufacturer), is a town of about 2,600 people located ten miles south of the United States–Canadian border. It is the hometown of former professional football coach Phil Bengston and Secretary of Agriculture Bob Bergland (Carter administration).

And hockey enthusiasts are very familiar with Roseau's celebrated history of seven state high school championships, thirty-four state tournament appearances (through 2015), and many ice hockey Olympians and professionals. Ruben Bjorkman was an integral piece of Roseau High School's first state tournament appearance, which resulted in a championship in the tournament's second year of existence (1946).

Born in 1929, Ruben played football his senior year in high school and ran the 400-meter dash in track, but the 5-foot-9-inch, 155-pound athlete called "the Masked Marvel" was best known for his prowess in ice hockey. Needing to wear glasses to improve his vision while playing hockey, it was not safe or practical for Ruben to play at the high school level until his coach, Oscar Almquist, devised some rubber-rimmed goggles to wear over the safety glasses that he wore during games. Looking like an early aviator, Ruben became known by his newly minted nickname with his dazzling play. "They fogged up," Ruben reports, "but I could see."

While Roseau did not qualify for the inaugural state high school ice hockey tournament in 1945, Ruben, some teammates, and Almquist attended the games as spectators at the St. Paul Auditorium. The tournament was a success and motivated the Roseau squad to make a return trip to St. Paul—as participants.

Known as the Green Wave (the team nickname is now the Rams), the Roseau team captured the regional title in 1946 with victories over Warroad and Thief River Falls. At the state tournament, the Masked Marvel seized the crowd and media's attention with his skating ability and deadly shooting. Ruben scored a hat trick (three goals) in a 6–0 win over Rochester as Roseau claimed the championship. "Playing in the state tournament was a defining moment," Ruben acknowledges. More extraordinary performances for the right wing were to come.

Roseau returned in 1947 and made a valiant effort to repeat as champions. They defeated another storied traditional power, Eveleth, in the semifinals. Ruben, named to his second consecutive all-tournament team, slapped two goals past goalie Willard Ikola, a future Olympian and longtime Edina High School hockey coach, who was in the nets for the defeated Iron Range team. Roseau then lost to St. Paul Johnson 2–1 in the finals. Jim Sedin, a Johnson player, recalls, "Rube was a great high school player. He had a smooth skating style and a great shot. And, of course, he then became a great college player." Sedin would later captain the University of Minnesota hockey team that Ruben played on, and the two would pair up again on the 1952 Olympic team.

Ruben explains playing in a simpler era: "Our games were outdoors. We did not have a youth traveling team. The farthest we ever went to play was Eveleth and Thief River Falls. I never lifted weights. Hockey was different then." Despite his state tournament heroics, Ruben was lightly recruited following graduation in 1947. He decided to enroll at the University of Minnesota even though he was not offered a scholarship. The selling point was that the coaches promised to get him an appointment with an eye doctor who could fit him with contact lenses! "It made all the difference in the world," the now Unmasked Marvel says in wonder. Still a pioneering concept in contact athletics, Ruben remembers "guarding them with my life" on his future forays overseas.

When Ruben enrolled at Minnesota, freshmen were not eligible to play varsity hockey, so he set his sights on the 1948 Olympic team. One of the most controversial and bizarre events in United States Olympic history followed. Two competing hockey organizations, the American Hockey Association (AHA), affiliated with the International Hockey Federation, and the Amateur Athletic Union (AAU) vied to field the ice hockey team representing the United States at the 1948 Olympic Games, to be held in St. Moritz, Switzerland.

"I participated in tryouts at the Minneapolis Arena on 2900 Dupont Avenue

South and won a place on the American Hockey Association team and later on the AAU team too, but I accepted the AHA spot first. I took an ocean liner to Europe and got very seasick," relates Ruben.

But the controversy was still brewing. The AAU team, sanctioned by the American Olympic Committee, also arrived at St. Moritz with a full hockey team, with both teams claiming "official" status as the United States ice hockey team. The International Olympic Committee finally decided to bar both teams, but the Swiss Olympic Committee defied the ruling and permitted the AHA team to participate on an "unofficial" basis. In an awkward compromise, the AAU team was allowed to march in the opening ceremony. Ruben describes the unprecedented discord this way: "No official team shows in the records, but I have an Olympic certificate saying that I was there."

After a pair of lopsided victories, the United States AHA team eventually lost to the three medal winners in the round-robin tournament to place fourth in the standings. Ruben, an Olympian at the tender age of eighteen, did not score, and records are murky about his playing time. However, since the AHA team's participation was "unofficial," the team is officially listed as "disqualified" in the Olympic record books. In an effort to not repeat the debacle in 1952, an independent group called the United States Hockey Committee would select the team for the next Olympic Games. Bob Ridder, a Minnesota media mogul, would become instrumental in resolving the raging conflict and restructuring hockey associations.

RUBEN BJORKMAN PLAYED FOR THE GOPHERS FROM 1947-51
Photo courtesy of University of Minnesota Athletics

Ruben returned to the University of Minnesota and had a successful collegiate career under coach Doc Romnes. Ruben is credited with scoring an impressive 22 goals and assisting on 25 others in 26 games during the 1950–51 season when Williams Arena opened for hockey.

"The 1952 Olympic Games in Oslo, Norway, was more organized," notes Ruben dryly. Based on his experience, "I was not tense about making the team."

He was joined by Gophers' teammates Sedin, Ken Yackel (the player Ruben says he most respected), and Allen Van. Other Minnesotans were on the team, including Minneapolis native Arnie Oss, a prolific scorer. Oss often played on the first or second line with Ruben. "Rube was a tremendous skater," Oss reports. "His terrific background at the high school and college levels made him valuable to the team."

The American contingent was known for their physical play, particularly the rugged Yackel, and the European spectators expressed their displeasure since body checking was not commonly a part of their finesse game. The outdoors games were sometimes played in foggy conditions and heavy snowfall. In the final game of the round-robin tournament, the American team needed a win over Canada to win the gold medal, but a loss would drop them into fourth, out of a medal.

The favored Canadian team led the Americans by the vast margin of 58–13 on the statistic of shots on goal. Ruben made one of the shots count, scoring unassisted in the second period. Trailing 3–2 with about two minutes remaining in the game, Sedin rifled in the tying goal. With the tie, the American team captured second place. Ruben had scored three goals in the tournament, and this time he had silver proof of being at the Olympic Games.

Again returning to the University of Minnesota, Ruben attained a degree in math and physical education in 1952. He was drafted into the United States Army in September; recalling his previous seasickness traversing the Atlantic Ocean for the 1948 Olympic Games, he dreaded the troop transport ship crossing. Serving in the infantry and one year in Korea after the armistice had been signed, he returned in time to join the national team and played in the World Championships in Germany. The team placed fourth, and another Olympics was forthcoming, but Ruben felt he needed to go to work.

Embarking on a career in coaching, Ruben's first job was at Greenway High School in Coleraine, Minnesota. "I liked the people on the Iron Range," he says fondly of his time there. "The people were very respectful of teachers and coaches." Another welcome part of the Iron Range was meeting his wife, Marilyn; together they had three children. Eight years later the Bjorkman family headed east—Ruben was offered a job as a college coach at Rensselaer Polytechnic Institute, a premier engineering school in Troy, New York. The first year, 1963–64, was an immediate triumph for the team, which placed third in the NCAA postseason tournament!

Ruben and the family moved farther east the next year, to a new coaching position at the University of New Hampshire. These were some of Marilyn's favorite years since there was less stress in coaching and their family was growing. Overcoming a disappointing start of 6 wins in 20 games, the team roared back three years later in the 1967–68 season with 22 wins out of 29 games and a 57–40 record over Ruben's four-year tenure.

Despite enjoying the Granite State, Ruben was seeking to return to the Upper Midwest. He accepted a job coaching at the University of North Dakota (UND) in Grand Forks. UND's Winter Sports Building, which hosted the hockey games, was famous for its frigid temperatures. Ruben began his coaching career in 1968 in the quonset-style metal roofed building referred to as the "Potato Barn" by Gophers coach John Mariucci. The team had a winning first season and continued winning until 1972, when the new (and warm) Winter Sports Center was constructed. Ruben coached six more seasons, but his collegiate coaching career ended at UND in 1978 with 224 wins, 234 losses, and 10 ties. "Coaching had become much more complicated. You need to be a good people-person. Kids have been raised in sophisticated programs with lots of training and travel. It has been a big change," Ruben acknowledges.

Warroad High School, neighbors and fierce rivals of his hometown Roseau Rams, offered Ruben a coaching job from 1980–83 while he also worked at Marvin Windows and Doors for nearly two decades in the personnel department of the large Warroad design and manufacturing facility. Ruben appreciates the company being a generous benefactor to the community and local hockey teams. Marilyn Bjorkman was also connected to hockey as an employee for nineteen years at another Warroad company, the hockey stick manufacturer Christian Brothers.

Ranked among Minnesota's greatest hockey players, Ruben has been the recipient of these awards: the 1982 Cliff Thompson Award from the Minnesota Hockey Coaches Association was presented to him for long-term contributions to hockey in Minnesota, and the 1997 John Kelley Award from the American Hockey Coaches

RUBEN BJORKMAN STANDS BY SOME OF HIS AWARDS AT HIS HOME IN WARROAD, MINNESOTA

Association, which is awarded to someone in the coaching profession who has contributed to the overall growth and development of the sport of ice hockey in the United States. While honored, Ruben solemnly says, "Our greatest pride is our children and grandchildren."

The protective Masked Marvel goggles are still in Ruben's possession, along with a 1952 silver medal and a certificate from the 1948 Olympics verifying his presence in St. Moritz.

Photo courtesy of USA Boxing

DUANE BOBICK

Still Fighting

AFTER BATTLING POVERTY, SOME OF THE WORLD'S best amateur and professional boxers, depression, and a horrific industrial accident, Duane Bobick is still fighting. And in this fight, he can't outmuscle his opponent, chronic traumatic encephalopathy (CTE), a progressive degenerative disease of the brain. Gaining widespread attention in recent years due to tragic deaths and the early signs of dementia in several famous athletes from the sports of football, ice hockey, and professional wrestling as well as boxing, CTE is a disease that is believed to be due to repeated head injuries and concussions. In fact, it was originally named pugilistic dementia because it was observed in so many boxers.

Duane is able to articulate his mixed feelings about his love of boxing and its turn on his health with an almost rehearsed answer. "If I'd have known back then about the effects of subconcussive hits to the head, I don't know if I'd have gone into the sport of boxing. But I don't regret it because I made many friends, learned a lot of discipline, and traveled the world—seeing every continent except the Antarctic."

Indeed, life has had many rewards for the affable former boxer, but it has not been easy. Born in St. Paul in 1950 as the second oldest of thirteen children (twelve boys and one girl), Duane's family had a hardscrabble existence and moved to Bowlus, a central Minnesota town with a population of less than 300 people, shortly after his birth. His father had a stucco plastering business and had his own battles with chemical dependency while raising the large family.

Attending Royalton High School, the same school as NFL Hall of Fame center Jim Langer, Duane participated as a 6-foot-3-inch, 180-pound lineman in football; played basketball; and was a pitcher and high-average hitter in baseball. He claims that he sometimes ran the six miles from his family home in Bowlus to high school, which proved he had more motivation and self-discipline than most student athletes. Duane also voiced his dream of going to the Olympics and credits teacher Mary Rose, a fellow Royalton High School Athletic Hall of Fame inductee, for encouraging him to pursue his dream.

As a high school sophomore, Duane started Golden Gloves boxing in Little Falls. He says simply, "I loved it." He won immediately, despite competing against many other good athletes testing out the sport. Brothers Rodney and Leroy joined him and experienced success too. Their first boxing coach, Roger Thielen, saw a promising future for Duane in the sport. "He had an impressive physique, a beautiful left jab, and was very coachable. The Bobick clan grew up fighting and had absolutely no fear. I saw a flame developing in Duane to realize that potential."

"He had an impressive physique, a beautiful left jab, and was very coachable."

Following graduation in 1968, Duane enrolled at Moorhead State in Moorhead, Minnesota. By his own admission, "I went to play football and soon realized college was not for me." It led Duane to enlist in the United States Navy and to start concentrating on boxing.

Assigned shore duty in Hawaii as a quartermaster, Duane signed up for the Hawaiian Golden Gloves Boxing Championships. Training six hours per day with ten-mile runs on occasion, he was strengthening not only his body, but his self-discipline and mind. Tough and powerful, he says that he lived by the brutal boxing maxim "kill the body and the head will die." Weighing between 200 and 215 pounds and using his 82-inch reach to his advantage, Duane proceeded to win the first of three all-Navy heavyweight championships and eventually became a two-time all–Armed Services boxing champ. Duane still seems astonished at the skyrocketing success he experienced, but he vividly remembers being defeated by United States Marine Percy Pride, a fighter he describes "like a block of cement."

A highlight that gained national attention was his 1971 Pan Am gold medal–winning performance as a heavyweight boxer in Cali, Colombia. In a hostile environment, Duane defeated the host country's representative in the first round, then marked a unanimous decision victory over future three-time Olympic gold medalist Teofilo Stevenson of Cuba in the semifinal match before claiming the gold medal by stopping Joaquin Rocha in round three of the title bout. It was part of a string of sixty consecutive boxing victories. Duane was suddenly hailed as a twenty-one-year-old celebrity in the sporting world. His picture adorned the cover of many magazines, and he was dubbed "the Great White Hope," a tag that he never embraced. The Olympics, a dream he had dared speak of as a schoolboy, was in sight.

Duane had earned the national Amateur Athletic Union (AAU) heavyweight crown in 1971 and followed that achievement with the 1972 national Golden Gloves title. He was certainly a favorite in the Olympic Trials based on his win at the Pan Am Games. The most famous bout of the trials in Fort Worth, Texas, was his semifinal match against future world champion Larry Holmes. Duane staggered his foe in the second round, and Holmes kept clinching despite repeated warnings to stop and was eventually disqualified. His finals opponent would be Nick Wells, the 1972 AAU champion and a native of the host city. The brawler from Bowlus would be in the championship contest seeking an Olympic trip to Munich, Germany. The fight was stopped after two rounds—Duane Bobick was an Olympian.

Being touted as a probable medal winner, Duane opened with a convincing 5–0 win over his Russian opponent. A much-anticipated rematch versus Stevenson didn't have the result Duane expected. A stunned American public watched as the referee stopped the match midway through the third round, declaring the young Cuban the winner. It should be noted, however, that Stevenson, who never turned professional, is certainly rated one of the best heavyweight boxers of his era. Duane also cites the tragic events unfolding before him at Munich as terrorists killed several Israeli athletes causing him to lose focus, an event he believes the Cuban team was isolated from by their coaches.

Duane returned to the United States determined to become a professional boxer. During his amateur career, Duane had fought men who would compete for the world boxing title while compiling a record of 93 wins, 61 by knockout (KO), and 13 losses. His first manager was Bill Daniels, and he was trained by Murphy Griffith, uncle of welterweight and middleweight champion Emile Griffith. He debuted as a professional in April 1973 with a first round KO over Tommy Burns in Minneapolis—it would be the start of 38 uninterrupt-

OLD GLORY

I'm proud of this country
Old Glory is my flag
Through the years she's had her knocks
I've seen her spirit sag
It was an honor to carry her
I tried to carry her tall
Into battle we went
I carried her for you all
The spirit of the colonies
And the soldiers of this land
With pride and courage carried
Old Glory to freedom's demand
In the sixties, I saw her burned
In the eighties, Iran did the same
I've had opportunity to carry her
She was with me in the Olympic Games
If opportunity does avail you
State your convictions out loud
Tell People you are an American,
And, of Old Glory you are proud

11-17-1987
©DUANE BOBICK, USED WITH PERMISSION

ed professional victories.

Now managed by boxing legend Joe Frazier and trained by Eddie Futch, Duane began inching his way up the rankings with notable wins over Mike Weaver and Larry Middleton, but it would be a match in 1976 against a fellow Minnesotan that would capture the attention of state boxing fans. Scott LeDoux, a slugging and gritty boxer from Crosby, Minnesota, and Duane fought before 13,789 people—a record crowd in Minnesota boxing history. The ten-round event, held at the Metropolitan Sports Center in Bloomington, ended in a unanimous decision favoring Duane. His analysis of the bout featuring the powerful punchers: "I had more speed in my feet."

DUANE BOBICK SCORES 8TH ROUND TKO VS SCOTT LEDOUX, JULY 28, 1977
Photo credit: St. Paul Pioneer Press

After wins over contenders Chuck Wepner and Fred Houpe later in the year, Duane would land the biggest professional payday and opportunity of his career against rugged and athletic Ken Norton in 1977. Duane uncharacteristically charged Norton at the opening bell instead of following his customary pattern of cautiously feeling out his opponent. Norton landed a pair of hard hits and then hit Duane in the throat with a devastating punch. The match, fought at New York City's Madison Square Garden, ended in a TKO a mere fifty-eight seconds into the first round. Duane received $250,000 for the fight, but he was stung by the criticism. Two months later, though, he rebounded with a victory in a rematch versus LeDoux back at the Metropolitan Sports Center.

In 1978 he lost to Kallie Knoetze in South Africa, signaling the beginning of the end of his boxing career. While Duane did reel off eight more straight victories, back-to-back losses to John Tate and George Chaplin, combined with a diagnosis of a severe case of bursitis in his shoulders, caused him to decide to retire from professional boxing with a record of 48 wins (42 KOs) and 4 losses in July 1979, one month shy of his twenty-ninth birthday.

Life then began spiraling out of control for Duane. He had impulsively married an artist-model from Arizona in 1973, and they divorced less than three years later. Duane's second marriage, to a restaurant hostess from Philadelphia, likewise ended in divorce. His brother Rodney, a sparring partner for Muhammad Ali, got killed in a single-car accident. Now living in Atlantic City, New Jersey, he had reached goals that most people never imagine, but he still felt at loose ends and became depressed. Finally he called his older brother Leroy and requested his help to pack up and move back home.

Duane, who married Debi Atkinson in 1986, became a security guard at the St. Cloud Reformatory in 1987. Welcomed stability occurred, and two children were born during his ten-year stint in his security position. Duane also served in the Minnesota Army National Guard for sixteen years. In 1997 he began to work at Hennepin Paper in Little Falls and suffered a dreadful industrial accident. Duane was cutting a roll of paper on a paper machine winder when the knife he was using got caught and both of his arms got pulled into the machinery. He was listed in critical condition with multiple broken bones and damage to his skin tissue, tendons, and blood vessels. "I think that he has had thirteen surgeries and underwent two years of intensive therapy," Debi reports. Duane has substantial scarring, lost an index finger, and fought to regain his incredible strength.

Boxing remained special to Duane—before and after the accident. He continued to serve as a referee and judge until 2011, when the effects of CTE became more apparent and he was forced to quit driving. Duane has participated in a day program at St. Otto's Care Center in Little Falls. According to Outreach Program Director Lisa Nelson, "Duane is very comfortable here since he also served as a longtime volunteer. He greets visitors and transports people around the facility. It is a time for him to socialize and participate in activities while offering respite for the family."

Duane Bobick was inducted into the Royalton High School Hall of Fame in 2010, the Minnesota Boxing Hall of Fame in 2011, and the Polish-American Sports Hall of Fame in 2014. The plaque he received from the 2011 induction has been donated to his hometown and joins posters of his boxing career on display at the Bowlus Community Center on the Soo Line Trail.

The man once ranked the number five heavyweight in the world, who knew, sparred, or fought boxing legends Ali (his favorite athlete), Frazier, Stevenson, Holmes, and Norton, laughs softly as he summarizes his avocation and vocation: "It was the best job in my life . . . beating people up for a living."

DUANE AND DEBI (ATKINSON) BOBICK AT
BOWLUS COMMUNITY CENTER, AUGUST 2012

HENRY BOUCHA AS WARROAD HIGH SCHOOL WARRIOR IN 1969
Photo courtesy of Warroad Heritage Center

HENRY BOUCHA

Bimiiwinitisowin Omaa Aiding

ONCE IGNORING HIS OJIBWE HERITAGE BECAUSE "IT was not cool," Henry Boucha now embraces it. Two of his grandfathers were chiefs, and he is a proud member of Northwest Angle Band Number 37. Henry writes that "Bimiiwinitisowin Omaa Aiding is a perfect definition of culture. We learn that we have everything that we need to survive and exist as a people."

Born in 1951, Henry began playing road hockey at age four or five with a taped snuff can, became an acclaimed player at Warroad High School, then was instrumental on national and Olympic teams before reaching the professional ranks with the Detroit Red Wings and Minnesota North Stars in the National Hockey League (NHL). In the brief span of twenty years, he undoubtedly has one of the most distinguished, yet compact, ice hockey careers of any American.

The eighth of nine children of a French-Canadian father and an Ojibwe mother, Henry is a dual citizen of the United States and Canada. As a child, he spent lots of time boating on Lake of the Woods with his father, a commercial fisherman. In winter, "if an extra player was needed for a hockey game, I would be asked. I played goalie. Shin pads were stiff and bulky. I wore a chest protector, but I didn't have a mask, and the skates that I wore were too big. My dream was to wear a uniform and make the peewee [ages eleven and twelve] team," Henry remembers.

The Warroad youth hockey teams experienced success. The bantam (ages thirteen and fourteen) team won the state championship in a spectacular upset in 1963–64 with Henry, age twelve, now playing defense. By eighth grade, Henry was playing junior varsity hockey with an occasional stint on the varsity squad. He continued to ascend in the sport and was eventually named all-state as a sophomore, junior, and senior in high school. He excelled in other sports, too. Henry loved football and played many positions including some running back and quarterback. The all-conference athlete was recruited by Notre Dame as a punter and kick placer. He was a third baseman and pitcher in baseball and participated in pole vault, long jump, relays, and the 440-yard run in track. A typical kid of the northwoods, he also fished and hunted—particularly partridge.

Annually, the path to the one-class Minnesota State High School League Ice Hockey Tournament in section 8 was blocked by a powerful Roseau team. Finally, in 1969, with Henry scoring sixty goals as a senior, the Warroad team qualified—albeit through the back door. Roseau once again won the section tournament, but the runners-up in sections 7 and 8 had a playoff game because there was not a representative in section 3. Warroad defeated Eveleth in double overtime as Henry rifled a shot into the net in the final second to earn the open spot. It was a personal highlight for Henry. "The state tournament was 'the Show.' Everyone wanted to go there. It took us five years to get there, but we finally did it with only two seniors and a great bantam team that joined us. The whole community came down to watch us."

Adding to the excitement was a fresh venue for the tournament: the new Metropolitan Sports Center in Bloomington, Minnesota. It is a tournament that lives in the memories of high school hockey fans more than four decades later. Tiny Warroad High School, with a student enrollment under 200 students, upset Minneapolis Southwest 4–3 in their first game. Paired against their northern rival Roseau in the semifinals, Warroad finally edged their antagonist 3–2. In both games, Henry scored the winning goal. His electrifying playmaking ability as a 6-foot, 180-pound skater won over the crowd.

Henry and the Warroad Warriors had captured the public's attention and affection with their storybook performances. Having played nearly every minute of every game, you would imagine that Henry would be incredibly fatigued, but he explains, "Remember, the periods then were only twelve minutes long. I played defense, and you could get moments of rest. The difficulty was that you didn't have a weight program or pay attention to your diet, so there would be some inconsistency in your performance—especially while trying to make adjustments to the noise and media attention."

Edina, a suburban school considered large and wealthy

Mike Antonvich
Greenway-Coleraine

Henry Boucha
Warroad

1969 MINNESOTA STATE HIGH SCHOOL LEAGUE ALL-TOURNAMENT TEAM MEMBERS (JEFF HALLETT AND ALAN HANGSLEBEN OF WARROAD WERE ALSO NAMED TO THE TEAM)
Photo courtesy of the Minnesota State High School League

compared to Warroad, would be their foe in the finals. During the game, with the team losing 4–2, Henry collapsed after a hard collision when he and an opponent raced for a puck in the corner. He was taken to a hospital and diagnosed with a concussion and ruptured eardrum; he would be hospitalized for three days. The scrappy Warroad team, buoyed by a crowd cheering their every move, made an astounding comeback to tie the game and force it into overtime before losing 5–4, an ice game for the ages.

Reflecting on his high school hockey career, Henry says, "Roseau always had a great group of players. My favorites, though, were Mike Antonovich of Greenway of Coleraine and Pokey (Steve) Traschel of Duluth Cathedral. You had to watch for them all the time because you really respected them."

Antonovich scored nearly two hundred goals in a long professional hockey career in the World Hockey Association (WHA) and NHL and served as a scout for the St. Louis Blues before returning to Coleraine and being elected mayor. "Henry was the best player I'd ever seen at our age level. He had the size and skating ability . . . that was what made him a great player. He was a big man at the time, but then, to me, everyone seemed big," laughs the 5-foot-8 Antonovich.

> *"Henry was the best player I'd ever seen at our age level. He had the size and skating ability . . . that was what made him a great player . . ."*

Steve "Pokey" Trachsel concurs. "We beat Warroad four to three when we were both seniors. Henry could skate better than anyone, and he was a tough, big guy. He only got bigger and better when I played against him when he was on the national team, and I played for University of Minnesota at Duluth [UMD]."

Following graduation, Henry passed on scholarship offers to UMD, the University of Minnesota, and Notre Dame. "I struggled a bit academically and would have had to improve my ACT scores," he states. Instead he joined the Winnipeg Jets junior hockey team and married his high school sweetheart in December of 1969. "I didn't realize it, but I was being scouted by the United States national hockey team. Murray Williamson [the coach] was recruiting players to represent US hockey to qualify out of Pool B and advance to the A bracket."

Working at Marvin Windows in Warroad during the off-season, Henry received a draft notice from the US Army in 1970. Although he acquired training as a military police officer, he was quickly given notice that he would be assigned to the national hockey team. "It was a godsend," Henry says of the moment. "Instead of going to Vietnam, I would play hockey and also develop my career." Stocked with many Minnesotans, including fellow Warroad resident Wally Olds, the team played many professional and top collegiate teams in their forty-seven-game schedule. The core group of players, counting leading scorer twenty-year-old Henry Boucha, would form the 1972 Olympic team under Williamson's direction. Critics had low expectations of the group as they headed to Sapporo, Japan.

"You must peak at the right time for the Olympics—including your mindset," Henry insists. Now cast as a center, Henry was paired with left wing Kevin Ahearn of Boston College and right wing Craig Sarner, a star at North St. Paul High School and the University of Minnesota. "All the lines were productive—ours was playing well," reports Henry. Following a vital 5–3 win over Switzerland to advance to the A pool, the line accounted for ten of the eighteen goals in final round play! The key victory was a stunning 5–1 win over the powerful Czech team, considered by most experts to be the only team that had a chance to defeat the dominant Soviet team. With another upset win, this time by a score of 4–1 over Finland (Henry scored one goal and had two assists), the surprising team was suddenly a medal contender. A 6–1 triumph over Poland, combined with Sweden's disarray and a Soviet win over the Czechs, cemented a silver medal for the young American team. Many people believe this amazing performance was a stepping stone to the successful strategy of the 1980 Miracle on Ice team.

HENRY BOUCHA WITH SILVER MEDAL AT HIS PARENTS' HOME IN 1973
Photo credit: Alice Boucha

Henry appreciates the exhilarating time and events. "It was a tremendous experience. I felt strong throughout the Olympics. We had a great crew—lots of camaraderie and practical jokes. Japan was beautiful, and the people were wonderful hosts." He also praises his linemates and other teammates. "Craig and Kevin really made things click. Tim Sheehy was an outstanding player, and

Lefty Curran was a great goaltender."

Ahearn remembers the time fondly too. "Henry was very talented and did great in the middle slot. We blended well. Everyone could motor. He was a quiet, strong, confident player . . . a great playmaker and good on face-offs too. Beating the Czechs was quite a thrill." Sarner chimes in saying, "Henry was an unbelievably gifted hockey player. He was a huge part of our success in Sapporo. He's a guy who made the game easy for you. He had quick hands, was strong, and a fierce competitor. The higher the stakes, the higher level he played. Nothing happens if you don't have the guy in the middle. That's critical."

The beneficiary of an early discharge from the army since the Vietnam War was winding down, Henry continued his hockey career for sixteen games as a member of the Detroit Red Wings, his favorite NHL team. As a youth he had won a trip to see the Red Wings play in an exhibition game in Winnipeg when he was a leader in candy sales. Star Gordie Howe played in that game, and his son, Mark, was a sixteen-year-old on the 1972 Olympic team with Henry. Now Henry, a second-round draft choice and sixteenth overall (there were fourteen teams in the league), could meet Gordie, a vice president with the Red Wings, in person. "He took me under his wing. We once visited a children's hospital and gave the kids Red Wings' memorabilia." In his first NHL game, Henry scored a goal.

The 1972–73 season results were mixed for Henry. He had a back injury midseason, split with his wife, and suffered from some depression. He was sent to a farm club in Norfolk, Virginia, for two weeks. "It got me motivated and jump-started my pro career," he says of the demotion. He returned to Detroit and was named the team's Rookie of the Year, scoring fourteen goals.

Although Henry had liked Red Wings coach Johnny Wilson, a coaching change the next year soured him on Detroit, and he felt blessed to be traded to his home state North Stars for Danny Grant before the 1974–75 season. His happiness proved to be short-lived.

Same venue, same player, tragic results.

HENRY BOUCHA IN NHL ACTION WITH THE DETROIT RED WINGS
Photo courtesy of the Detroit Red Wings

That's what happened to Henry Boucha on January 4, 1975, a mere six years after stirring fans at the Metropolitan Sports Center when starring for Warroad High School. Having scored 15 goals in the first 51 games of the season, Henry was having a good year and topping $100,000 in salary. In a physical game against the Boston Bruins, Henry was hit violently in the face with the butt end of a hockey stick by Dave Forbes. "It was devastating and affects me to this day," Henry says sadly. "It required thirty stitches, three surgeries, blew out my cheekbones, and I suffered double vision. It took me a long time to get over my resentment and anger." Forbes was suspended for ten games and charged with aggravated assault by Hennepin County. The nine-day trial was followed closely by the media and professional sports. It resulted in a hung jury and was declared a mistrial. A protracted civil suit was settled about five years later.

The next several years were a struggle for Henry. A comeback in hockey in the NHL and WHA was thwarted, and he retired from the sport at age twenty-five. A second marriage was rocky and would soon end in divorce. "I moved to Idaho and hunted, fished, drank, and partied too much," he admits. "I was a bit lost. I didn't have a sense of purpose until my daughter, Tara, called wanting to live with me—but she wanted me to return to Warroad." It was a positive spiritual and motivational reawakening for Henry.

> "I was a bit lost. I didn't have a sense of purpose until my daughter, Tara, called wanting to live with me—but she wanted me to return to Warroad." It was a positive spiritual and motivational reawakening for Henry.

Back in Warroad, Henry had a variety of occupations: real estate agent, working in Indian education through the public school for five years, and coaching various levels of hockey players for twenty years, including two sons, Henry and JP, who would later pursue junior hockey. More recently he moved to Anchorage, Alaska, for part of each year, originally to help with a US hockey diversity program. Henry then established a nonprofit called Kah-Bay-Kah-Nong (Ojibwe for "the trail leading west

Photo courtesy of the Detroit Red Wings

from Lake of the Woods," which became a common path for Native Americans heading into battle, or "War Road"). He has also authored a book on Ojibwe Native Americans. Henry was inducted into the United States Hockey Hall of Fame in 1995, the first Native American so honored. He is rated fifth in the *Minneapolis Star Tribune's* ranking of the top one hundred all-time Minnesota high school hockey players on its Minnesota Hockey Hub website.

As a father of four children and grandfather to five, Henry knows that his life has been marked "by deep canyons and mountain peaks. I am happy to have made it through it all. I like to help people on their journeys."

Henry Boucha has learned he has everything he needs to survive and exist as a person.

MATT SCHNOBRICH AND MICAH BOYD
Photo credit: Shivani Parmer, www.shivspix.com

MICAH BOYD, MATT SCHNOBRICH

Same Origin, Different Paths, Same Destination

ST. PAUL IS THE CITY MICAH BOYD AND MATT SCHNO-brich both call home. Their paths had many similarities, which then diverged and finally dovetailed together when they rowed in the 2008 Olympics in Beijing, China. They were one seat apart in the eights, a rowing event with each member using one oar as a sweep, with a coxswain.

Micah, born in 1982, grew up in the St. Anthony Park neighborhood of St. Paul where he was, in his words, a "fat, uncoordinated kid." At the urging of his identical twin brother, Anders, he decided to give rowing a try in 1997 as a sophomore at St. Paul Central High School. "Rowing is a very inclusive sport—it had no cuts. You can work hard and move up the performance ladder so quickly. It's what happened to me." They rowed at the Minnesota Boat Club on Raspberry Island in St. Paul. To Micah's surprise, he experienced some quick success being part of the winning four-man rowing team at a junior race in Thunder Bay, Ontario. Nevertheless, it was not love at first sight with the sport. Remembering the race, he says with a grimace, "It was the most intense pain I'd ever felt. It was absolutely awful."

Less than five miles away, Matt Schnobrich, born in 1978, was growing up in the shadow of the campus of St. Catherine University in the Highland Park neighborhood. While he felt he was on the smaller side at 5 feet 11 inches tall and 160 pounds, he participated in soccer and cross country skiing at St. Thomas Academy. His nordic ski coach and physics teacher, Mark Westlake, cited by Matt as an influential person in his life, recognized his athleticism and willingness to reach his full potential. "Matt was a super-hard worker and senior captain who provided great leadership. At nordic sections, he broke his pole and began using both arms to pull on one pole. Despite the lack of equipment he placed second and the team qualified for state. He is a genuinely nice guy who now gives back to the school." Following a dramatic growth spurt after he graduated from high school, Matt received encouragement to try rowing from Matt Rose, a resident assistant in his dormitory at St. John's University in Collegeville, Minnesota, "because he was tall." Since the labs in his science courses interfered with the possibility of trying soccer, he decided to try the college's club sport on a lark.

Meanwhile, Micah enrolled at a rowing powerhouse, the University of Wisconsin (UW); he is convinced that he was accepted in part because of the background he had in the sport. It is the only Big 10 school that has men's rowing as a varsity sport, but Micah reports that hundreds were invited to try out for the team. Coaches sent hundreds of students who had participated in high school sports an invitation to attend an informational meeting on rowing. "About three hundred might attend the meeting, perhaps a hundred would come for the first practice, and maybe fifty would still be there after the first week," Micah smiles. Invitees soon learned what a grueling sport rowing could be with eight to ten practices per week. His freshman team placed fifth nationally, and as a varsity member and junior co-captain on the 2002–2003 team, the varsity eight—which usually races two kilometers—won the prestigious Eastern Men's Sprints for the first time in more than fifty years and rowed to a runner-up finish at the Intercollegiate Rowing Association Championships. While at Wisconsin, Micah became known for wearing a Minnesota Twins hat with the M script while competing. And despite being on a Badger varsity team, he remained a Gophers fan! A favorite memory of his senior year was reuniting with Anders, who was also attending UW, on the varsity eight.

The atmosphere was much more relaxing for Matt rowing on

MICAH, FRONT, AND ANDERS BOYD, HEAD OF IOWA RACE, 2003
Photo courtesy of Micah Boyd family

pastoral Lake Sagatagan at St. John's. He was comfortable at the college, which his father and many of his relations had attended. The team had no coach, and the rowers primarily seemed to enjoy the exercise and each other's company. Gradually, the informal group improved and competed against formidable club teams from Notre Dame and Michigan. But the rowing seed was firmly planted in Matt's mind to take the sport a bit further based on coaching and encouragement received from others at the Minneapolis Rowing Club during summer breaks.

In 2004, with a degree in wildlife ecology from UW, Micah migrated east after serving as an assistant freshman coach at UW for one year and began rowing at Penn Athletic Club (Penn AC) while working part-time. At 6 feet 3 inches and 210 pounds, Micah became a two-time member of the national rowing team and was a member of the 2005 bronze medal–winning crew at the World Rowing Championships. Achievements continued to accumulate for Micah, culminating with him being named US Rowing's Male Athlete of the Year in 2008. Micah Boyd was ready to compete for a spot on the Olympic rowing team.

MICAH BOYD, TEAM CAPTAIN, WITH JABLONIC CUP IN 2003 WIN OVER BOSTON UNIVERSITY
Photo credit: UW Athletic Communications

Although he graduated from college three years earlier than his fellow St. Paulite, Matt, now 6 feet 5 inches and 205 pounds, remained in his home state, working for Cargill for one year and then enrolling in graduate school at the University of Minnesota to become an environmental engineer. During that time he was still rowing four to five times per week at the Minneapolis Rowing Club before he decided to head east too in 2004. Finding a job in Philadelphia with Arcadis as an environmental engineer, Matt also joined the Penn AC and improved rapidly through more intense training and thirteen practices per week, highlighted by a victory in the pairs at the National Team trials in 2005 with Pat O'Dunne. That victory launched him onto the national team for the next four years. More victories in the pairs followed, along with being a member of the eights that won the 2006 and 2007 Head of the Charles in Boston. In 2007, Matt and Beau Hoopman, a teammate of Micah's at UW, did not lose a pairs race. "Things were really clicking," he reports. Matt Schnobrich was equally ready to compete for a spot on the

Olympic rowing team.

The lengthy, physically exhausting, and mentally draining trials for the rowing team took place over four years with the intensity building as the 2008 Olympics approached, first at Clemson University on Lake Hartwell in South Carolina, then with the finalists on Lake Mercer in West Windsor, New Jersey. The coach was hard-driving Mike Teti, a veteran of three Olympics and a bronze medal winner as a member of the eights in 1988. Teti lavishes praise on the Minnesotans. "In some ways they were very similar; in other ways they were quite different. Micah and Matt were both good, respectful Midwest guys. They blended in well with the other guys; everyone liked them. They had good values. They were not a surprise to make the team. The boat got better with them aboard."

> *"In some ways they were very similar; in other ways they were quite different. Micah and Matt were both good, respectful Midwest guys. They blended in well with the other guys; everyone liked them. They had good values. They were not a surprise to make the team. The boat got better with them aboard."*

Micah felt uncertain about his status. Constantly being paired with different rowers and never knowing how many pieces (races) they would be doing in practice each day, Micah did not originally make the most select group. He persevered, however, and later was always in a boat that performed well and had extremely high scores in cardiovascular tests. Coach Teti remarks, "Micah is a tough guy. He has no fear. He is a relentless competitor who got the best from what he had. He became part of our power section in the middle of the boat."

Matt felt more confident. Josh Inman and Matt won the pairs trial and were guaranteed that spot. They accepted the place with the understanding that they could continue in the trials with the possibility of being selected for the eights team. Both continued to row well, and the time came when Coach Teti called their names as selected members of the eights, which they quickly accepted, relinquishing their place as qualifiers for the pairs. Teti declares, "Matt is cerebral in his approach to rowing. Technically, he is very good, and he got in good shape in a hurry at training camp."

Micah and Matt, rowers from the same city in the same state, had never teamed together until the Olympic Trials. And now, they were not only teammates, but one seat apart on the long 18.5 meter (60-plus feet) boat. Matt would take the bow position in the two seat looking at Micah's back in the three seat (rowers have their backs to the finish line).

Micah was to be a workhorse. He summarized his skills this way: "I have a nervous energy that I try to harness as a strength. I believe I have a strong aerobic base. I probably am more mentally tough than I am physically gifted."

Matt was comfortable in the more technical bow position. He believes his responsibility was "to be a stabilizing factor because balance is key. I sat bow almost exclusively while on the national team. I enjoyed it and was accustomed to that place."

Canada was a known entity and the favorite to win the eights at Shunyi Rowing Park, an hour's drive from Beijing, in the 2008 Olympics. Great Britain was another force to be reckoned with at the Olympics. "We had not been competing internationally," relates Matt, "but we felt we were quick and confident after posting some of the fastest times ever on Lake Carnegie at Princeton. The group came together as a boat about three weeks before the Olympic Games and gained extra speed. We wanted to ascend throughout the races at the Olympics."

Micah, who had worn his trademark Minnesota Twins' hats throughout college, national regattas, and the trials, would not be allowed to wear it in the Olympic Games since all team members' apparel must be uniform. He was appreciative of the opportunity to participate at the highest level of the sport, though. "To be part of the eights—the most prestigious rowing event—in the most renowned sports game of the world is a highlight."

" To be part of the eights—the most prestigious rowing event—in the most renowned sports game of the world is a highlight."

In the first heat at the 2008 Olympics, the eights team finished second to Great

Britain and was relegated to the repêchage, a second opportunity to advance to the finals. The team rowed strongly and claimed first place to join Great Britain, Canada, and three other teams for the finals.

Matt fondly recalls almost every second of the nearly eighteen minutes (total time for three heats) that he rowed in the Olympics. "It was not a great start," he admits of the finals, where they began in last place, "but our strategy was to pour it on in the final thousand meters." They did exactly that and were edged out of second place by Great Britain by less than one-fourth of a second. The men originally from St. Paul, who took different routes, then joined together near Beijing, had won a bronze medal.

MATT SCHNOBRICH WITH BRONZE MEDAL AT THE 2008 OLYMPICS IN BEIJING, CHINA
Photo courtesy of Matt Schnobrich

The rowers savored the opportunity to view many of the Olympic events since their competition ended after the first week. Micah and Matt both remarked on the immense size of Dwight Howard, the basketball star who was one of the few professional athletes to live in the Olympic Village. "The guy must have been five feet wide!" exclaims Matt. Another Olympic memory is witnessing sprint sensation Usain Bolt and the Jamaican 4 x 100 meter relay team slam down cheeseburgers two hours before the Olympic relay final.

Both Micah and Matt married women in the biological sciences field. Micah is married to Jo, a physician. They have two children and live in Chapel Hill, North Carolina, where he now serves as coach of the men's club rowing team at the University of North Carolina. Matt is married to Maria Raymond, a Division I All-American rower from Brown University (her father, Peter, was a two-time Olympic rower) who is an equine veterinarian. They live in Lexington, Kentucky, with their sons, Macpherson and Patrick, where Matt continues to work as an environmental engineer for Arcadis.

Both Micah and Matt proudly recall their time at the 2008 Summer Olympics in China. "I was most impressed with people who appreciate the true Olympic experience," Micah says. "The most powerful experience—the closest to my heart—was to represent our country at a time when people from all corners of the world come together," echoes Matt. "It's a shared experience where you are a part of something much bigger."

MATT SCHNOBRICH FISHING WITH OLDEST SON, MACPHERSON, ON POTATO LAKE (NORTH OF PARK RAPIDS, MINNESOTA), JULY 2014
Photo courtesy of Matt Schnobrich family

"It's a shared experience where you are a part of something much bigger."

It appears that the rowers from St. Paul had the same destination in more than one way.

JESSIE DIGGINS CAPTURES THE SILVER MEDAL AT THE 2015 WORLD
CHAMPIONSHIPS 10-KILOMETER INDIVIDUAL EVENT ON FEBRUARY 24,
2015, IN FALUN, SWEDEN
Photo credit: ©Hendrik Schmidt/Corbis Images

JESSIE DIGGINS

It Takes a Village

JESSIE DIGGINS BELIEVES IN COMMUNITY, WHETHER it is a family, school, sport, city, region, state, or nation. Starting with the family community, Jessie is the daughter of Clay and Deborah Diggins of Afton, Minnesota, a picturesque area along the St. Croix River on the eastern edge of the state. Born in 1991, she and her sister, Mackenzie, a theater student, are part of an active family that loves to camp, canoe, swim, and cross country ski. She remembers being in her father's backpack as a toddler and calling out, "Faster, Daddy, faster!" as he would ski along the cross country trails.

Another community that Jessie has fond memories of is the Minnesota Youth Ski League—especially when the group shared hot chocolate after skiing. Her parents led a club of the ski league that skied at Willow River State Park near Hudson, Wisconsin. "I loved the people I met in sports," she declares. It showed as a youth and continued into her years at Stillwater High School. Jessie played soccer, participated in dance, tried all of the events except discus in high school track and field, and swam a variety of races for the Stillwater Ponies' swim team.

CLAY AND DEB DIGGINS WITH JESSIE IN A BACKPACK, 1999
Photo courtesy of Clay and Deb Diggins

The sport of cross country skiing was where Jessie excelled, though, and she continues to have greater success than any other woman nordic skier from the state of Minnesota. The exuberant athlete began competing in the sport at Stillwater in seventh grade as part of the junior varsity team until a varsity member suddenly got sick on the day of the conference meet. Jessie was chosen to replace her and did very well—finishing second on the team. "All of my teammates were so good to me. They taught me how to warm up and helped me feel comfortable," she says of the team community.

The times of two styles of nordic skiing, classic and freestyle (skating), are combined to determine the place of the skier at the high school state meet, so it is important for a skier to become proficient in both techniques. In 2006, Jessie did exactly that and qualified as an individual for the state meet as an eighth grader and placed thirty-seventh overall despite suffering from a case of food poisoning. "The day before the state meet Jessie began vomiting due to mango food poisoning and continued vomiting throughout the night," her mother says, remembering the call she received from Jessie's coaches. "She staggered around the next morning and announced, 'I can ski.'" The Stillwater nordic team and Jessie only got better as the team took runner-up honors the following year when Jessie won with an impressive time of 34 minutes 39.2 seconds (34:39.2). In 2008, her sophomore year, everyone celebrated championships as the Ponies won the state team trophy and Jessie repeated as the individual champion by a comfortable margin of one and a half minutes ahead of the second-place finisher.

Stillwater coach Kris Hansen, a huge and positive influence on Jessie according to the Diggins family, states that Jessie "is strong, coordinated, and has exceptional cardiovascular capacity. But while these physical strengths are important, what sets Jessie apart is her attitude. Jessie sees obstacles as a challenge for her to master, opportunities to push herself harder. Jessie never makes excuses." For part of the 2008–09 season, Jessie made the difficult decision to compete at the Junior National Championships with "girls from all over the country." It would become a lifestyle for the future.

Returning to the Stillwater High School nordic team for her senior year, Jessie and the team capped off a stellar season. The team won the championship and Jessie was victorious in a rousing sprint to the finish with Annie Hart of St. Paul Academy and Summit. "It was so close," Jessie says of the end, where the competitors exchanged the lead. Jessie edged Hart by 1.5 seconds. "It's always good for the sport when it stirs such excitement." Hart would attend Dartmouth College and is now a Stratton Mountain School T2 club team member with Jessie. "It's fun to have Minnesotans on the team," Jessie says of sharing another bond with Hart.

Following high school graduation in 2010, Jessie decided to delay entering college and a full academic scholarship offer at Northern Michigan University and focus on nordic skiing. "It was a tough decision—kind of scary—but I'll only be able to train at this level for a certain number of years. I wanted to give it my best shot." Deb Diggins concurs and provides this perspective from a parent's point of view: "It was one of the toughest decisions we had to make. We signed on as parents if the scholarship would be deferred one year—it had to be in writing." Jessie experienced immediate success and made the B team, but her personal expenses were not funded by the

US Ski Team. Her home and regional communities helped bridge that gap by hosting fundraisers.

Remarkable stories about Jessie's effort and competitiveness flow from those who have witnessed her in action. High school coach Hansen states that the freestyle sprint at the 2011 US National Championships in Maine is one she enjoys recalling. "The sprint is a short, high-energy race. Coming down the final stretch, Jessie was in the lead. She got a bit ahead of herself sprinting toward the finish line and tripped herself on her own pole. She fell to her knees and the field moved past her. Lots and lots of skiers would have given up at that moment. Jessie jumped to her feet and restarted her charge to the finish line. She dug in as hard as she could, repassed the field of competitors to become the national champion." Jessie's heroics didn't end there.

Later that year, at age nineteen, Jessie made a memorable debut in the 2011 World Championship in Oslo, Norway. "It was really an eye-opening experience. Tabloids follow the sport; up to fifty thousand fans are there. People were chanting my name! It's the place to be—the birthplace of the sport." Nicknamed "Sparkle Chipmunk" by her national teammates for her habit of adding glitter to face painting on her cheeks before competition, Jessie won a gold medal in the team sprint relay with Kikkan Randall in Quebec City, Canada, in 2012. Jessie later achieved her first individual podium finish in 2014 in the skate sprint with a silver medal at the Under 23 Nordic World Championships.

The training regimen is demanding. Jessie, 5 feet 4 inches tall, often trains for up to five hours per day with skiing, lifting weights, running, and other conditioning—not counting the stretching, psychological aspect, and driving time. "Training is a twenty-four-seven job," states Jessie. "Everything affects you. You have to eat healthy and get enough sleep. It's an endurance event—not just a skills event." The training takes place from May to November at different locations for national team members. Then they race from November through March. "Travel on the World Cup circuit is like a traveling circus," she says about the experience, which is a mixture of

JESSIE DIGGINS COMPETING FOR STILLWATER HIGH SCHOOL
Photo credit: Stuart Groskreutz/Stillwater Gazette

excitement and exhaustion. "But it's also a cool way to see the world."

A personal and team highlight came in the 2013 World Championships in Val di Fiemme, Italy, when Jessie and Randall, a four-time Olympian and legend in women's nordic skiing, paired up in the team sprint (in this event each team member races three alternating laps). Jessie held a slight lead when disaster struck. "On my final lap, a competitor stepped on my pole and I lost it. I swung empty-handed until a coach running along the course later handed me a men's classic pole. The poles were different lengths, but I gritted my teeth and gave it my best." Randall describes the mishap from the perspective of a proud teammate. "Jessie was surging up the hill when the skier behind her stepped on her pole and it was pulled out of her grasp. She didn't lose any speed; in fact, she even accelerated and tagged me with a two-second lead." Randall increased the lead and crossed the finish line seven seconds ahead of the Swedish team. "We looked at each other in disbelief. It was a special moment when we won the first United States gold medal in women's nordic skiing at a World Championship."

Jessie's father, Clay, summarizes the order of the nordic ski circuit this way: "The World Cup is every year, the World Championships are every other year, and the Olympics punctuate an athlete's career." And the 2014 Olympics were on the horizon. The nordic ski team is picked based on a point system accumulated over the past year of races. Since every course is different and snow conditions vary, the selection process takes a lot into account. All seven members of the women's national team made the Olympic team. At age twenty-two, Jessie Diggins was the youngest team member going to Sochi, Russia.

While in Sochi, "I had my room decorated with posters and cards from home," Jessie says with a mixture of pride and gratitude. "It was really cool that I have such

JESSIE DIGGINS AND KIKKAN RANDALL WITH THEIR WOMEN'S CROSS COUNTRY TEAM SPRINT GOLD MEDALS AT THE NORDIC SKI WORLD CHAMPIONSHIP IN VAL DI FIEMMIE, ITALY, ON FEBRUARY 24, 2013
Photo credit: ©Yves Herman/Corbis Images

a loyal support base in Minnesota and Wisconsin."

Despite being exhausted and being surrounded by a throng of spectators, Jessie once again detected support as she raced to an impressive eighth-place finish out of sixty-one competitors in the 15-kilometer skiathlon, a race combining classic and skating styles. "On the final hill, I heard my parents cheering me on—that was so cool!" Other events were not as successful, but inspire Jessie for

JESSIE IS KNOWN FOR WRITING INSPIRATIONAL MESSAGES ON SIGNED POSTERS
Photo credit: Stuart Groskreutz/Stillwater Gazette

the future. She also placed fortieth in the 30-kilometer race, captured thirteenth in the sprint, and ninth place for the team in the 4 x 5 kilometer relay that Jessie anchored. Nevertheless, Jessie reports, "We held our heads up high—we gave it one hundred percent."

Coach Jason Cork of the United States Skiing Team offers this information about the sport and Jessie: "Cross country skiing requires aerobic endurance and muscular strength, and Jessie obviously has them. The thing that makes her even better is that she is so tough. Her future looks pretty bright. She's so young—she could do three more Olympics."

In February 2015 at Falun, Sweden, Jessie made history in US women's cross country skiing by becoming the first woman to win an individual medal in a long-distance race at the FIS Nordic World Ski Championships. Her 10-kilometer freestyle race time of 25:49.8 in snowy and windy conditions catapulted her to a silver medal. Adding to the celebration, teammate Caitlin Compton Gregg, of Minneapolis, placed third. Two American women teammates standing on the podium at a world cross country championship truly caught the attention of the skiing world.

Jessie brims with optimism and a cheerful spirit. "My coaches have been incredible. My sister has been my biggest fan. My role models are my teammates. There are a lot of people responsible for me being an Olympian. It takes a village . . ."

Lots of communities, small and large, consider Jessie Diggins a credit to them too.

Skating

OFFICIAL MAGAZINE OF UNITED STATES FIGURE SKATING ASSOCIATION

VOL. 28, NO. 5

MARCH 1951

JANET GERHAUSER AND JOHN NIGHTINGALE APPEARED ON THE COVER OF SKATING MAGAZINE, MARCH 1951

Photo credit: U.S. Figure Skating

JANET GERHAUSER AND JOHN NIGHTINGALE

Pair's Friendship Still Skating Along Famously

A GIRL FROM MINNEAPOLIS AND A BOY FROM ST. Paul bridged the distance across the Mississippi River that separated the two in the 1940s to forge a lifetime friendship that included many memorable trips together, including one to Oslo, Norway, where they performed as young adults in figure skating pairs at the 1952 Winter Olympics.

Janet Gerhauser, the girl, began figure skating at five years old at Lynnhurst Park three blocks south of Lake Harriet in Minneapolis. John Nightingale, the boy, was recovering from scarlet fever at his home in the Macalester-Groveland neighborhood of St. Paul when an aunt gave him a pair of black skates with yellow laces at age ten.

More than six decades after their Olympic appearance, Janet and John still speak in warm, glowing terms of their skating partnership and friendship. "John was like a brother to me. He is just the nicest guy you could imagine. He was funny, yet hardworking," Janet says, complimenting the skating partner she met at age thirteen. John has equally high praise for Janet, saying, "She was the ideal pair partner. We had complete cooperation—we never argued or fought. She's a nice person all around and a very special friend."

Born in 1932, Janet remembers her father having speedskates, but her Mississippi-native mother never

JANET GERHAUSER WITH HER FATHER, FRANK, AT WILLIAMS ARENA IN MINNEAPOLIS
Photo courtesy of Janet Gerhauser Carpenter

went near the ice. She and her sister Cokey took group lessons through the Figure Skating Club of Minneapolis at the old Portland Avenue rink and at the Minneapolis Arena in South Minneapolis (just east of Lake Calhoun on Dupont Avenue) from ages seven to nine. Janet then advanced to private lessons through the St. Paul Figure Skating Club (SPFSC) located at the St. Paul Auditorium, one of the few places in the country that had summer ice in the 1940s. "I wore boots on Oberhamer Skates made in St. Paul," Janet recalls. "They were a top customized bootmaker that provided boots all over the country." The blades were furnished by Olympiad or Strauss Skates, similarly respected manufacturers also located in St. Paul. Apparel supplied by Minneapolis Knitting Works called Kumfortites, advertised as stylish, comfortable, and warm tights, was another local article contributing to her outfit. Janet took lessons for a brief time from Minnesota's first two figure skating Olympians, Margaret Bennett (women's single, 1932) and Robin Lee (men's single, 1936). At the SPFSC, she watched a future World Championship qualifier, Janette Ahrens. "I looked up to her and aspired to be like her," says Janet humbly.

John's introduction to figure skating resulted in a scar above an eyebrow that is still visible. He was born in 1928 and raised one block north of St. Catherine University in St. Paul. Due to health concerns from scarlet fever, a doctor had recommended that John not have too much physical contact and limit his exertion. Maybe figure skating would provide exercise while still fulfilling the doctor's suggestion. More familiar with ice hockey skates, John tripped during his first attempt on a nearby rink at Macalester College, and the fall resulted in a bloody gash. His mother never dreamed that he would continue the sport. He did though, and enjoyed the activity so much that a friendly neighbor named Betty Schalow (she later became a star soloist for more than ten years with the Ice Follies) asked John's parents if she could take him to the St. Paul Figure Skating Club. John was

ROBIN LEE, A 1936 OLYMPIC FIGURE SKATER, SITS BETWEEN JOHN NIGHTINGALE AND JANET GERHAUSER AT WILLIAMS ARENA IN MINNEAPOLIS
Photo credit: Virginia Murphy

awestruck. "I was amazed at the talent of the skaters." Staying on the periphery of the rink, he would imitate the other skaters. The next year he became a member of the club and began to take an occasional lesson. John could not get enough of his new-found sport. He placed third in the novice division at the Midwestern Championships and earned second place in junior pairs with partner Joan Erickson in 1945—and the pair repeated the accomplishment the next year. A memorable time at a unique ice skating event would trigger Janet and John becoming a pair.

"We skated to live music. Stanley Judson produced and choreographed our performances. He was exceptional . . . ahead of his time."

Both figure skaters fondly remember the summer St. Paul Pops concert series. Beginning in 1945, the concerts were inexpensive entertainment for the public in a cooled environment. Performed by the seventy-piece Minneapolis Symphony (forerunner to the Minnesota Orchestra), concerts were scheduled three nights per week for six weeks at the St. Paul Auditorium. Janet learned to skate all three disci-plines: fours, pairs, and singles. "We skated to live music. Stanley Judson produced and choreographed our performances. He was exceptional . . . ahead of his time. The skating was interspersed with musical pieces. It was wonderful training ground since we got used to performing in front of crowds," says Janet. John echoes this sentiment: "The Pops Concerts gave us a lot of confidence and were a wonderful opportunity to perform."

ST. PAUL FIGURE SKATING CLUB WITH THE HARNED TROPHY AWARDED TO THE CLUB FOR THE MOST POINTS SCORED AT NATIONALS IN 1947; (LEFT TO RIGHT) MARLYN AND MARILYN THOMSEN, JOHN LETTENGARVER, JANETTE "DEE DEE" AHRENS, HARRIET SUTTON, JANET GERHAUSER, AND JOHN NIGHTINGALE
Photo credit: St. Paul Pioneer Press

John goes on to say, "In 1947 Janet and I formed the St. Paul Four with the Thomsens, brother-sister twins named Marlyn and Marilyn [also from the SPFSC]. That was the beginning of everything." The fours, or two mixed pairs, is not an Olympic event, but was popular at the midway point of the twentieth century. The foursome won the national fours championship in Berkeley, California, not only that year, but defended the title in 1948 and 1950 and won the North American championship in 1949. "It was great fun," recalls Janet. "We were invited to carnivals all over the country. It also offered instant exposure."

Only entering high school, Janet was already touring the United States for competitions and amateur figure skating club shows. To practice in Minnesota, her father, Frank, gave her a ride to the Minneapolis Arena to skate before school. She then took a streetcar to Washburn High School to attend classes and sometimes traveled a second time on a streetcar after school to the St. Paul Auditorium. "The principal, Leonard Fleenor, recognized the opportunity and need for girls to participate in sports and allowed a flexible class schedule for me," Janet says gratefully. "Patty Berg graduated from Washburn in 1937, and she may have blazed a path." In 1950, Janet joined the famous golfer as an alumna—and later as an inducted Washburn Hall of Fame member (2010). For ten years, Janet took ballet lessons from Judson at a St. Paul studio. Additionally, she served on the school's student council and was the National Honor Society secretary. She would later enroll at the University of Minnesota (U of M) following graduation.

Nearly four years older, John had graduated from Cretin High School, then a military school, in 1947. He attended St. Thomas College (now University) with his sights set on a preengineering program while also participating in the Reserve Officer Training Corps (ROTC) program. He decided to transfer to the U of M one year later since Williams Arena, an on-campus basketball and ice hockey facility, offered more skating opportunities. Continuing his affiliation with the ROTC program while also balancing a job, John switched to less-demanding coursework, pursuing a major in physical

BANNERS HANGING AT THE ST. PAUL FIGURE SKATING CLUB FEATURING THE CLUB'S NATIONAL CHAMPIONS

education.

The Minnesotans won the national junior pairs figure skating title in 1950 and had immediate success, claiming silver medals in the 1951 North American Championships behind Peter and Karol Kennedy, a brother-sister pair from the state of Washington, the reigning world champions. With more practice time necessary to compete at the elite level, Janet took leave of her studies at the U of M during the winter quarters, and John took a minimal class load that still permitted him to retain his ROTC status. They trained in Colorado during the summers of 1950 and 1951 under the tutelage of Eugene Turner. The pair also performed between periods at U of M ice hockey games in exchange for free and, generally, unlimited ice time as they struggled to coordinate practice schedules. Due to their finish at the nationals, Janet and John were invited to the 1951 World Figure Skating Championships. Janet says they were "pleased" with their performance, and John touts it as "a big boost for us" when describing their eighth-place finish in Milan, Italy.

"Our goal was to skate our best," reminisces Janet. "We were just so thrilled to be there. We were not nervous, actually confident.

In the US Figure Skating Championships of 1952, the Kennedys again captured first place, and nineteen-year-old Janet Gerhauser and twenty-three-year-old John Nightingale claimed second place and would be skating at the Winter Olympics in Oslo, Norway. As often happened at the time, their parents would not be able to afford the transatlantic expenses and would not see them perform. In fact, John's father only saw him compete once outside the Twin Cities—in Rochester, Minnesota!

Nevertheless, the enthusiastic pair was excited to travel and compete on the world stage. Dick Button, now a famed skating television analyst, was the featured figure skater as a returning Olympic gold medalist. Tenley Albright, a female skater in the singles, had suffered a polio attack as a child. She also had star power and would win a silver medal and capture a gold medal in 1956. It is astonishing to know that there were only thirteen women on the 1952 US Winter Olympic team representing two sports, figure skating and skiing. Bislett Stadium served as an outdoor stage for figure skating and speedskating, and the figure skating competition consisted of a single free skate program. Janet describes the planned five-minute program: "It was a balance of spins separately and together, single jumps, some lifts, and footwork in unison. There were no throws—that would have been considered too theatrical at the time." The events were held in the center of the large oval speedskating track—a long distance from the crowd. The rink did not have boards, only a snowpack to define the boundaries. The figure skating events were scheduled for the evening, a time when the winds calmed.

"Our goal was to skate our best," reminisces Janet. "We were just so thrilled to be there. We were not nervous, actually confident. We were very pleased to finish sixth—it was a great achievement." John agrees, saying, "We were happy to be there and did well. My job was to show her off—and with her good looks and talent, it was easy!" The pair had ascended two spots during the brief time since the 1951 World Championships.

> *"None of us have ever seen the pair skate better. It was their best effort at the crucial time and they never faltered for an instant. A grand job by a hardworking pair of wonderful kids."*

A treasured report filed by team manager Ted Patterson reads: "None of us have ever seen the pair skate better. It was their best effort at the crucial time and they never faltered for an instant. A grand job by a hardworking pair of wonderful kids."

Their time was limited in Oslo due to a commitment to skate at the 1952 World Championships, hosted in Paris, France. They were not able to stay for the closing ceremonies, but they have many memories. Janet has a meticulously organized scrapbook that holds many souvenirs, newspaper articles, pictures, and programs, which serves as a wonderful record of the marvelous experience. It has many articles about Olympic teammates Peter and Karol Kennedy winning a silver medal in the figure skating pairs. John reports watching Dick Button, saying, "He was heads above everyone else." John was thrilled to be seated on the bench with the ice hockey team for one of their games, but wary of the crowd expressing their displeasure with the physical style the Americans played. An enchanting event occurred when some teammates and John went to a Norwegian school and watched the kids rush to their skis after school and zip through a narrow lane downhill and homeward. It was their transportation home and miraculously conducted without an accident!

Still appreciating their showing at the Olympics, the relaxed pair moved up another notch to fifth place at the competition in Paris. They went on an exhibition tour with other figure skaters around Europe and continued to enjoy their time together. Medalist Peter

STEPHEN, JOHN, AND GREGORY NIGHTINGALE CELEBRATE WITH HELEN AND JOHN ON THEIR 60TH WEDDING ANNIVERSARY IN 2012
Photo credit: Mary Kerr-Grant

Kennedy cherished the time too saying, "John and Janet were fun to be around. They were nice, unassuming people. Janet became my sister's best friend as we toured. They carried themselves so well."

The pace did not slacken for John Nightingale. In September of 1952 he went to St. Louis, Missouri, for the first time in his life. He traveled there to marry Helen Geekie (with Janet as a bridesmaid), an accomplished figure skater who finished fourth at the Olympic Trials but did not attend the games in Oslo because alternates were required to pay their own expenses. John then continued in the ROTC program and—with Helen—taught figure skating lessons at Ann Arbor, Michigan, while also being trained in radio intelligence and taking classes in communications. He became a commissioned officer for the US Army in 1954, and his first duty assignment was at a base in the state's Upper Peninsula near Sault Ste. Marie. It was the start of a twenty-year military career in air defense artillery and public affairs that included stops in Germany, Belgium, Korea, France, and Vietnam, as well as numerous assignments around the United States. During his military service time, John and Helen had three sons: John, Stephen, and Greg. None of the boys pursued figure skating, but Greg was an excellent hockey player who learned the basic skills of the sport when his father was stationed in Minnesota.

Returning to a more subdued pace after the tour, Janet Gerhauser resumed her studies at the U of M. She retired from competitive figure skating and began coaching figure skaters, losing her amateur status since coaches were considered professionals in the sport. Still able to graduate in four years, Janet earned a degree in sociology and married her college boyfriend, Don Griffiths, in 1955. The couple had four children: Kim, Dale (died of spina bifida at six months old), Jill, and Guy. While raising the children, Janet refrained from coaching, regained her amateur status, and was encouraged to consider judging in the early 1960s. There is no financial compensation for figure skating judges. "The appeal was to stay involved with the sport and get in touch with old friends," she comments. The new viewpoint has led Janet to another fascinating career in the same sport. Janet advanced in the judging levels to the degree where she was judging national champion-

SKATING'S MANY FORMS: JANET GERHAUSER CARPENTER WITH GRANDDAUGHTERS (LEFT TO RIGHT) SY LI GRIFFITHS (FIGURE SKATING), SEAN DALA (HOCKEY), AND JIA GRIFFITHS (SPEEDSKATING) AT THE MINNEAPOLIS DEPOT RINK IN 2010
Photo credit: Jill Griffiths

ships. In 1984 Janet was named team leader of the US Olympic figure skating team competing at Sarajevo, Yugoslavia. "It was a very satisfying experience," relates Janet. "You are a support system and advocate for the members."

In 1988 Janet was selected as one of the four US figure skating judges for the Olympics in Calgary, Canada. The men's figure skating championship was billed as "The Battle of the Brians," referring to American Brian Boitano and Canadian Brian Orser, the World Champion. With a sensational free skating performance, Boitano edged Orser to win the gold medal. Janet is inclined to agree with the final outcome. To her surprise, Janet was named as an Olympic judge again in 2002, her final year of eligibility as an international judge since they face mandatory retirement from judging at age seventy. Twice an Olympic judge, sixteen times a national judge, and a judge countless times at other levels, Janet still fields requests to judge despite being over eighty years old. Obviously she is respected throughout the realm of figure skating.

Following retirement from the military with the rank of lieutenant colonel, a career that ended at a base in Duluth, Minnesota, John and Helen moved to the St. Louis area in 1974. They started a thirty-five-year career teaching figure skating lessons, primarily at Creve Coeur Figure Skating Club. Among the students they had was Lea Ann Miller, a 1984 Olympian. John also worked in security administration for Hussmann Corporation, an international refrigeration company for twelve years.

Janet and Don Griffiths had divorced by the time their children were adults. She then married Bob Allen, who died in 1998. Besides being named a figure skating judge for the Olympics in 2002, the year proved to be notable in her personal life when she married longtime friend Norm Carpenter, whom she had served with on a YMCA board. She now goes by the name Janet Gerhauser Carpenter.

Along with her supportive children and scores of other well-wishers, John and Helen Nightingale were present at Janet's 2008 induction ceremony (she was officially named in 2007) to the US Figure Skating Hall of Fame in St. Paul to congratulate her. The bonds of friendship didn't miss a glide.

**KARA (GRGAS-WHEELER) GOUCHER WINS THE 2000 NCAA
DIVISION I CROSS COUNTRY CHAMPIONSHIP**
Photo courtesy of CU Athletics

KARA GOUCHER

Continental Competitor Calls Minnesota Home

"I FEEL REALLY LUCKY THAT I GREW UP IN MINNE-
sota. When I say, 'I am going home,' I mean Minnesota," says elite
long-distance runner and two-time Olympian Kara (Grgas-Wheeler)
Goucher who now resides in Boulder, Colorado. The home Kara refers to is Duluth,
the largest American city on the shoreline of Lake Superior and the fifth-largest city
in Minnesota. Due to the city's strong heritage in hockey, ski jumping, and nordic
skiing, Duluth is home to many Olympians, but Kara is a rarity from the port city in
representing the United States at the Summer Olympic Games.

Born in Queens, New York, in 1978 to Mirko and Patty Grgas, Kara is the middle
child of three girls. Tragically, Mirko was killed by a drunk driver when Kara was four
years old, and Patty, Kara, and her sisters, Kelly and Kendall, soon moved to Duluth
to be with extended family. Patty credits her parents for their phenomenal support
during the relocation and trying time. Later Patty would marry Tom Wheeler, a local
financial advisor, and the three girls would take the surname Wheeler.

Kara had many passions during her youth: ballet, tap, and jazz dance; playing
the French horn in orchestra and pep band; student government; a variety of sports;
and in her sister Kelly's words, "lots of time playing with dolls." About the future Olympian, Kelly, a soccer star at Ottawa University (Kansas)—the same school and sport
where her birth father was a three-time All-American—and now an assistant soccer
coach at the University of Minnesota–Duluth, says, smiling, "Kara is not known for
her hand-eye coordination." Patty chimes in with a memory of an athletic event that
illustrates the point. "One of my favorite stories about Kara is when she played softball
in fourth or fifth grade. A ball was hit, and she stuck her glove out and caught it. She
didn't even know she had it until she looked inside her glove!"

A passion that Kara developed later was running. Patty had doubts that her
daughter would stick with cross country when Kara requested permission in 1990

to try the sport as a seventh grader, but Kara quickly caught the attention of Duluth East High School coaches with her early performances. And Kara embraced running quickly too. "I loved running from the beginning. I liked the way it felt." Kara would be running varsity track the following spring. Her participation in cross country would help launch Duluth East as a power in cross country and claim Minnesota State High School League championships for seven consecutive years, 1992–98. Duluth East had several topflight runners on the team besides Kara, one of them being younger sister Kendall. Coach Dick Skogg enjoyed the Duluth East cross country championship teams he coached to the first five state championships, and he has accolades for the team's number-one runner. "Kara really had great endurance. She took well to training. She had high-end distance speed. She set a torrid pace and could maintain it. She was very coachable—I worried about her overtraining. Everyone in the region looked up to her. She's just what you want in a runner."

Individually, Kara won the 1993 Minnesota State High School League cross country championship (a two-mile course at the time) with a time of 11 minutes and 42.3 seconds (11:42.3), and she was a close runner-up to Carrie Tollefson, a five-year state cross country champion and future 2004 Olympian, in 1994. Teammates Amy Hill, Casey Cherne, Kami Iverson, and Jami Miller all finished among the top twenty-five runners, sweeping the team to a dominant victory. Kara has her own fond memories of the four years she participated on the state cross country championship teams. "The greatest friends of my life were through running. We were so innocent, loved what we were doing. We were proud of how we did and just had so much fun. The team still tries to get together annually." In track, Kara won championships her freshman and sophomore years in the 3,200-meter race with a personal best of 10:48.47 in 1993 and her senior year in the 1,600-meter run with a time of 5:00.92.

Actively recruited by many Division I schools, Kara used all five of her allotted official visits (the colleges paid for her travel expenses) and thought all of them were acceptable, but she hadn't fallen in love with any school or athletic program. When her mother offered to pay for a sixth—and final—visit at the family's own expense, Kara decided to travel to the University of Colorado (known as CU). The tour proved to be everything Kara was hoping for, and she made the decision to become a CU Buffalo following her high school graduation in 1996.

Running varsity collegiate cross country as a freshman was a big step for Kara—everyone on the team had a running resume similar to hers. She placed 135th at the NCAA Cross Country Championships, but the competitive fire that her sisters, coaches, and teammates had observed in high school still reigned, and she set a goal to become the NCAA Division I cross country champion. Her rise in finishes was significant. In 1997, Kara finished 56th before redshirting (withdrawing from varsity competition for one year to extend eligibility) the following year due to injury. The 1999–2000 year was Kara's breakthrough year in collegiate competition. She rose to ninth place in the NCAA cross country championship in the fall of 1999, won the 2000 NCAA outdoor track championship in both the 3,000- and 5,000-meter running events, and wonderful news would keep coming.

Younger sister Kendall, who had eclipsed most of Kara's school running record times at Duluth East, would be joining Kara at CU for the 2000 fall season. Also, Kara's success and times resulted in an invitation to the 2000 Olympic Trials. Kara ran well and qualified for

KARA GRGAS-WHEELER AS A MEMBER OF THE DISTANCE MEDLEY RELAY AT THE 2000 HAYWARD RELAYS
Photo courtesy of CU Athletics

the finals in the 5,000-meter run. She finished eighth with a time of 15:34.47, the top collegian in the elite field of runners. However, the winner of the 2000 Olympic Trials in the men's 5,000-meter event was CU graduate Adam Goucher, the 1998 NCAA Division I men's cross country champion. Adam, the man Kara would marry in 2001, made the finals and placed thirteenth at the Olympic Games in Australia. And then Kara realized the goal she had dared speak only to family members four years earlier . . . she won the 2000 NCAA women's cross country championship in Ames, Iowa, with a time of 20:30.5 on the 6-kilometer course as the CU Buffaloes also captured their first national women's team championship.

After Kara graduated with a degree in psychology in 2001, she and Adam were determined to pursue careers in running, which included sponsorships with Nike. Both experienced injuries and disappointment at the 2004 Olympic Trials. The couple moved to Portland, Oregon, to train under the guidance of famed runner and coach Alberto Salazar. Before the 2008 Olympic Trials, Kara had remained healthy and burst strongly onto the international racing scene by becoming the first American woman to win a medal in the 10,000-meter run at the World Championships in Osaka, Japan, closing with a hard sprint to claim a bronze medal in 32:02.05. Kara was "shocked" and giddy at the finish. "The race played out perfectly for me. I was in fifth place when I made my move with two hundred meters to go. Later I held up the flag wrong—I had never held the flag before. The race changed my life." Later that year, Kara also ran the Great North Run in England in 1:06:57, setting an American best in the half-marathon that still stands. In February 2008, she won the Millrose Games mile in New York City with a personal best time of 4:36.03. Kara was poised to make her first US Olympic team in three attempts. Adam would also be in the hunt to make the 2008 Olympic team.

The 2008 Olympic Trials were at nearby Eugene, Oregon. Again Kara realized a dream—she took second in the 10,000-meter run behind Shalane Flanagan, which qualified her for a trip to Beijing, China, as a member of the American women's Olympic team. But she wasn't finished. Kara had also qualified for the 5,000-meter run and—now assured that she was an Olympian—she decided to go with gusto and qualify in two events. Kara proceeded to win the race in 15:01.02. Nevertheless, she experienced some disappointment. Although Adam ran a personal best in the 10,000-meter run, he finished seventh and failed to qualify for the Olympic team.

KARA GOUCHER IN THE PACK EN ROUTE TO WINNING THE BRONZE MEDAL AT THE 2007 WORLD CHAMPIONSHIPS IN JAPAN
Photo credit: Kirby Lee, Image of Sport

Kara finished in the top ten of both Olympic races. She finished tenth in hot, humid conditions, breaking thirty-one minutes in the first final running event, the 10,000-meter run. A week later, she placed ninth in the 5,000-meter run, the top American woman. "Making the Olympic team was very emotional," says Kara. "I thought the Olympics would be my highlight, but there have been more memorable moments: running the major marathons, being a bronze medalist at the 2007 World Championships, and the Great North Run half-marathon when I defeated the world champion." Yes, Kara would soon turn her attention to marathoning.

Less than three months after the completion of the Olympics, Kara made her debut in the New York City Marathon—and what a splash she created! Kara finished third overall in the women's division and became the first American on the podium in fourteen years with a sensational time of 2:25:53, a record for a woman's first marathon. She repeated her third-place finish in 2009 at the Boston Marathon and placed ninth at the World Championship in Berlin, Germany.

There was joyful news in the personal lives of Adam and Kara Goucher in 2010. A son, Colton Mirko, was born in September. Naturally Kara limited her training, planning to resume it in 2011. By April she was strong and ready to compete in the Boston Marathon. The comeback was wildly successful— Kara set a personal best time of 2:24:52; she was the fifth woman to cross the finish line. Now she had her sights on going to Europe—

KARA GOUCHER WINS THE 5000-METER RUN AT THE 2008 OLYMPIC TRIALS
Photo credit: Kirby Lee, Image of Sport

specifically London—in 2012 to compete in the longest running event in the Olympics.

And Kara did qualify for her second Olympic team. She finished a strong third at the Olympic Trials in Houston behind winner Shalane Flanagan, now her training partner in Portland. In London the race started in a heavy rain, but Flanagan and Kara carved out times at 2:25:51 and 2:26:07 respectively while finishing tenth and eleventh out of more than one hundred competitors.

The Goucher family returned to Colorado—Adam's home state—in 2013, to train with their college coach, Mark Wetmore. Kara switched her professional running affiliation to Oiselle, a manufacturer of women's running apparel. She is excited about the future association with her new sponsor.

In the running world, Kara has great respect for fellow runner Lynn Jennings and cites world-class runners Paula Radcliffe and Joan Benoit Samuelson as influential people in her life. With strong performances in Asia (2008) and Europe (2012), Kara continues to train and be among the world leaders in marathons as she looks toward running in an Olympics on a third continent, at Rio de Janeiro, Brazil, in South America in 2016. But the continental competitor thinks of home often and says, "My family is my rock."

BURDETTE HALDORSON IN ACTION VS KANSAS
Photo courtesy of CU Athletics

BURDETTE HALDORSON

He Has Been to the Mountaintop

BEING A GOLD MEDALIST IS A RARE FEAT, BUT A PERson not known to many Minnesotans has been to the mountaintop twice as a member of a gold medal–winning Olympic basketball team.

Burdette "Burdie" Haldorson's humble roots originate in rural Austin, Minnesota, where he was born on a farm about seven miles southwest of the city, which is home to the famed meat product Spam. The only child of a single parent, Burdie doesn't know how he obtained his unusual first name. He did not attend kindergarten and began first grade at five years old. He and his mother, Dorothy, a teacher, moved to town when he was in fifth grade. Former neighbor and high school teammate Dale Hamilton met Burdie at Sumner Elementary; he remembers him as "a gangly guy. He did not really develop until later in high school."

Basketball was the only sport that Burdie participated in during his school years at Austin High School. Burdie shot up to 6 feet 7 his senior year in high school. "My height had a lot to do with it," he says matter-of-factly about being recruited for the team, "and there was some peer pressure to pursue basketball. Coach Ove Berven was an influential person in my life, too." Austin was an athletic powerhouse in multiple sports, which included six state appearances between basketball championships in 1946 and 1958 (including a runner-up finish in 1957) of the single-class state tournament. While Burdie received substantial playing time as a fifteen-year-old junior, it was his senior year that proved pivotal in his athletic career.

The Austin High School boys' basketball team entered the 1951 state tournament undefeated after claiming the regional crown with a thrilling victory over Rochester (which had only one public high school at the time). In the first game, Austin was paired against Gilbert High School, which had its own center standout, 6 feet 9½ Bill "Boots" Simonovich. Gilbert won the game—and the tournament—with Bur-

BURDIE HALDORSON AND DALE HAMLILTON ON THE 1951 AUSTIN HIGH SCHOOL TEAM
Photo courtesy of the Minnesota State High School League

die fouling out and being outplayed by Simonovich, who would later play for Hamline and the University of Minnesota. Austin would rebound in the consolation bracket with Burdie leading the team to a win against St. Paul Monroe before losing to Hopkins in the consolation finals.

Burdie's dominating performances throughout the season brought many college coaches calling. He was most intrigued by Butler, Indiana University, and the University of Colorado, but it was the last that most appealed to Burdie. "I liked the coach, Bebe Lee, the program, and the environment. I had never seen a mountain before my recruiting visit to the campus." High school teammate Hamilton joined Burdie at Colorado on a football scholarship.

It proved to be an auspicious choice for Burdie. He was eligible to play his first year since many players were being drafted for military service due to the Korean War. His early success continued through a fulfilling and celebrated career with the Colorado Buffaloes from 1951–54. Burdie scored more than 1,000 points while also hauling down more than 700 rebounds, pulling in 31 in one game (still a Colorado record). He led the Big 7 Conference in scoring in both his junior and senior years with averages of 21.3 and 23.9 points per game (ppg) respectively. The highlight of his collegiate career was playing in the 1955 NCAA Final Four. Burdie recalls, "We lost to the University of San Francisco sixty-two to fifty in the semifinals. They were led by Bill Russell and K. C. Jones, who became part of the great Boston Celtic tradition. We later beat Iowa seventy-five to fifty-four for third place in the tournament." Being selected as an Amateur Athletic Union (AAU) first-team All-American his senior year capped his athletic career at Colorado.

Drafted by the St. Louis Hawks of the National Basketball Association (NBA), still a struggling professional sports organization at the time, Burdie spurned their offer to play for the Luckett-Nix Clippers in the National Industrial Basketball League. The following year he joined the Bartlesville Phillips 66ers and teamed up with Chuck Darling, an All-American center from Iowa, to power the perennial contender to the AAU National Championship. The pairing would continue for three years. "I was impressed with Burdie's versatility," Darling recalls. "He was a good natural post player who could rebound and score, yet he could also hit the jump shot from outside. I really enjoyed playing with him."

Selection for the 1956 Olympic men's basketball team was determined by a round-robin tournament between eight teams. A team composed of college all-stars and several AAU teams played in the tournament. The winning team would have five members and their coach on the squad, and the balance of the Olympic team would be selected from players on other teams in the tournament. In a clash of centers, Darling outdueled Russell to lead the Phillips 66ers to a four-point victory. Coach Gerald Tucker, Burdie, and the other four starters of the team, including Colorado teammate Bob Jeangerard, were automatically chosen to be Olympians. Of course Russell and Jones, future Boston Celtic stars, were a welcome addition to the team, which would be playing in Melbourne, Australia.

BURDIE IS CREDITED WITH 31 REBOUNDS IN ONE GAME, STILL A UNIVERSITY OF COLORADO RECORD
Photo courtesy of CU Athletics

Due to the reversal of seasons in the Southern Hemisphere, the summer Olympic Games began in November. "It was an amazing experience. The country embraced Americans," says the Austin native. "After the team was chosen, we trained for two weeks and played exhibition games for two weeks, including one at Austin High School! Then we took a propeller plane to Hawaii and were there for four days—we didn't even practice. But we were a real team headed by Bill Russell, the number-one player in the country. He was really dominant in Melbourne." In fact, the entire team was dominant—they won every game by 30 points or more—and knocked off the Soviet Union eighty-nine to fifty-five in the championship game. With Russell and Jeangerard leading the scoring parade, Burdie was a solid contributor, finishing sixth on the team by averaging 8.6 ppg. Burdie was the first Minnesotan to receive an Olympic gold medal in basketball. "It is the highlight of my career," he says proudly. "It's at the top of your resume. A gold medal is with you the rest of your life."

Burdie and Darling triumphantly returned from Australia and rejoined the Bartlesville Phillips 66ers basketball team, and Burdie resumed working in the marketing department for the Oklahoma petroleum company. Burdie's string of AAU All-American awards continued in the 1957–58 and 1958–59 seasons. Notable names joining him on the squad were K. C. Jones and Adrian Smith, a guard who had a solid career with the Cincinnati Royals.

The 1960 Olympic basketball squad was chosen in a similar fashion as the 1956 team. The College All-Stars richly deserved to win the tournament and did so in convincing fashion. Oscar Robertson and Jerry West, two names that became synonymous with NBA all-star performances and helped catapult the league to fame, were the starting guards. Other players named to the team were Jerry Lucas, Terry Dischinger, Bob Boozer, and Walt Bellamy, who all continued in the sport to have successful NBA careers. The 1960 American Olympic basketball team is routinely recognized as the greatest amateur team ever assembled. Considering the wealth of talent, Burdie confesses, "I was uncertain that I'd get picked." He was added as an at-large choice by Coach Pete Newell of the University of California. This time the team trained harder and played games throughout Europe to prepare for the Olympic Games in Rome, Italy. The Soviet Union seemed to be playing with more authority, and the American team wanted to be ready.

"I had just finished my collegiate career. It was quite an honor to be an Olympian. Everybody treated us great. The people in Italy were very courteous."

As expected, the United States team breezed through the preliminary games, and still defeated the Soviet Union handily 81–57 behind the exploits of Robertson, West, and Lucas. Burdie's best game was when he scored ten points in a 108–50 trouncing of Uruguay. Burdie enjoyed his cast of teammates and refers to West and Robertson as "real class guys." Robertson gives his Olympic teammate credit for his role too. "Burdie was a perennial AAU all-star who served as backup to Walt Bellamy and offered stability in the position." Burdie and Robertson loved the experience too. Robertson adds, "I had just finished my collegiate career. It was quite an honor to be an Olympian. Everybody treated us great. The people in Italy were very courteous."

Eventually the entire 1960 Olympic basketball gold medal team would be inducted into the Basketball Hall of Fame in Springfield, Massachusetts, in 2010 for their achievement. Burdie was standing among the famed class with seventeen family members in attendance. "We had a ball! The people organizing the event treated us very well," he comments.

Burdie's draft rights in the NBA had been exchanged to different teams, and he was tempted to sign with the New York Knicks at one point. Married in 1959 to Kaye Sivinski, a native of St. Cloud, Minnesota, he decided not to pursue professional basketball after the 1960 Olympics and settled into his career with Phillips 66 Petroleum Company.

Later, Burdie and a business partner formed A-B Petroleum (the letters A and B stand for Archie

BURDETTE HALDORSON JERSEY RETIRED ON SEPTEMBER 17, 1994 AT FOLSOM FIELD; THE UNIVERSITY OF COLORADO DEFEATED NO. 10 WISCONSIN, 55-17
Photo courtesy of CU Athletics

and Burdie, the co-owners), a series of gasoline service stations started in Colorado Springs. He and Kaye had three children, including a son, Brian, who played one season of basketball for the Colorado Buffaloes and now operates the business. Burdie continues to follow the sport, and he and Kaye now enjoy nine grandchildren.

Besides being a member of the 1960 Olympic basketball team inducted into the esteemed Naismith Memorial Basketball Hall of Fame, Burdie was named to the Colorado Springs Sports Hall of Fame in 2011, added to the Pac-12 Men's Basketball Hall of Honor (successor to the Big 7) in 2012, and inducted into the University of Colorado Athletic Hall of Fame in 1999, which also retired his #22 basketball jersey a few years earlier. Statewide, Burdie was listed thirty-third on *Sports Illustrated's* list of Minnesota's fifty greatest sports figures of the twentieth century.

Burdie enjoys living in Colorado Springs and having been to the mountaintop twice.

SARA HILDEBRAND ON 10-METER PLATFORM
Photo courtesy of Indiana University Athletics

SARA REILING HILDEBRAND

101 Bathing Suits

FLIPPING AND TUMBLING HAVE BEEN AN EXTENSIVE part of Sara Hildebrand's life. The results have been topsy-turvy too, ranging from frightening medical reports to All-American achievements for the woman from Roseville, Minnesota.

"My mother was an acrobat," says Sara. "I followed her around a lot." Born in 1979, Sara and older brother Scott are the children of Ray Reiling, a self-employed carpenter, and Sandy Reiling, a nurse. Sara dove into a variety of activities throughout her childhood: dance, softball, tennis, soccer, and piano during her elementary school years, but gymnastics was the sport she devoted most of her time and energy to. Practicing at Flips Gymnastics Center and the YMCA in White Bear Lake, she began competing at age five and qualified for Level 10 before suffering a serious lower-back stress fracture. Sara remembers receiving the bad news. "I was told that being in a wheelchair at age thirty was a very real possibility."

The injury triggered a change to another sport where she could capitalize on her gymnastics skills while also relieving the worry of a potential catastrophic injury. "I switched to diving in 1994. In diving there were no hard, immediate stops like gymnastics," explains Sara. Under the guidance of Mike Martins and Scott Smith, Sara experienced success while diving with the Twin City Diving Club at the University of Minnesota Aquatic Center. Rather than join the swimming and diving team at Cretin-Derham Hall High School, the school she attended, Sara remained in club diving because she preferred 3- and 10-meter diving, which is offered through Minnesota State High School League competition.

While at Cretin-Derham Hall, Sara received another diagnosis. "Reading, writing, and spelling-related subjects were difficult and I was prone to making mistakes. Coupled with the pressure of timed exercises in the classroom, anxiety and errors

SARA HILDEBRAND WAS NAMED BIG 10 DIVER OF THE YEAR, INDIANA UNIVERSITY FEMALE ATHLETE OF THE YEAR, AND US DIVING ATHLETE OF THE YEAR IN 2003
Photo courtesy of Indiana University Athletics

became more frequent. I was diagnosed with dyslexia and a reading comprehension and expression disorder. There were ways to cope with it. My grades were not bad—it was just that I had to work very hard," Sara says. Having these experiences would eventually assist Sara in her chosen career. Sara finished high school in Irvine, California (where she moved to improve her diving), and received diplomas from both high schools in 1998.

Sara landed a spot on the national diving team at the age of seventeen, barely three years after she began the sport. College coaches were well aware of her abilities and the successes Sara had at the junior level, and she was heavily recruited by premier swimming and diving teams. While Auburn, Miami, Ohio State, and Texas were considered, the difficult choice was between the University of Tennessee and Indiana University (IU). She chose the latter, based on the following factors: "It was a school that I felt would understand how to meet my academic needs. Additionally, I had attended a diving camp there under coach Jeff Huber's direction, and I felt we worked really well together."

Sara's years at the Big 10 school with a high-profile swimming and diving team would be both demanding and memorable in numerous ways. "My time at IU was eventful. I was constantly in athlete mode, trying to be a better diver while also working very hard on my academics. I was not home much because of the number of meets I was competing in. We'd leave as early as Wednesday and sometimes be gone a full week or more—sometimes up to two weeks for nationals." Training included lifting early in the morning a minimum of three times per week and being in the water twice each day for a total of three to four hours. Cardio workouts on top of those workouts only added to the time commitment. Preparation for the Olympic Trials and Olympics increased that total.

An encounter with a student in a world geography class would become a lasting relationship. Always arriving to class in sweats and with wet hair following diving practice, Sara noticed a student with a backpack that had Big 10 Wrestling Championships lettering. When she asked whether he was a wrestler, the brusque answer she received from the muscular man, "That's what the bag says," annoyed the 5 foot 1 inch, 110-pound diver. She later confronted him about his response. "An easy friendship developed after the initial rudeness," Sara says. Butch Hildebrand, the IU wrestler in the world geography class, fell hard for the wet-haired diver, and the couple married in 2002.

Accumulating enough points to qualify for the 2000 Olympic Trials at King County Aquatic Complex in Federal Way, Washington, Sara planned to "use it as a learning experience. I was very happy to have qualified, but it was a huge surprise to compete as well as I did and make the Olympic team!" Yes, the petite dynamo finished second behind Laura Wilkinson and claimed the only other spot on the women's 10-meter platform diving team. After spending only six years as a diver, Sara Reiling would be going to Sydney, Australia, as an Olympian.

> ## "I won the one-meter springboard, which was a surprise, won the three-meter [springboard], then a lot of media asked whether I could win the ten-meter [platform], and I did!"

Competitors at Sydney with the top eighteen qualifying scores from the first round of diving advanced to the semifinals in the Olympic competition. After the fourth of five dives, Sara was in twenty-fourth place, and chances of moving to the next round seemed slim. She then scored the third-highest score of all competitors on her final dive, climbed to sixteenth place, and advanced to the next round. The top twelve qualifying scores of the semifinals then moved forward to the finals. Sara got as close as possible, finishing thirteenth overall. Teammate Wilkinson shocked the diving world, becoming the first American woman diver to win a gold medal in the 10-meter platform event since 1964.

Returning to IU a semester later since the Olympics had been held in September, Sara racked up an impressive list of achievements that would eventually include being a three-time Academic All-American, an eight-time Big 10 Champion, and an eleven-time Division I All-American. She was gaining notoriety for her signature dive: 1½ somersaults and 2½ twists out of a backward armstand on the platform.

It was a banner year for Sara in 2003 as she was named Big 10 Diver of the Year, Indiana University Female Athlete of the Year, and US Diving Athlete of the Year. Her most memorable collegiate meet also occurred that year at the Big 10 meet hosted by Purdue when she won every diving event. "I won the one-meter springboard, which was a surprise, won the three-meter [springboard], then a lot of media asked whether I could win the ten-meter [platform], and I did!"

Despite the awards and accolades in 2003, Sara started to lose faith in herself and found diving stressful and no longer fun. She wanted to quit. But Coach Huber and Butch were not supportive of her desire and—through some tough love—convinced her to continue her

SARA HILDEBRAND (FOREGROUND) AND CASSANDRA CARDINELL
PERFORM IN THE FINAL ROUND OF THE WOMEN'S PLATFORM
SYNCHRONIZED DIVING AT THE 2004 US OLYMPIC TEAM TRIALS
ON JUNE 9, 2004
Photo credit: AP/Tom Gannam

diving career. It was less than six months to the 2004 Olympic Trials, and Sara had serious doubts.

Sara and IU teammate Cassandra Cardinell were pairing together for synchronized diving, in addition to the 10-meter platform competition at the trials in St. Peters, Missouri. "I was extremely fortunate. Cassandra and I matched up well and attended the same school, so it was easy to train. We felt confident we could win synchro [synchronized]." And they did—outdistancing the team of Laura Wilkinson and Kimiko Soldati by more than thirty points. Due to their first-place finish in synchronized diving, one member of the pair would also qualify for a spot as an individual. Sara placed a disappointing fifth in the 10-meter platform diving, but ahead of Cardinell, so she also made the team individually. This leapfrogged Sara ahead of other competitors, including St. Paul native Brittany Viola, daughter of former Minnesota Twins' pitcher Frank Viola. This time Sara was going to the original home of the modern Olympics: Athens, Greece.

Sara was also taking some luggage, which caught the attention of some in the media. "I always traveled with at least twenty different bathing suits," Sara begins. "I took over a hundred suits to Athens," she says, starting to giggle. "We were there for over six weeks—that's a long time! I needed options!" she laughs heartily.

> *"I took over a hundred suits to Athens," she says, starting to giggle. "We were there for over six weeks—that's a long time! I needed options!"*

Promising prospects for a medal in synchronized diving were dashed on the very first dive when her diving partner, Cardinell, clipped the bottom of the platform. The score was so disastrous that it became a struggle for the pair to climb out of last place to finish seventh. Sara fared better in the individual event on 10-meter platform diving. She finished the qualifying round in fourteenth place to advance to the semifinals and moved up to eleventh place in that stage to make the finals. Her dives were steady and solid, placing Sara tenth out of the twelve finalists. The finals at her second Olympics would be Sara's last competitive dives.

Sara and Butch moved to Fort Myers, Florida, after the 2004 Olympics. Sara was a dual major in elementary education and special education and completed her student teaching in the Sunshine State, earning her degree from IU in 2005. Sara taught for six years in Florida beginning in 2006; she currently teaches at National Trail Elementary School in New Paris, Ohio. Butch is employed by the local government and acts as the chief deputy for the Preble County Engineer's Office.

Sara and Butch are parents of two girls: Liliana, born in 2005, and Delaney, born in 2007. Both daughters enjoy competitive gymnastics and soccer. Sara and Butch own a facility for wrestling where the girls have insisted on having a pink balance beam. The couple spends a lot of time planning camping trips with their daughters and two dogs, Sebastian and Zeke.

Photo courtesy of Georgetown Athletics Department

STEVE HOLMAN

Premier Miler

POSTING THE FASTEST MILE TIME EVER RUN BY A Minnesotan, Steve Holman is appreciative of his Richfield High School coaches instilling a love of the sport of track that became a major part of his life. The son of a Baptist minister, Clyston, and a high school counselor, Janet, was born in Indianapolis, Indiana, in 1970. He moved to Richfield, an inner-ring suburb of Minneapolis, at the age of two. Neither parent was a runner and knew little about the sport. They also did not know that their "busy" son had more running talent than any other student. Janet does remember Steve requesting money to enter a Richfield Fourth of July fun run when he was in fifth or sixth grade. She gave him a dollar, but with the fee being only a quarter, Steve put the change in his sock. He won the race with the coins rubbing his foot as he ran.

He recalls his serious introduction to running while a middle school student: "You always had to run around the fence of a field in phy ed, and I usually won." This success encouraged Steve to join the cross country and track teams in ninth grade. "I was mostly motivated by wanting to be the first ninth grader to earn a varsity letter—and I did," Steve laughs. "I was about five feet-three inches and eighty-nine pounds."

A year after being exposed to cross country, Steve qualified for the Minnesota cross country meet in 1985 as a sophomore and finished fifty-first. His coaches recognized his talent but wisely did not burn out the driven young athlete. While he continued to improve in long-distance running and placed fourth in the 1987 state cross country meet, the middle distances in track were Steve's forte. "My times really started to come down when I matured [grew]." As a junior he won the Class AA 1,600-meter run in 4 minutes 20.49 seconds (4:20.49), a five-second margin over the runner-up. Steve also demonstrated his speed with a third-place finish in the 800-meter run won by Mark McConnon of Monticello, a future college teammate.

College recruiters came calling in 1988, when Steve posted some of the fastest times in the nation in track as a senior. He won both the 800- and 1,600-meter runs

STEVE HOLMAN WON THE 1600-METER RUN AT THE MINNESOTA STATE HIGH SCHOOL LEAGUE TRACK AND FIELD CHAMPIONSHIPS IN 11TH GRADE
Photo credit: Gene Niemi

at the Minnesota State High School Track & Field Championships with times of 1:53.12 and 4:11.08 respectively. Steve names Donovan Bergstrom, another highly recruited runner who accepted a scholarship to the University of Wisconsin, as the Minnesota runner he most liked watching run because of his fluid style. However, Bergstrom ran at the Class A level for Elgin-Millville High School, so they never competed against each other.

Articulate and intelligent, Steve decided to accept a scholarship offer to be part of the Georgetown University Hoyas because a high school trip to Washington, DC, had piqued his interest. He admits the public's fascination with the Hoyas' successful basketball team and alumnus star center Patrick Ewing made him consider the college too. "I thought there was a bigger world out there. I was also part of a great track recruiting class—what became a golden era of track at Georgetown." State champions and record holders John Trautmann and Rich Kenah were other members of Coach Frank "Gags" Gagliano's prized class.

By his sophomore year, Georgetown and Steve were qualifying for national meets. In 1989 Steve placed seventy-first in the NCAA Cross Country Championships. His senior year he climbed all the way to tenth place—quite an accomplishment for someone whose prowess was in track. "Cross country is an endurance event. I considered myself more of a middle-distance runner," Steve acknowledges.

Indeed, Steve won multiple Big East Championships and rose from finishing eighth in the NCAA Outdoor Track & Field Championships in the 1,500-meter run as a sophomore to running to the title in 1992 ahead of Bob Kennedy of Indiana, the 1990 champion, with a time of 3:38.39 as a senior, his first collegiate individual championship. And better things were still to come.

"June 1992 was the greatest month of my life until I got married," proclaims

Steve. Besides the NCAA title, he also graduated with a degree in English and then ran in the Olympic Trials—competing against the biggest and most veteran middle-distance stars in America. "I felt like I might be about fourth going into it. I was hopeful, but I was a bit surprised to make the Olympic team," he confesses. Steve won his first qualifying heat, took third in the semifinals, and then finished second to Jim Spivey in the finals. Coach Gagliano remembers watching his pupil with pride. "Steve making the Olympic team at age twenty-two was a tremendous high." Steve then capped off his stellar weeks of running by becoming the 186th American to run a mile under four minutes with an incredible

STEVE HOLMAN PLACED TENTH IN THE NCAA CROSS COUNTRY CHAMPIONSHIPS IN 1991
Photo courtesy of Georgetown Athletics Department

time of 3:53.31 at the Bislett Games in Oslo, Norway, on July 4. It was the fastest debut mile by an American-born man in track history.

Steve Holman was still soaring when he got to Barcelona, Spain, for the Olympic Summer Games. He advanced to the semifinals of the 1,500-meter run when he placed second in his qualifying heat with a time of 3:38.38. Then inexperience surfaced, and, combined with being unable to maintain peak physical shape, Steve took ninth and failed to make the finals. Nevertheless, it seemed like a promising start in international racing for a young middle-distance runner now standing 6 feet 1 and weighing 155 pounds.

For nearly the next decade, Steve trained diligently with Coach Gagliano and raced around the globe. "In college I tended to run a longer distance—eighty to ninety miles per week—than most middle-distance runners. I trained with 5K [kilometers] runners during the indoor season and then eight-hundred-meter runners later. It was the Gags's philosophy of strength before speed." Gagliano alters the statement slightly, saying it was "strength plus speed." Through endorsements and earning prize money, Steve was able to meet living expenses.

> *" My career had some highs and some lows. I am very proud of the times and records but very disappointed to bomb out in the 1996 trials—I just put a lot of pressure on myself."*

Steve was now among the most accomplished American 1,500-meter runners and a contender for any championship race. He was the 1996 USA indoor champion in the mile and was keying in on the 1996 Olympic Trials. Not only was Atlanta, Georgia, hosting the Olympic Summer Games, but it was also the site for the track and field Olympic Trials. Steve won the first qualifying round and followed with a victory in the semifinals, but disaster struck in the finals when he placed thirteenth in very hot conditions. It was devastating. "My career had some highs and some lows. I am very proud of the times and records but very disappointed to bomb out in the 1996 trials—I just put a lot of pressure on myself," Steve says of the experience.

Still competing, Steve had a personal best time of 3:31.52 in the 1,500-meter run in 1997. Two years later, he was victorious in the USA Track & Field Outdoor Championships. He states, "It led me to believe I was in pretty good shape going into the 2000 Olympic Trials." Then Steve suffered

STEVE AND HIS WIFE, TERESA GILLIAMS, WITH CHILDREN CHLOE AND CAMILLE AT STEVE'S INDUCTION TO THE GEORGETOWN ATHLETIC HALL OF FAME IN 2014
Photo credit: Rafael Suanes/Georgetown University

a stress fracture and had to limit training. He did make the finals but narrowly missed a spot on the Olympic team when he placed fifth—a scant 0.3 of a second away from a trip to Sydney, Australia.

In 1999 Steve married Teresa Gilliams, a college English professor from Connecticut whom he met in Washington, DC. Another stress fracture ended Steve's competitive running career by the time they moved to Minnesota for the 2001–02 academic year when Teresa taught at Hamline University. They decided a more moderate climate beckoned and returned to the East Coast the following year. Steve attended the Wharton School of Business at the University of Pennsylvania, where he earned a master's degree in finance. Upon graduation in 2004, he accepted a position with Vanguard, the largest mutual fund company in the world. He is currently a principal with the company. Steve and Teresa are the proud parents and mentors of daughters Chloe and Camille and live in the Philadelphia metropolitan area.

> *"Steve Holman is a very, very good man and very good student athlete. He was very driven. The reason he was good was because of his work ethic. No doubt he was a premier American miler in the 1990s."*

Steve's track exploits are very impressive. Among his feats are holding the Minnesota 800-meter record for eight years, being a ten-time collegiate All-American, running the anchor leg for the Georgetown University 4 x 800 meter relay team, and setting a personal best of 3:50.6 in the mile (in 1996 in Oslo, Norway). He is listed as one of the most decorated male athletes in Georgetown University history and was inducted into their Athletic Hall of Fame in 2014.

Frank Gagliano, Steve's longtime coach, is another proud mentor. "Steve Holman is a very, very good man and very good student athlete. He was very driven. The reason he was good was because of his work ethic. No doubt he was a premier American miler in the 1990s."

MIKE HOUCK ON THE PODIUM AS THE GOLD MEDALIST
AT THE WORLD CHAMPIONSHIPS IN 1985
Photo courtesy of USA Wrestling

MIKE HOUCK

Blazing the Trail to World Champion

AT HIS INTRODUCTION TO GRECO-ROMAN WRES-tling (a style of wrestling allowing only holds above the waist) in 1977 at the University of Minnesota (U of M) wrestling room, Mike Houck was in awe, profoundly affected by the presence of five 1976 Olympic Greco-Roman wrestlers from Minnesota: Brad Rheingans (Appleton), Dan Chandler (Anoka), Bruce Thompson (Prior Lake), and Pat Marcy and Gary Alexander (Hopkins). Mike had no idea that he would be the person from that distinguished group who would blaze the trail to become the first American individual Greco-Roman world champion less than a decade later.

Born in 1959, Mike is the oldest of three children of Marilyn, an employee at General Mills, and Dick Houck, a tool-and-die maker. Each of the children exhibited athletic ability: daughter Heidi won many trophies as a speedskater, and son Chris became captain of the high school gymnastics team. Although Mike sang in the choir and played guitar, his primary interest was sports, and he had dreams of playing in the NFL. He played linebacker for the Robbinsdale High School Robins (the high school closed in 1982 and is now a middle school) football team and served as a captain his senior year. The powerful Robins squad had tied or won eight state titles in wrestling and had a strong tradition in the sport. Mike qualified for the Minnesota state high school wrestling tournament in his junior and senior years but did not place in the sport that he started before entering fifth grade.

Despite being an integral player on the suburban high school team north-west of Minneapolis, Mike was not recruited for college football upon graduating in 1977. "I had great passion for the sport, but I did not have the size [six feet] or speed," he reports. Mike's disappointment was softened somewhat when he did well in a national junior wrestling tournament and received an invitation to a three-month training camp in Squaw Valley, California, as a "prospect." It was at the camp that he approached 1972 Olympic freestyle wrestling gold medalist Ben Peterson about at-

MIKE HOUCK WRESTLING FOR MARANATHA IN 1980
Photo credit Maranatha Baptist U Athletics

tending college at Maranatha Bible College in Watertown, Wisconsin, where Peterson was the wrestling coach. Peterson, a man of deep faith, became very influential in Mike's life.

Due to his concerns about possessing low academic skills, Mike did not enroll at Maranatha until 1978 and left after a single year. "As long as I was engaged and productive, my parents were supportive of my struggling years," he says appreciatively. Those years became not only more productive, but more successful in wrestling as he made the national junior Greco-Roman wrestling team in 1979. Mike now had a goal of becoming an Olympic gold medalist.

Mike trained and practiced nearly full-time on the national team under the guidance of the 1976 Olympians whom he admired, particularly Rheingans and Chandler, along with national champion Gary Pelcl, another Hopkins High School graduate. Mike's ascent was swift—in 1980 he was the 90 kilogram (kg) national Greco-Roman wrestling champion. He remained on the national team for ten years and was national champion three more times in 1981, 1983, and 1984. Mike was primed to become an Olympian in 1984 and battle for the gold medal.

A constant competitor at Mike's weight class was Steve Fraser, a two-time All-American at the University of Michigan. Each match brought out the best efforts of both wrestlers. "We contributed to each other's success," states Mike.

Fraser returns the compliment in more detail. "He was a true stud! Every match we had was a full-out brawl. Mike was a very respected guy. He had a great cardio-vascular system, he could grind with the best of them. As a person, he was a very nice guy. We were fierce competitors, but off the mat we could be cordial."

The 1984 Olympic Trials finals at 90 kg (198 pounds) predictably paired up Fraser and Mike. Early in the first match (of three), Fraser caught Mike in a headlock and gained three points as Fraser nearly pinned him. Mike expended a lot of energy struggling to avoid the pin and battled back but still lost 3–2. Mike won the next bout

2–0, so the third and final match would decide the American representative at the 90 kg weight class. The final ended in a 3–3 draw, so each wrestler had one win, one loss, and a tie. Based on tie-breaking scoring criteria at the time, the wrestler that had the higher point move would be declared the winner. Fraser's near fall was the highest point score, and he was declared the US Olympic Trials champion. "The sun did not rise the next morning," Mike recalls of the devastating loss.

The US Olympic Greco-Roman wrestling team won their first gold medal of any Olympics in Los Angeles, California, in 1984. The first gold medal was won by Steve Fraser. "One big reason I won an Olympic gold medal is because I had a guy like Mike Houck pushing me at the national level," is Fraser's assessment. A day later, superheavyweight Jeff Blatnick took the top spot on the podium in a memorable victory as the country witnessed him win a gold medal after battling back from Hodgkin's lymphoma diagnosed only two years earlier.

Mike decided to return to Maranatha Bible College in 1984 while also remaining a member of the national Greco-Roman team. In 1985 he blazed the trail for American Greco-Roman wrestlers in the nonboycotted (the 1984 Olympics were boycotted by fourteen Eastern Bloc countries) World Championships at Kolbotn, Norway. Mike defeated a Korean by technical fall, then won a match against a Bulgarian and upset three-time gold medalist world champion Frank Andersson of Sweden before losing to a Czech wrestler. "I found myself in the finals because contenders had eliminated each other in the double-elimination tournament," relates Mike. This time Mike was vindicated and won the first gold medal by an American Greco-Roman wrestler in the World Championships as he surprised another world champion, Igor Kanygin, a two-time gold medalist from the Soviet Union. Mike then experienced "unsolicited emotion, and my teammates lifted me up and threw me into the air." It was a special moment and the highlight of Mike's wrestling career.

Training under Peterson's tutelage and "hands-on" approach, Mike also became a two-time Christian College national champion in freestyle wrestling while at Maranatha. Remembering their many years together, Peterson writes reflectively, "From the first day I met Mike, he impressed me as someone who was

MIKE HOUCK MOBBED BY TEAMMATES AFTER GOLD MEDAL VICTORY AT THE 1985 WORLD CHAMPIONSHIPS
Photo courtesy of USA Wrestling

MIKE HOUCK WITH WORLD CHAMPIONSHIP GOLD MEDAL AND BELT IN 1985
Photo courtesy of USA Wrestling

able to discipline and focus himself for a serious task. As we worked through his college career and his Greco-Roman training with the Minnesota Wrestling Club, there was a continual advancement and maturing. He just always wants things to be better and works to that end. Mike is a special friend, and his tough, competitive nature and his gracious, thoughtful perspective have continued to be a blessing to many."

Mike's grades improved, and he is thankful for the patience and assistance demonstrated by many staffers. He was nearing a degree in elementary education and felt he received a "tremendous education." Despite having back surgery early in 1987, Mike thought he had another shot at the Olympics on the horizon, so he decided to train full-time for the 1987–88 academic year in an effort to make the 1988 Olympic team.

Mike moved to Robbinsdale and trained two to three times per day six days per week. He worked on improving his cardiovascular system every day. Mike is convinced that the Minnesota Wrestling Club and Peterson were leaders in Greco-Roman training. Believing that he was a better wrestler and in better shape than he had been in 1984, Mike was ready for the challenge and confident he would make the 1988 Olympic team. Two Mikes would be grappling for the championship: Mike Houck and Mike Foy, a former U of M wrestler. "Mike Foy was the most physically talented wrestler I ever faced," notes Mike. "He was tall, lean, and explosive, with great leverage." Foy used those physical gifts to his advantage and had a spectacular tournament defeating Mike. "I have no regrets because I had unwavering, phenomenal effort," says Mike, summing up his aspiration of becoming an Olympian. He retired from wrestling and obtained his degree at Maranatha.

But Mike was not retiring fully from the sport. He was named the second full-time national Greco-Roman wrestling coach in 1990. Mike especially enjoyed coaching Matt Ghaffari, Randy Couture (of mixed martial arts fame), and Jim Gruenwald. There were no assistant coaches during his five-year tenure, and the team trained in an old military base in Colorado Springs that had been sold to the US Olympic Committee for one dollar. A first-class training facility is now available for the team.

Mike also has favorite wrestlers that he watched or competed against. "Dan Gable inspired a generation of wrestlers. He is the Babe Ruth of wrestling," declares Mike. "Frank Andersson of Sweden was a favorite. He was so technically sound."

Since 1999 Mike has been a technology teacher at Chaska Middle School. He also serves as wrestling co-coach with Ned Shuck and names Pat Smith, a 2009 graduate of Chaska High School, as another favorite athlete that he has had the privilege to coach. Smith wrestled at the U of M and placed second in the 2014 national Greco-Roman championships. Smith pays this tribute to his former coach: "Mike has been a huge mentor to me more ways than as a wrestling coach. He made me realize that wrestling is bigger than just me and the glory and accomplishments that go along with it. It involves family, community, and God. He is a great role model—he coaches life."

In 2004, at the age of forty-five, the lifelong bachelor married Bonnie, an English teacher in the Chaska School District. They are proud grandparents of step-daughter Jessica Means's three children. Mike also manages many of the buildings of a property management company that he has in partnership with his brother and father.

Mike was inducted into the National Wrestling Hall of Fame in Stillwater, Oklahoma, in 2008. A year later, he was a member of the inaugural class inducted into the Alan and Gloria Rice Greco-Roman Hall of Champions of the Dan Gable International Wrestling Institute and Museum in Waterloo, Iowa. But those accolades and awards don't mean the trailblazer and world champion has always been immune to embarrassment. The technology teacher says that a student who wasn't doing what he was supposed to be doing in class announced to classmates that Mr. Houck was a wrestler. He had found a video of their teacher in a wrestling match, and a crowd quickly gathered around to watch. The video was of the 1984 Olympic Trials finals against Fraser, and there was Mr. Houck on his back! "They were watching the absolute worst minute of my life!" he laughs.

MIKE HOUCK RECEIVES U. S. WRESTLING HALL OF FAME AWARD
Photo courtesy of Mike Houck

**GEORGE HOVLAND STANDING OUTSIDE SNOWFLAKE
SKI CENTER, FEBRUARY 2009**
Reprinted with permission of the Duluth News Tribune

GEORGE HOVLAND

Life Is Fun, by George

FOR A MAN BORN IN 1926, GEORGE HOVLAND SHOWS amazing quickness in action and wit. A visitor immediately notices his bright blue eyes and how George bounds up steps, rifles through a sheaf of documents, and has you laughing within five minutes of meeting him. Meet George Hovland, a skiing legend from Duluth, Minnesota.

George was born in his family home near Chester Park, where "all activity of skiing in Duluth occurred. There have probably been two dozen national ski champions that lived within a one-mile radius of Chester Park," claims George. The setting proved vital to his athletic and personal success. At age two, George was already on homemade wooden skis. By age seven, George took the next leap in skiing by jumping off small hills, graduating to larger and larger ones when he and some friends—terrified and half daring each other—decided to try jumping off the "big one" (more than fifty meters—the biggest in Duluth at the time) at age eleven. "The most pliable guy got pushed down the jump and didn't die," he reports with a straight face, "so we all jumped." It became a daily winter routine to take some jumps (Chester Park's two iconic ski jumps were demolished in 2014 over the strenuous objections of George and a nucleus of ski jumpers) and ski the two cross country trails around Chester Park after school. "It was just what we did," George says simply. "It was an idyllic place to live. We had a wonderful resource."

> *"The most pliable guy got pushed down the jump and didn't die," he reports with a straight face, "so we all jumped."*

The budding Duluth Ski Club founded in 1905 was already hosting its second national ski jumping championships in Chester Park ten years later. Over 12,000 spectators came to watch the competition. George became a member of the thriving club, joining Peter Fosseide, a Norwegian immigrant who inspired him. Fosseide, the 1940 champion in national cross country and nordic combined (cross country and jumping), won the 1938 Arrowhead Ski Derby on an unmarked route from Duluth to St. Paul to celebrate the St. Paul Winter Carnival. Using Northland Skis made of hickory, Fosseide completed the challenging five-day endurance competition that had no prepared track in less than thirty hours. "The gravel and pavement had worn down the hickory until the groove on the bottom of the ski had disappeared," marvels George.

George attended Duluth Central High School, the downtown building with its landmark 230-foot clock tower, and was the 1943 Minnesota State High School League champion in both slalom and cross country skiing at sixteen years old. Duluth Central dominated the decade: the team won every nordic state high school championship in the 1940s except 1948 (Cloquet won) and claimed five state championships in slalom skiing during the same era. Norman Kragseth, a two-time state high school champion in ski jumping, slalom, and cross country skiing for the powerful

JOHN BURTON AND GEORGE HOVLAND, 1952
Photo courtesy of the John Burton family

Duluth Central Trojans who earned an incredible twenty-three varsity letters in seven different sports at the school in the 1940s, remembers George. "I had a lot of respect for George," says Kragseth, a longtime Hopkins High School teacher and coach who became the first NFL referee from Minnesota. "I couldn't compete with him in cross country, but I could compete with him in jumping." In fact, Olympic coaches would make a worrying observation about George's jumping style in a few years.

George joined the US Navy after graduating from Duluth Central in 1943. He served on an auxiliary geodetic survey ship that took soundings in harbors to determine safe landings for marines in World War II. At the end of his two-year commitment, George was summoned by the ship's commanding officer, who encouraged him to continue serving in the military and offered George a rise in rank and pay. George remembers his response clearly: "I said, 'Thank you, captain, but I want to go skiing.'" And so he did.

Combining his passion for skiing with an education at the University of Minnesota (U of M), George joined Minnesota notables John Burton (Minnetonka) and Fred Lang (Minneapolis) on the college club team that was never beaten as it competed throughout the Midwest. Burton, who died in December 2014, is remembered fondly by George. "John Burton was a dear friend. His record is remarkable. He was a heckuva athlete and tough competitor, yet he was a total gentleman," he says in tribute to his Olympic teammate. George graduated from the U of M in 1949 with a BA degree in engineering. That year he placed third in the national combined ski event—behind Peter Fosseide, now in his midforties.

"There has never been a fatality in American Olympic ski jumping, and we're not going to start with you."

Trying to make ends meet, George displayed early signs of his entrepreneurial spirit by doing "a number of imaginative, but borderline legitimate schemes" while still skiing whenever possible. A US Ski Association (USSA) official saw him ski and invited him to train with other candidates for the national ski team. George, now twenty-five years old, showed more promise in nordic skiing than alpine or slalom and made the 1952 US Olympic nordic combined team and the cross country team. Before participating in the Olympics in Oslo, Norway, the team trained in Sweden. It was there that nervous American coaches approached George about his ski jumping—they were not sure he was ready for the daunting Holmenkollen Ski Jump in Oslo. "They said, 'There has never been a fatality in American Olympic ski jumping, and we're not going to start with you,'" laughs George. Instead of jumping, George would be the prestigious lead leg (earned from the sprint trials) on the 4 x 10 kilometer (km) cross country relay team and also race the 18-km cross country event.

With a crowd of 140,000 people watching the relay race, George zipped out to second place on the heels of Heikki Hasu, an admired Finnish skier who would lead his team to the gold medal. Again George's humor surfaces: "Sooner or later I got to the relay area. The coach, Leif 'Swede' Odmark, asked me, 'George, are you all right? We thought you broke a ski!' None of the American team was really competitive," he admits.

After the 1952 Olympics, George traveled to Sweden in an effort to become the first non-European to complete the Vasaloppet in Sweden, the oldest (established in 1922), largest, and longest (at the time) cross country ski race in the world. Odmark, thinking George could not complete the 90-kilometer endurance race, tried to discourage him from entering. Nevertheless, when a Norwegian failed to show, George received the absent competitor's form and proudly skied in the historic race, cheered on by Norwegians in the crowd who believed George was one of their nation's skiers!

Reprinted with permission of the Duluth News Tribune

Returning to Minnesota, George continued to ski, but he became an entrepreneur, starting or operating several businesses involved with his passion. He opened the first ski shop in Duluth and started the first alpine ski area in Duluth, Ski Kenwood Inc. (SKI) near Chester Park in 1954. After searching for the ideal location for years, George founded Spirit Mountain Recreation Area in Duluth, designing and managing construction of the original cross country ski trails. Continuing to be sought for his expertise in trail design, he ultimately completed the design and planning of the cross country trails in Superior, Wisconsin, and—at the request of contractor and former teammate Al Merrill—Giants Ridge in Biwabik, Minnesota. In addition to these accomplishments, George was also heavily involved in designing and developing unique home construction.

Despite juggling his many business interests, George remained an avid skier who competed in dozens of races locally and around the world. His most notable achievements include: earning one of only two spots (via cross country ski trials at Lake Placid, New York) to represent the United States at the World Championships in Sweden in 1954; winning the Central USSA four-event championship four times (re-

JANE (COVEY) AND GEORGE HOVLAND, JUNE 2015
Photo credit: Ann Treacy

quiring proficiency in ski jumping, slalom, cross country, and down-hill); becoming the first American to complete a "Worldloppet" race, a series of long races around the world (including Canada, Europe, and Australia); and completing the American Birke-beiner (established in 1973 when George was forty-six years old) thirty-two times—the final time at age eighty-five.

George and Jane Covey, a psychology professor at the U of M Duluth, married in 1981. They developed, own, and have operated Snowflake Nordic Ski Center, one of the most popular ski centers in the Arrowhead region, the past quarter century. Through a previous marriage, George had three children: Julie, an innovator who married actor Telly Savalas (together they had two children); George III, vice president of hospitality for Brutger Equities based in St. Cloud; and Lee (deceased).

Throughout the past sixty years, George has inspired and encouraged young and old with his enthusiasm to enjoy life and the healthy benefits of cross country skiing. If you listen to him for five minutes, you will know and believe that he practices what he preaches, by George.

TONI AND TAMI JAMESON
Photo courtesy of Toni and Tami Jameson

TAMI AND TONI JAMESON

Twins Always Wanted to Do a Doublemint Gum Commercial

IDENTICAL TWINS TAMI AND TONI JAMESON HAVE NOT had many times of separation during their lifetime. The first break occurred when Tami was born a scant twelve minutes before Toni on April 13, 1968. The pair remained together as they starred in high school and college athletics and eventually made the same Olympic team in the same sport in 1996, the fast-paced game of team handball.

The daughters of divorced parents, Tami and Toni were raised by their mother, Regina, who worked in customer service for AT&T while their brothers Tory Kitchen and Stacy Jameson were brought up in Minneapolis by their father, Eddie, a truck driver who served the Midwest area. The parents shared responsibilities collaboratively, and the twins had a close relationship with their brothers.

Tall and athletic, Tami and Toni attended public schools in St. Paul and had immediate success in multiple sports. The 5-foot-10-inch Tami was a two-year starter in basketball, played tennis one year, and was on the softball team a few years for the Highland Park Scots. Toni went a slightly different path as she competed two years each in volleyball, track and field, and softball. One inch taller than her sister, Toni excelled at basketball and was a four-year starter. The twins were both All-City in basketball for two years, and Toni was also All-Metro her junior and senior years and considered among the top five recruits in Minnesota girls' basketball. The Scots qualified for the state basketball tournament both of those years and placed as runner-up in 1986 to St. Louis Park. Toni also experienced great success individually in track and field by competing in both shot put and discus throw at the state meet; she garnered second place her senior year in the shot put. The culmination of Toni's year was being named the recipient of the David Winfield Student Athlete of the Year Award

TAMI JAMESON STARTED FOR THE ST. CLOUD STATE UNIVERSITY WOMEN'S BASKETBALL TEAM FOR TWO YEARS
Photo courtesy SCSU Athletic Media Relations

and its accompanying scholarship. The achievements and athletic skill set of the sisters caught the attention of recruiters from many colleges.

Tami and Toni were excited to go on their first airplane flight for a recruiting visit to nearby Madison, Wisconsin, where Edwina Qualls, the first African American Big 10 women's basketball coach, had been coaching for a decade. It was also the day Coach Qualls was fired. "It was heartbreaking," says Toni. "That's how St. Cloud State University (SCSU) came into play. They pieced together enough academic and athletic scholarships that it paid for college." An additional enticement of attending SCSU was the relationship to a redshirt quarterback, their brother Stacy. The three siblings would enjoy being together on campus for the next four years.

Their first experiences at SCSU were a bit uncomfortable for the girls from the more diverse Twin Cities. They believe that there were only four other African American women athletes on campus. "It really helped having our brother on campus," notes Toni. She also appreciated support from their basketball coach, Gladys Ziemer, a tough taskmaster but "very influential in our lives. She was a pioneer in women's sports."

"I played softball and basketball my first year," Tami reports, "and then joined track my sophomore year in addition to basketball." She would be a power forward (four position) and end her career with more than 700 points—almost all scored her final two years when she earned a starting role.

Toni diverged slightly. "I played volleyball, basketball, and track, but my main focus was basketball and track." Toni was a starter in basketball all four years of her eligibility (1986–1990) and was named All-Conference three times as a versatile guard. She snared more than 1,000 rebounds and scored more than 1,500 points during her remarkable collegiate career. Her talent in basketball earned her a tryout that would eventually expose her to team handball, a sport in which she'd become a future Olympian.

TONI JAMESON SCORED MORE THAN 1,500 POINTS AND GRABBED OVER 1,000 REBOUNDS AS A FOUR-YEAR STARTER AT SCSU
Photo courtesy SCSU Athletic Media Relations

"In 1989 only two Division II players were invited to Colorado Springs for the World University basketball trials. I survived the first cut, but I didn't make the team. That's where I met Derrick Heath, a member of men's team handball. He said they were looking for tall women," recalls Toni. One year later, the Olympic Festival was hosted in the Twin Cities, and not only did Toni make the team, but so did her twin sister, and her brother Stacy made the junior men's national team (he briefly played as the goalie on a trip to Canada)! "They threw balls at Tami and she didn't blink, so they made her a goalie," Toni says, assessing the tryouts.

"They threw balls at Tami and she didn't blink, so they made her a goalie."

Team handball is wildly popular in Europe and combines elements of basketball, soccer, and ice hockey in its skills and physicality. The game consists of two thirty-minute periods played on a 40 x 20 meter (approximately 44 x 22 yards) court. The object is to throw a ball that is approximately 55 centimeters in circumference (21½ inches—larger than a softball, but smaller than a volleyball) into a net 3 meters long and 2 meters high (about 10 feet x 6½ feet) high past a goalie. Each team has six

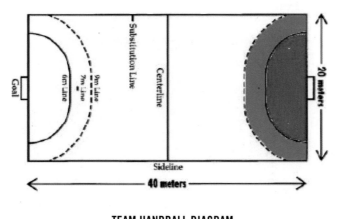

TEAM HANDBALL DIAGRAM
Reprinted with permission from USA Team Handball

other position players besides the goalie: two wings, three backs, and a circle runner (or pivot). A 6-meter near-semi-circle in front of the net is solely the goalie's domain. There are penalties similar to ice hockey and warnings and suspensions like soccer. A player is allowed to take up to three steps without dribbling or passing the ball but must move the ball within three seconds. The dribbling and passing that American basketball players have developed are primary reasons they are prized candidates for the sport. It is accepted that players on men's teams have thrown the hard leather or synthetic ball at speeds surpassing seventy miles per hour.

Two years later, Tami and Toni were trying out for the US Olympic team handball squad. In another rare bout of separation, Toni found the trials very stressful and left the team for a while to return to St. Paul before rejoining the group in Colorado Springs. The departure may have been the reason for her to be the final cut on the 1992 Olympic team. Tami would be going to Barcelona, Spain, without her twin sister. "It was a humbling experience," confesses Toni. "I was always the star, the better athlete, but Tami was faithful to the team." Toni has, in fact, been inducted into the Highland Park and SCSU Athletic halls of fame.

> *"It was a humbling experience," confesses Toni. "I was always the star, the better athlete, but Tami was faithful to the team."*

The adventure turned out to be a mixed experience for Tami. "I loved the opening and closing ceremonies. I loved the Olympic Village and travel." What was disheartening for the goalie was not playing a minute of any game. And since only twelve of the sixteen team members suit up for each game, Tami was especially disillusioned when she was not even chosen to suit up. The team got sixth place out of eight qualifying teams.

The twin sisters decided to return to SCSU to complete their degrees, and in 1994 Tami graduated with a major in mass communications and a minor in speech. Toni graduated with a degree in physical education and minors in health and coaching. A year later, they were traveling around the world with the American team handball squad as it went undefeated at the Pan Am Games in Argentina. Winning the gold medal also qualified the team for the 1996 Summer Olympics, which would be hosted on American soil in Atlanta, Georgia. And this time Tami and Toni would not be separated.

Now living in nearby Marietta, Georgia, the sisters held part-time jobs at JC Penney through a program sponsoring athletes. They also received a $208 per month stipend for being on the team. Their routine included a two-hour morning practice, working five to six hours at their job, taking a short nap, and then returning for two more hours of practice. The team would scrimmage on Saturdays and go to tournaments around the world. They spent about twenty-four hours per week practicing and conditioning while working.

TONI AND TAMI JAMESON AT THE 1995 PAN AM GAMES IN ARGENTINA

Photo courtesy of Tami and Toni Jameson

" I went to eat and saw Vice President Al Gore was having breakfast with the Olympians one day. A person invited me to present him with an Olympic jacket. Cameras were everywhere! "

TORY JR (TJ), TAMI, TORY KITCHEN, BRITTANY KITCHEN, STACY JAMESON, AND TONI, AT THE 1996 OLYMPICS IN ATLANTA, GEORGIA
Photo courtesy of Tami and Toni Jameson

Both sisters were named starters at their respective positions: Tami as the goalie, Toni as the circle runner, a position where she would take some punishing hits on her 160-pound frame. Also on the team handball unit were former University of Minnesota basketball players Carol Peterka and Laura Coenen, both celebrating being on their third Olympic team. At the Olympic Village, Tami was bestowed a unique honor that was not planned. "I went to eat and saw Vice President Al Gore was having breakfast with the Olympians one day. A person invited me to present him with an Olympic jacket. Cameras were everywhere!"

The first game pitted the American team against Denmark, the eventual gold medalist. The American team lost 29–19, and a second loss followed to a Hungarian team that would claim the bronze medal. Tami was removed as goalie despite playing well against strong competition. She did not play in the third game and did not suit up for the fourth and final game. Toni scored ten goals through the four games, five of them versus China in an unexpected 31–21 loss in the third game. The final blow was a loss to Angola by the score of 24–23. Sadly, neither the men's nor women's teams have qualified in team handball for the Olympic Games since those losses. "Team handball requires strength, agility, jumping, throwing, and good hand-eye coordination. This country could pick this sport up and become very good," laments Toni. Her favorite Olympic memory is "sharing fifteen minutes with someone from another country. They are all people and athletes trying their best."

Leora "Sam" Jones, a three-time Olympian and legend in American women's team handball who scored thirty-two goals in the 1984 Summer Games, remembers Tami and Toni well and still keeps in contact with the twin sisters. "Tami was very competitive. She had the ability to see the ball and had a very quick first step. Toni was versatile, so strong, was good at spotting players and anticipating what would happen. She was one of the fastest players on the team," Sam says. "They were both athletic and driven. They were also friendly and very family oriented."

Tami and Toni remained in Georgia for the next two years, Tami as a police and security officer and Toni as a teacher, coach, and security officer. Tami also became a team handball official and briefly played professionally in Norway. She returned home eleven days later; she admits to being homesick. They would soon return to Minnesota.

Toni Jameson married Eric Hall in 2005. Eric has multiple sclerosis and is now on disability. They have a cat named Bella and reside in the Twin Cities after living in Hastings for two years. Tami is single, has a boxer-mix dog named Ginger, and resides in St. Paul after also living in Hastings for two years. Yes, they lived together for support and the financial benefits.

"My experience from Highland Park to Saint Cloud State University to national and Olympic teams—everything was meant to be. I may never have been introduced to team handball and all these experiences," Toni summarizes.

"We would like to thank our parents for all their support and sacrifices. We never had any major injuries. We are just so grateful. We took a spiritual journey and want to thank God for everything."

"We would like to thank our parents for all their support and sacrifices. We never had any major injuries. We are just so grateful. We took a spiritual journey and want to thank God for everything," twin sister Tami concludes.

After appearing in a Coca-Cola commercial filmed by famed director Michael Apted before the 1996 Summer Games, the identical twin sisters were hoping to someday be featured in a Doublemint gum commercial. Alas, it was not to be.

When Tami returned to Minnesota in 1999, she began working in the insurance department for the company now known as Ameriprise Financial in the downtown Minneapolis home office. A few months later Toni joined her, working in the same department for the same company in the same office, where they continue to work today. Where do they work in a large corporate office? "Right next to each other!" the identical twins exclaim in unison. Naturally.

Photo courtesy of Ken Johannson

JIM JOHANNSON

Family History Subject: USA Hockey

THE NOW-BOOMING CITY OF ROCHESTER, MINNESO-
ta, had a population barely nudging north of 40,000 people when two-time
Olympian ice hockey player Jim Johannson was born in 1964, a century
and a year after Dr. William W. Mayo had moved to the city. Phenomenal growth,
primarily due to the expansion of medical care facilities in the Olmsted County city
located on the south fork of the Zumbro River, has elevated Rochester to the rank of
third-largest city in Minnesota. Rochester often receives high marks for its quality
of life and is noted as a favorable place to retire. The city's internationally acclaimed
Mayo Clinic currently employs more than 35,000 people—one of the famed clinic's
employees having been an administrator named Ken Johannson.

Ken Johannson, a native of Canada, was a prolific scoring forward for the University of North Dakota ice hockey team from 1950–53. He had a lengthy professional
career with the Rochester Mustangs of the United States Hockey League and played
two years on the US national team. Ken and Marietta Sands married in 1958 and had
three children: Judy, John, and Jim. While Judy became active in diving, John and
Jim were playing hockey by the age of four. The entire family became heavily invested in hockey, and Ken eventually became a founder of the USA Hockey Coaching
Education Program, writing a manual on the subject in 1975.

By the time Jim began playing varsity hockey on Rochester Mayo High School's
hockey team as a sophomore, John was having an illustrious senior season and being
recruited by the University of Wisconsin (UW) Badgers. In 1982, the year Jim graduated, the Mayo Spartan hockey team made their first appearance at the Minnesota State
High School League tournament. The Spartans lost in the consolation finals, but it
was an exciting and memorable season for the team. Known as a cerebral player who
played the game hard, Jim, at 6 feet 1 inch and 180 pounds, was not only on the recruiting lists of the Universities of North Dakota, Northern Michigan, Minnesota, and
Wisconsin, but he was also drafted in the seventh round by the NHL. Corey Millen,

a fleet skater from Cloquet, joined Jim on his recruiting visit to Madison, Wisconsin. The head coach, "Badger Bob" Johnson, had a long history with the Johannson family through competition and hockey camps, so it almost seemed predestined that Jim would become reunited with John in Madison, Wisconsin. Johnson told Jim bluntly, "You're comin'," and the deal was sealed.

In an unexpected twist, Johnson resigned from UW as the head coach after sixteen years to take a similar job with the Calgary Flames in the NHL. Jeff Sauer, the head coach at Colorado College, would replace Johnson and experience immediate success. "The real first true self-challenge was my freshman year in college and trying to learn [my] teammates. You had to make your mark your first year," reflects Jim. Evidently, Jim did make his mark as the team marched to the NCAA title for the 1982–83 season with a 6–2 victory over Harvard in the finals at Grand Forks, North Dakota. He capped off the season by being named to the US National Junior hockey team in 1983 and again in 1984. When his brother graduated from UW in 1984, John played five games for the New Jersey Devils in the NHL before beginning a career in real estate.

Sauer, who has known the Johannson brothers since they were in kindergarten, says, "Jim was a great leader and very committed to the game. He got a lot out of what he had. Bottom line, he has been an integral part of every team he has played on. He is now one of the best hockey administrators in the world."

While at UW, Jim scored 63 goals and proved his versatility by playing center and left and right wing. He graduated with a degree in recreation and resource management in 1986 and headed to Germany to play professional hockey. Invited to participate on one of four Olympic Sports Festival teams, Jim was not selected for the national team training camp, but head coach Dave "Pete" Peterson, the veteran coach of Minneapolis Southwest High School and several national teams, asked him to join the team nevertheless. Jim's response? "I'll be there," he answered directly. "Playing all three forward positions

JIM AND JOHN JOHANNSON PLAYED TOGETHER ON THE UW BADGERS MEN'S HOCKEY TEAM FROM 1982–84
Photo courtesy of Ken Johannson

probably helped me make the Olympic teams. I kept surviving the cuts. We were young, and I think Coach Peterson trusted me." Jim Johannson would be playing in the 1988 Winter Olympics in Calgary, Alberta, Canada.

There was a very familiar team-mate on the men's Olympic ice hockey team: defenseman Guy Gosselin, a 1982 graduate of Rochester John Marshall. Gosselin and Jim's parallel paths included being on some Rochester teams together as youths, competing against each other in college (Gosselin played for the University of Minnesota–Duluth), being on the same Olympic teams, and later working professionally for USA Hockey. Gosselin credits his roots for his hockey

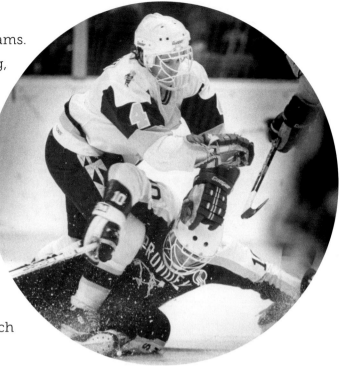

GUY GOSSELIN PLAYED FOR THE UNIVERSITY OF MINNESOTA–DULUTH AND ON THE 1988 AND 1992 US OLYMPIC HOCKEY TEAMS
Photo courtesy of UMD Sports

success, saying, "The Rochester Mustangs created a culture where they gave back to the community. We played because we loved the game and had a passion for the sport. We had some awesome mentors."

Ben Smith, an assistant on the 1988 Olympic hockey team, pairs up the Rochester Olympians, commenting, "Jim and Guy are solid, wonderful human beings. They are cut from the same cloth: gritty players who are grinders shift in and shift out. Jim was a cerebral, intelligent player who could see plays develop. Guy was tough as nails. He gave our team real backbone."

While the 1988 Olympic men's hockey team repeated its 1984 performance by finishing in seventh place, the team won two of five games and had very respectable performances against the perennially potent teams from the Soviet Union and Czechoslovakia in losing by identical 7–5 scores. Jim centered the line with Kevin Stevens and Todd Okerlund, a Burnsville, Minnesota, native, and had one goal in a 10–6 win over Austria. Of his teammates, Jim particularly appreciated Corey Millen's speed and watching Brian Leetch (a defenseman paired with Gosselin). "To see him play every day in practice was special," says Jim about Leetch, who would win the Calder Trophy as the NHL Rookie of the Year in the 1988–89 season and twice be awarded the Norris Trophy as the NHL's top defenseman.

For the next three years, Jim played in the International Hockey League (IHL) and won the Ironman Award while playing for Indianapolis Ice in 1990–91, for playing in all the team's games and displaying outstanding offensive and defensive skills. Jim was then released from his contract in order for him to try out for the 1992 Olympic team. "In 1988 I was still figuring myself out as a player and improving my skating, play, and endurance. A core tenant of the Olympic training got you ready for the event. In 1992 I felt more confident in my play." Yet Jim felt uncertain about his status at the training camp despite his previous experience and improved play. "Coach Pete [Peterson was again named the Olympic hockey coach] put both hands on my shoulders and said, 'You're right on the bubble. Just keep being who you are.'" Jim did make the squad and would be paired primarily with Ted Drury on the penalty-killing team. "Our role was more of keeping things in check," Jim reports.

> *"In 1988 I was still figuring myself out as a player and improving my skating, play, and endurance. A core tenant of the Olympic training got you ready for the event. In 1992 I felt more confident in my play."*

The 1992 Olympic hockey competition would be at Méribel Ice Palace, about thirty miles from the host city, Albertville, France. "We had an unheralded team full of gamers," says Jim. The team proved it by winning four games and one tie in their group to advance to the final eight teams. Jim scored a goal in the first game, a 6–1 victory over Italy. The American team defeated France in the quarterfinal but then squared off against the Unified Team (the former Soviet Union without the Baltic States) and lost 5–2. In the bronze medal match, the American suffered a disappointing 6–1 defeat to Czechoslovakia.

Returning to the IHL, Jim played for the Milwaukee Admirals, then an independent team, for two seasons and one season in Germany before accepting a position to coach the Twin City Vulcans at the age of thirty-one in 1995. "It was a great experience. The timing was good," Jim remarks of his three years of coaching the Vulcans to 68 victories in 156 games. Afterward he devoted himself to duties as the team's general manager.

Jim then joined USA Hockey and has had a series of positions with the organization since 2000. Beginning as manager of international activities and serving as team leader for the silver medal–winning 2002 men's Olympic hockey team, Jim is now assistant executive director of hockey operations. He is responsible for daily hockey operations, schedules, and fulfilling team and staff needs. "We try to field the best team we can. If self-assessment is off, you're going to continually have challenges." He encourages hockey players who want to make Olympic teams to be versatile because it can help them not only make the team to fill a need, but it will also advance their professional career. In 2011 he married Abigail Tompkins, an employee in international relations on the US Olympic Committee.

Photo courtesy of USA Hockey

Striking hockey memories run the gamut for the Minnesota Olympian. Jim was in disbelief when he saw Jay North of Bloomington Jefferson score a goal while his team was shorthanded two players in the section finals against Mayo in 1980. Jim expresses awe at how Dave Tippett, an NHL coach since 2002, "could single-handedly disrupt a team" when Tippett played at the University of North Dakota. And he marvels at Phil Housley (South St. Paul High School), "the most special player from a pure hockey point."

Having grown up around hockey, Jim was familiar with USA Hockey through his father, who played a role on the 1980 Miracle on Ice team when he served as general manager in addition to being an educator, coach, and administrator at many levels of the sport. It has a family history—and its subject is USA Hockey.

**BOB KEMPAINEN RUNNING A
CROSS COUNTRY RACE IN 1990**
Photo courtesy of Dartmouth Athletics Communications

BOB KEMPAINEN

The Minnesota Distance-Running Tradition Continues

LED BY OLYMPIANS LEONARD "BUDDY" EDELEN (1964) of St. Louis Park, Van Nelson (1968) and Ron Daws (1968) of Minneapolis (Washburn and Central, respectively), Garry Bjorklund of Proctor (1976), and Steve Plasencia (1988 and 1992) of Robbinsdale Cooper, male distance runners from Minnesota have been prominent at the national and international levels of running for over half a century. Other notable runners who have achieved success as premier distance runners include Steve Hoag and Mark Nenow of Anoka, Mike Slack of St. Paul Harding, Don Timm of Burnsville, Bruce Mortenson of St. Louis Park, Tom Heinonen of Robbinsdale, and Dick Beardsley of Wayzata.

Throughout his life, Bob Kempainen of Minnetonka has been familiar with Minnesota's storied history in distance running. "I was aware of the precedent of distance runners from Minnesota. It aided in my consideration of attempting to become an Olympian. It seemed that they would hunker down, work hard, and show up when it counts." The recipe proved successful for Bob as well; he qualified for the 1992 and 1996 Summer Olympics in the longest distance-running event of all, the marathon.

Bob was born in 1966, and followed older brothers Todd and Steve, both of whom experienced great success, into competitive running. Until his junior year at Hopkins High School, Bob had sandwiched ice hockey between fall cross country season and spring track season. "It was a tough transition to play hockey after eight to nine months of running," Bob admits. As a result he switched sports for the winter season by participating in nordic skiing.

Bob credits his coaches at Hopkins Public Schools, Pat Lanin, Paul Noreen, and Gerald Metzler, a trio of University of Minnesota (U of M) runners, for his success in high school. Metzler speaks about the brothers and a particularly demanding workout at a track when Bob was in tenth grade and Steve was a senior. "They were very intelligent and coachable. Just wonderful guys to have on the team, and they had very supportive parents. The time I remember best is a private practice. It was raining, and we were on a dirt track. Steve and Bob ran five eight-hundred-eighty-yard runs with only a three-minute jog recovery time between runs. They ran each interval under two minutes, twenty seconds! That was when I knew they were going to be something special." Todd had become a member of the national nordic ski team, and Steve did win the 3,200-meter run at the Minnesota State High School Track and Field Championships that spring. Bob would duplicate that feat in a memorable race in 1984.

As a junior, Bob placed fourth in the 3,200-meter run with a time of 9 minutes, 27 seconds (9:27) at the state meet and set his sights on a championship for his senior season. In the fall of 1983, he was the runner-up to John Wodny of Esko/Cloquet at the state Class 2A cross country meet. At the 3,200-meter run at the state track and field meet, Bob would eclipse his performance of the previous season by more than ten seconds. He won by the thinnest margin possible: 0.01 seconds over a hard-charging Ben Husaby of Eden Prairie. "The race was virtually a dead heat," Bob concedes. He names Wodny and Husaby as the competitors he most respected in high school: "They were so strong." Wodny would become a collegiate cross country conference champion at the University of Wyoming, and Husaby would compete in cross country skiing at the University of Colorado.

"It was a classic duel. The next day we competed in the 1,600-meter championship, but I think we were so spent [Wodny and Steve Lumbar of Bemidji also ran in both finals] that we placed fifth and sixth. We knew each other socially as well as competitors. I admired Bob's quiet leadership. He was well spoken, humble, and respected."

Husaby, a 1992 and 1994 Olympian in nordic skiing and now a director at Bend Endurance Academy in Oregon for nordic skiing, biking, and rock climbing, remem-

BOB KEMPAINEN (NUMBER 100) AND THE DARTMOUTH COLLEGE CROSS COUNTRY TEAM AT A MEET
Photo courtesy of Dartmouth Athletics Communications

bers the race as a poignant moment. "It was a classic duel. The next day we competed in the 1,600-meter championship, but I think we were so spent [Wodny and Steve Lumbar of Bemidji also ran in both finals] that we placed fifth and sixth. We knew each other socially as well as competitors. I admired Bob's quiet leadership. He was well spoken, humble, and respected."

Bob decided to enroll at Dartmouth College, the smallest Ivy League college, in Hanover, New Hampshire, after consulting his brothers, who had left Minnesota for college (Todd had attended the University of Vermont, and Steve was at the University of Alaska in Fairbanks). "I was interested in a smaller liberal arts college and wanted to go somewhere new," Bob reports. "I was a nonscholarship athlete and liked the coach, Vin Lananna. He was very charismatic. He could sell you anything, and he could back it up." Bob was not confident that he could compete at the Division I level, but he did manage to be the number-five runner on the cross country team as a first year student athlete. "Dartmouth had a few runners on the cusp of greatness. There was quite a separation between the top four and me," he says in his low-key manner. Dartmouth's team was on the upswing, and the team won its first of eight conference (referred to as the Heptagonals) titles. The leap to Division I running proved exhausting, however. "The tank was empty at the end of the year," Bob confesses.

After an abbreviated trial at nordic skiing and one full track season, Bob blossomed in cross country as a sophomore. He usually finished second to teammate Frank Powers and concluded the season by finishing fourteenth at the NCAA meet. Powers, a 1986 graduate, watched Bob's growing strength and maturity. "Bob was a supersmart guy, always seeking input from others. It was fun watching him develop as an efficient runner. He is a likable, humble, hardworking, and disciplined person. Sometimes he seemed disorganized—probably because he was trying to pack so much into every day. I know that he once missed the start of a race! He really took off, though, when he tried marathon running. His natural talent and work ethic lent itself to longer distances."

DARTMOUTH COLLEGE CROSS COUNTRY TEAMMATES BOB KEMPAINEN, PAUL CHALLEN, AND RONALD FAITH
Photo courtesy of Dartmouth Athletics Communications

In 1986 Dartmouth qualified as a team for the NCAA Cross Country Championships and surprised the competition with a runner-up finish as Bob surged to a fourth-place finish. The team proved it was not a fluke by repeating as runner-up in 1987 when Bob placed eleventh overall individually. His senior season was completed with a strong third-place showing in the 10,000-meter run in 28:53, surpassing his sixth-place finish the previous spring, at the NCAA Track and Field Championships at Hayward Field in Eugene, Oregon. Bob's modesty continues: "It all came together at the end."

Graduating with a biochemistry degree in 1988, Bob did participate in the 10,000-meter event at the Olympic Trials in Indianapolis, Indiana. "I got lapped, but I was cheering for the Minnesota runners ahead of me. Plasencia qualified by placing second [Nenow finished fourth—two seconds away from being the final qualifier]. Beardsley, Bjorklund, Nenow, and Plasencia . . . they had a mystique that you could train on your own outside the hub." The inspiration led to the next step in Bob's quest to be an Olympian.

Continuing to train under Lananna's guidance, Bob worked in a biology lab at Dartmouth and had modest support from Nike. "I feared that I didn't have the necessary speed for a much better ten K because I didn't have the kick for such a tactical race," Bob says. That analysis led him to consider running a marathon. He was also applying (and being accepted) annually to medical school at the U of M and decided to enter in 1990. That same year, he won the USA Cross Country Championships at Van Cortlandt Park in the Bronx (a challenging course he had run often as a collegian), ending Pat Porter's (born in Wadena, Minnesota) streak of eight consecutive victories. Granted a one-year leave from medical school, Bob then upped his training to 150 miles per week for a brief time to prepare for the Twin Cities Marathon in 1991. He also lived with the Bjorklund family in Fort Collins, Colorado, during part of that year while training. In one of his personal highlights, Bob placed second with an astounding time of 2 hours, 12 minutes, and 12 seconds (2:12:12) in his first attempt at a marathon! The remarkable result and demanding training came with a price, however. Bob had a stress fracture in his patella and adjusted his training regimen to pool workouts and cross-training using nordic equipment.

At the tender age of twenty-five, with only one marathon under his belt, Bob was a decided dark horse candidate to qualify for the 1992 Olympics. A pair of runners at the marathon trials in Columbus, Ohio, had built a commanding lead that slowly dissipated as Ed Eyestone, Steve Spence, and Bob gained. "We pretty much ran the race together," Spence recalls. "We reeled the two leaders in at mile twenty-three, and they had no response. Bob was a very patient runner who showed determination running after suffering an injury prior to the trials." Bob finished as the third and final marathon qualifier for the 1992 Olympics in Barcelona, Spain.

> *At the tender age of twenty-five, with only one marathon under his belt, Bob was a decided dark horse candidate to qualify for the 1992 Olympics.*

"The United States training center was in Narbonne, France, and it also served as a staging center," says Spence. "We ran the majority of the Olympic race together and had a good team performance. As a team, we were third and would have received a bronze medal if running teams were recognized." Spence finished twelfth, Eyestone thirteenth, and Bob was seventeenth with a time of 2:15:53. "At first I was disappointed, but in retrospect I ran a solid race," Bob says.

Continuing his medical school studies full-time in 1992–93, Bob expresses his appreciation that the U of M then allowed him to take three years to complete his final two years of medical school requirements: "They were very flexible and deserving of kudos." His best marathon running would be during the years 1993–94 as he balanced training, competing, and rotations at hospitals.

In 1993 he placed second in the New York City Marathon with a time of 2:11:03, more than a minute below his personal record and more than one and a half minutes ahead of the next American runner, Keith Brantley. It was another personal highlight for Bob. "The number of people cheering as you came back into Manhattan is mindboggling." Bob next finished seventh in the prestigious Boston Marathon in 1994 while achieving another personal best time of 2:08:47.

Bob and Lananna, coaching at Stanford at the time, would collaborate and meet in blocks of time to review training. "Bob was a very unpolished runner when he enrolled at Dartmouth, but he had great endurance from the beginning. He was motivated and determined as he rose to become our top runner. His strengths were his intelligence, efficiency, being able to utilize his resources and maximize his time. As a person, Bob is one of the premier athletes I ever coached. He is thoughtful, caring, and respectful. You hope for your children to be like him," Lananna says appreciatively. "He was in fantastic shape for the 1996 Olympic Trials."

> " *As a person, Bob is one of the premier athletes I ever coached. He is thoughtful, caring, and respectful. You hope for your children to be like him.* "

DR. ROBERT KEMPAINEN
Photo courtesy of Fairview-University Hospitals

It showed in Charlotte, North Carolina. Legendary among long-distance runners, Bob's running on that chilly and gusty day is famed for the film footage showing him vomiting six times around the twenty-three-mile mark while maintaining his pace—if not increasing it. "I felt queasy after drinking some fluids. For some reason my body was not absorbing them. I didn't cramp and felt better after vomiting." He actually broadened his lead over the last four miles with mile times of 4:42, 4:33, 5:06, and 4:59, winning convincingly in a time of 2:12:45. Brantley and Mark Coogan were the other two qualifiers. Bob also claimed a $100,000 prize for the championship. Plasencia, still racing strong at age thirty-nine, finished fourth—just missing becoming a three-time Olympian.

Battling tendinitis in both legs, Bob lost two months of running training after the trials. He thought the course in Atlanta, Georgia, host of the 1996 Summer Olympics, fit his strengths, but the lost training time took a toll. For a while he doubted that he could compete, but a couple of better weeks of running shortly before the Olympics provided some optimism. He decided to compete but struggled to a thirty-first-place finish with a time of 2:18:38.

While disappointed that he hadn't been able to compete at his peak, the future was full of promise. Bob married Sarah, a woman from Wisconsin whom he'd met in medical school, in 1997. They lived in Seattle, Washington, for a few years while Bob received specialty training in pulmonary and critical care at the University of Washington. They returned to Minnesota in 2002, where Bob now teaches at the U of M Medical School and practices at Hennepin County Medical Center, and Sarah practices internal medicine. They are parents of two children, Nora and Louis. Bob still runs a moderate twenty miles per week while balancing family, professional, and community responsibilities.

Bob Kempainen has now become an integral member of the elite Minnesota long-distance running corps that he observed and has perhaps unknowingly served as role model to many other aspiring runners who identified with the heritage he valued.

**JANIS AND BARNEY KLECKER WITH THEIR CHILDREN (LEFT TO RIGHT)
JAMES, JOE, JOHN, MARY, SARAH, AND ELIZABETH ("BIT")**
Photo courtesy of Janis and Barney Klecker

JANIS KLECKER

Gold Medal Family Runner

A CONVERSATION WITH JANIS KLECKER QUICKLY leads a person to understand that her family life is not only important to her, but also an integral part of her success as a runner. Her mother, Mae Horns, encouraged her to run; her husband, Barney Klecker, strongly supported her running; and the running spirit is now alive and active in her six children.

The route Janis took to becoming an elite long-distance runner is unusual. Born in 1960, Janis, the middle child of five children of Norman and Mae Horns, did not run competitively for the cross country or track teams at Edina West High School. Beginning in her senior year, Janis jogged about a mile a day in the spring solely as a means of staying physically fit. Previously, the only sport she had participated in was softball.

Enrolling in the University of Wisconsin at Madison in 1978, Janis considered engineering as a major and continued her running for fitness and recreational purposes. It was then that her mother contacted Janis and surprised her with the announcement that she was going to train for a marathon in Duluth, Minnesota, the following year.

In the spring of 1979, Mae Horns and her friend Pat Wiesner, a physical education instructor who started Macalester College's women's cross country program and was advising Mae on training, joined Janis in running a 10-kilometer (K) race in Madison, Wisconsin. Pat and Janis both won their age group in the race and won a trip to Kansas City to participate in a regional 10K race. It was the turning point in her running career. "The victory caused running to take on a new meaning," explains Janis.

In the fall of 1979, Janis transferred to the University of Minnesota–Twin Cities campus and asked Gopher women's cross country coach Mike Lawless whether she could train with the team without the commitment of competing and traveling. Lawless agreed to the request. Janis considered it a wonderful experience. "I learned the process of training with the team," she notes. Lawless, the women's cross country coach from its inaugural varsity season in 1974 until 1985, believes it was beneficial for the team as well. "Janis was an accomplished road racer who set a good example for the team. She was open-minded, positive, and found it interesting to be on a team and, perhaps, a valuable experience."

> "Janis was an accomplished road racer who set a good example for the team. She was open-minded, positive, and found it interesting to be on a team and, perhaps, a valuable experience."

That same fall, Janis and Mae ran the City of Lakes Marathon (forerunner of the Twin Cities Marathon). "At the start of the race Mom said, 'If you feel good, just keep going.' We separated after one half mile," laughs Janis as she finished third in the women's division at the tender age of nineteen. The overall winner of the marathon was Barney Klecker, posting his second victory in the event. While Barney and Janis were obviously at the same race, it was not until a later race in Bloomington that they actually met and soon started to date. The pair of long-distance runners became engaged in 1980—the same year Janis won her first City of Lakes Marathon—and married in 1981. As you might suspect, a lot of their time together revolved around running.

Continuing to train with the Gophers cross country team, Janis eventually became a varsity runner, but her success was limited due to suffering from asthma-related problems from running on cut grass. Rocky Racette of St. Louis Park was the top runner on the team with Janis generally being the sixth or seventh team member of the squad to finish. Racette tragically died in October 1981 from injuries sustained in a car accident. A foundation, scholarship, and annual meet (Rocky's Race) hosted by the Gophers are named in her honor.

With the continued family support that Janis treasured, she became a vital part of the burgeoning of women's marathon running and qualified for the 1984 American women's inaugural marathon Olympic Trials hosted by the city of Olympia, Washington. Trying to recover from a stress fracture, Janis placed twenty-sixth with a time of 2 hours, 38 minutes (2:38), about three minutes slower than her personal

**JANIS KLECKER WINS THE 1990
ST PATRICK'S DAY 8K IN 26:05**
Photo credit: St Paul Pioneer Press

best at the time.

Janis was also deciding on a professional career. "I became interested in the health field, but I did not want to be a nurse or a doctor, so I drifted toward dentistry by default." Janis graduated from dental school at the University of Minnesota in 1987 and is very satisfied with her career choice.

Although Janis again qualified for the 1988 Olympic marathon trials in Pittsburgh, Pennsylvania, complications with another stress fracture derailed her plans, and she did not compete. Before the trials, Janis won the women's division of the 1987 Grandma's Marathon in Duluth with a time of 2 hours, 36 minutes, and 12 seconds (2:36:12). In 1990, after recovering from the injury, she earned her second marathon victory in the San Francisco Marathon (the first was in 1983).

Houston, Texas, was the site of the 1992 American Olympic marathon trials and Janis's crowning achievement. Seeded fourth, Janis was healthy, confident, and well prepared. She had won the Twin Cities Marathon women's division in 1991 (2:30:31) just three months after her victory in San Francisco and would win again in 1992 (2:36:50). Her training included running in California for the three weeks preceding the trials after years of two-a-day workouts (a long run in the morning and cross training in the afternoon) in Minnesota. Her running mileage was between seventy and one hundred miles per week.

Coming from behind in the last mile to overtake the leader, Janis won the Olympic Trials in a personal best time of 2:30:12. It proved to be a very exciting and competitive race with Cathy O'Brien (who qualified for two US Olympic teams) and Francie Larrieu Smith (who qualified for five US Olympic teams) finishing within thirty seconds of Janis's winning time. A very modest person, Janis admits to it being a personal highlight of her running career.

Returning to Minnesota, Janis trained under the guidance of a few trusted coaches, but her husband Barney had become her closest advisor. Barney Klecker, renowned in running circles for his accomplishments in ultra-distance running,

JANIS KLECKER WINS THE 1991 TWIN CITIES MARATHON IN A TIME OF 2:30:31
Photo credit: St Paul Pioneer Press

had won several marathons and other long-distance races. A University of Wisconsin–Stout graduate, Barney was also a very successful snowshoe racer.

While the trip to Barcelona, Spain, for the Olympic marathon competition did not result in a medal for any American, Janis does have fond memories of the experience. Obtaining tickets for the opening ceremony was extremely difficult, but the track team manager was able to procure extra tickets and gave them to Janis. "It was great fun just to be present. Having Barney, my parents, and two close friends attend the opening ceremony was spectacular. They saw so much that we athletes did not see before marching into the stadium."

The race itself was difficult for Janis. The first half of the course wound along the Mediterranean coastline, but then it entered the city and ended with a challenging uphill climb for the last five kilometers. The race began at 6:30 p.m.—a poor choice of time in Janis's opinion because traffic had increased the level of pollution—and when entering the urban portion of the race, Janis was hit by many factors complicating her race strategy to run from behind. "Barcelona was hot, humid, and polluted. I have asthma, so I was really struggling. The gold medal–winning time was 2:32:41, a slow time for an Olympic championship." Janis finished twenty-first with a time of 2:47:17.

"Ron Daws [a 1968 marathon Olympian from Minneapolis] said, 'This will change your life.' Being an Olympian gives you credibility. It has been a platform, and people get glimmers of your faith and what drives you," Janis reflects.

Janis continued to run, practice dentistry part-time, and balance those workloads with the start of a family. She qualified for both the 1996 and 2000 Olympic marathon trials held in Columbia, South Carolina. She participated in the 1996 trials run even though it was not long after the birth of the Kleckers' third child, but she did not qualify for the Olympic team. In 2000 she decided not to participate in the trials because she was pregnant. Here is the scorecard: US Olympic marathon trials qualifications, five; children, six.

Athletes that Janis most admires tend to run in the family. The bonding between Mae and Janis went far beyond running (the Twin Cities Marathon in 1999 was the last marathon they ran) and sometimes competing as a mother-daughter duo—they were literally part of each other's daily life. Her father, Norman, was an athletic and disciplined runner who ran under 2:50:00 for the marathon after the age of fifty. Her husband, Barney, has held several American and even world records in long-distance. Other athletes that Janis has great respect for are the pioneers of women's long-distance running such as Joan Benoit Samuelson.

JANIS KLECKER, SARAH AS AN INFANT, AND MAE HORNS AT THE 1996 US OLYMPIC TRIALS
Photo courtesy of Janis and Barney Klecker

Today Janis runs in a way that is familiar to most parents: to keep up with her children's activities. The five oldest children all competed for the cross country and track programs in Hopkins. All the running Kleckers are disciplined and self-directed in the sport, and the oldest four continued at the collegiate level. They have also been involved with soccer, baseball, and karate. Janis sometimes thinks that the children's running is her mother's legacy. Mae Horns died of ALS in 2001.

Friend and long-time running partner Bonnie Sons, an All-American cross country and track runner at Iowa State, says of Janis, "She is one of the most genuinely nice and humble people you will ever meet. She is dedicated and has a very strong faith life. Her focus enables her to accomplish whatever task is at hand. It is obvious that her children and husband mean much to her. We always end up chatting about family throughout our runs, and the miles fly by."

Janis concludes, "In my life, running has been the faith journey vehicle by which God has shown me who He is. I have journals full of incredibly clear answered prayer." After a long run a few days after her return from the Olympics, Janis was feeling discouraged with running and not having medaled when her spirits were bolstered by a young neighbor girl who brought her a gift: a shiny plastic gold medal with the name Janis Klecker emblazoned on it.

KRIS KUEHL AT THE 2002 NATIONAL TRACK AND FIELD CHAMPIONSHIPS
Photo credit: Kirby Lee, Image of Sport

KRIS KUEHL

A Genuine Thrower with an Artistic Flair

DISCUS THROWING IS MORE THAN TWENTY-FIVE hundred years old. Ancient statues celebrating the sport show a muscular man bent low in a twisting motion, highlighting the strength and flexibility of his body. Discus throwing was one of five athletic (track and field) events that debuted for women in the modern Olympics in 1928. It's a technical sport that requires not only strength, but rhythm, balance, acceleration, and a precise release point while spinning one and a half times around inside a ring with a 2.5-meter diameter. In a sports oddity, the women's disc is the same weight, one kilogram, regardless of the level of competition (junior high school through the Olympics). In the twenty-first century, seventy-two years after discus was introduced as a women's sport in the Olympics, a woman from Minnesota was slinging the disc at the Summer Olympics in Sydney, Australia.

Kris Kuehl (pronounced Keel), the middle of three children of Kornell and Gisela Kuehl, was born in 1970 and grew up on a farmstead in southwestern Minnesota. "Our mailing address was Heron Lake, I was born in Windom, lived nearest to Storden, graduated from Storden-Jeffers High School, and went to track and field practice in Westbrook for the last two to three years of my high school career. So it might be most accurate to say I'm from Cottonwood County. Such is life in rural areas," explains Kris.

Playing basketball and participating in track and field throughout most of junior and senior high school, Kris was more known for her basketball prowess as a 6-foot frontcourt player than as a discus-throwing standout. Her improbable start to becoming an Olympian in discus throwing began on the third day of track practice. "The first day we ran two miles. The second day we ran farther. On the third day we had the option to run or try throwing the discus. I opted for throwing the

KRIS KUEHL JUST RELEASING THE DISC AT THE MINNESOTA STATE HIGH SCHOOL LEAGUE TRACK AND FIELD CHAMPIONSHIPS IN 1988
Photo courtesy of Dave Fjeld

discus," laughs Kris. She qualified for the state high school track and field championships her sophomore year but did not place. In 1988, her senior year, she again qualified and this time placed second—becoming one of the better throwers in the state. That same year, the Storden-Jeffers High School girls' basketball team was runner-up in the state basketball tournament to Tracy-Milroy, led by Kansas State–bound Mary Jo Miller. "We were deep and could run. We had soundly defeated Tracy-Milroy earlier in the year," Kris remembers. In 1989 Storden-Jeffers was crowned Class A state champion, but Kris had joined older sister Ann at Concordia College in Moorhead, Minnesota.

While initially disappointed that she did not draw major college attention or recruiters, Kris now believes choosing a Division III school may have been for the best. "The Concordia coach, Doug Perry, was enthusiastic. He kept it simple and taught the basics during my freshman year. I was still scrawny. I liked the size of Concordia, and it felt like a good fit." An art education major, Kris, growing stronger and more familiar with the disc, qualified for nationals her first collegiate year. She did not place, but she liked the sport. "Throwers are very genuine people. Men and women train together and become a family. They look out for each other—even at nonteam events."

The jump to quick college success was surprising, but what followed was astounding: Kris proceeded to capture three consecutive NCAA Division III titles in discus throwing! Her senior year, she had a discus

KRIS KUEHL PLAYING BASKETBALL FOR STORDEN-JEFFERS HIGH SCHOOL IN 1988
Photo courtesy of Kris Kuehl

throw that qualified her for the 1992 Olympic Trials, and she was also an All-American in the shot put. Evonne Vaplon, Concordia's throwing coach at that time, remembers Kris as a top scholar and athlete. "She was the type of person who wanted to excel at everything she did. She also had a great sense of humor and a curious mind—particularly for random, odd facts she liked to share with her teammates. One memory I have is trying to keep the discus from going onto the track

KRIS KUEHL
Photo credit: John Borge, courtesy of Concordia College Archives

during a meet at Moorhead State University (now Minnesota State University–Moorhead) so it wouldn't hit the runners. She was throwing it so far it became a hazard, and I would try to stop it with my foot after it hit the ground and bounced!"

At this point, Kris had not considered pursuing throwing discus postcollegiately. That changed dramatically when she placed eighth in the trials at hot and humid New Orleans, Louisiana, with a throw of 177 feet 11 inches (54.24 meters). Still one month shy of her twenty-second birthday, Kris was the top collegian at the trials and considered young in the sport. The result spurred her decision to continue training and compete nationally and internationally until the 1996 Olympic Trials.

Kris and Vaplon devised a training schedule based on the time of year and the success she was having at meets. Remaining under Vaplon's tutelage, she trained six days per week, sometimes twice a day. Kris would throw the discus five days per week but decreased it to three times per week later in her career. Putting her art degree to use, she made stained-glass windows and mosaics at an art studio in Fargo, North Dakota.

Placing third at the 1995 Pan Am Games was the first major international event where Kris medaled. Fouling (stepping over the ring or throwing out of bounds) plagued Kris, though, and in the 1996 Olympic Trials at Atlanta, Georgia, she fouled on all three qualifying attempts and received no mark. "I was depressed only briefly; then I was mad and determined," Kris reports. She never considered quitting despite the frustrating experience. Kris resolved to make the 2000 United States Olympic team.

Kris was considering a move to Kentucky in 1998 to connect with a new coach when back pain due to a ruptured disc halted the plan. It was a few months before she tried throwing a discus. The results were satisfactory, and Kris was cautiously optimistic about continuing her career. She opted to move to the Twin Cities instead of Kentucky and was coached by Loreena Anderson at Hamline University in St. Paul. She worked part-time for Target Corporation in their fraud prevention division to pay the bills as she continued training. Performances where Kris stood on the awards podium the next two years included a bronze medal at the Goodwill Games and a silver medal at the 1999 Pan Am Games in Winnipeg—an event that she had set her mind to win. The perseverance and effort she poured into the sport paid the ultimate dividend when she placed third behind Seilala Sua and Suzy Powell in the 2000 Olympic Trials at Sacramento, California, with a throw of 202 feet 7 inches (61.74 meters). At age thirty, Kris was headed to Sydney, Australia, for the XXVII Summer Olympiad.

> *"My back flared up, and it required a couple visits to the local hospital. I was in tears, could barely walk, and was very stressed out. The epidural I received on the second hospital visit allowed me to compete."*

Unlike the 1956 Summer Games, which were held in the months of November and December due to the seasonal changes in the Southern Hemisphere, the 2000 Games were held at the end of September. "We were outfitted with a variety of gear because of the season," Kris notes. While the 2000 Olympic Games received acclaim for their organization, volunteers, the friendliness of the citizens, and facilities, the most vivid memory for Kris is the excruciating pain she experienced days before the discus event. "My back flared up, and it required a couple visits to the local hospital. I was in tears, could barely walk, and was very stressed out. The epidural I received on the second hospital visit allowed me to compete." Kris hurled the disc 195 feet ½ inch (59.41 meters), finishing eighteenth of thirty-two competitors. "I was disappointed, but did pretty well, all things considered," Kris summarizes.

The next year Kris qualified for the finals for the first time in a major international competition when she placed eighth in the prestigious World Championships in Edmonton, Canada, with a throw of more than 61 meters and her parents witnessing the event. The incremental progress, a genuine enjoyment of the sport, and the hope of medaling prodded her to continue training for the 2004 Olympic Games. During 2003 Kris had broken a bone in her foot and still competed in the 2003 World Championships. The injury didn't heal properly, and eventually Kris had surgery a few months before the 2004 Olympic Trials. Although it severely limited her training time, Kris still was second in the qualifying round at the trials with a solid throw of 197 feet 1 inch (60 meters), but her best throw in the finals was a full meter less, and she ended in fifth place in the competition.

KRIS KUEHL IS A PHYSICAL THERAPIST AT PHYSICAL THERAPY ORTHOPAEDIC SPECIALISTS, INC (PTOSI)
Photo courtesy of Kris Kuehl

Kris wrapped up her athletic career working with Lynne Anderson, throws coach at the University of Minnesota, in 2005. Kris continued to work for Target and became a personal trainer, but discovered her interest was drifting toward physical therapy. She enrolled in the University of Minnesota doctoral physical therapy program as a full-time graduate student in 2009. "I was a nontraditional student and the oldest person in my class," she vouches. She enjoyed the three-year program and finds her work at Physical Therapy Orthopaedic Specialists, Inc. satisfying and fulfilling.

A lifelong Vikings fan, Kris names Ahmad Rashad, a wide receiver with the team from 1976–82, as a favorite athlete because of his spectacular acrobatic catches. Discus thrower Connie Price-Smith served as an unofficial mentor, and Kris found her very approachable. Kris admired another discus thrower, Olympic gold medalist Mac Wilkins, for his perfect throwing form. Wilkins appreciated Kris seeking pointers to improve her throwing. "I was able to train with Kris a few times. She was technically astute. She had a yearning to learn more all the time about how to perfect a throw. In my view, she was very creative in her approach. She was able to tie abstract concepts to the technical aspects of her throw. It added to her sense of humor that was very endearing and refreshing."

Photo credit: David Carmichael Photography

MARK LADWIG

Good Things Happen in Pairs

BOASTING SOME OF THE RICHEST AGRICULTURAL land in the world, the Red River Valley was formed from silt deposits as giant Lake Agassiz melted ten millennia ago. Moorhead, located adjacent to the North Dakota border and the largest city in northwestern Minnesota, also boasts two colleges, Minnesota State University–Moorhead and Concordia, and many professional hockey players. In addition to the outstanding athletes playing in the NHL, there is another athlete who has had great success on the ice: Olympic pairs figure skater Mark Ladwig.

John and Carol Ladwig are very proud of the diverse careers their three children have pursued. Oldest child Todd is a commander in the United States Navy; youngest child Erin is a dentist; and middle child Mark, born in 1980, realized his dream of being an Olympic figure skater. John, a physician practicing internal and geriatric medicine, and Carol, a medical technologist and longtime Moorhead Public Schools board member, remember that Mark was involved in many activities and into a bit of mischief. "You could call him strong-willed when he was young. He had a big heart, but he needed to buckle down," admits Carol. Mark had gerbils and chameleons, participated in wrestling and gymnastics (Mark Cullen, a former NHL player, was in the same class), became proficient in swimming and diving, and at various ages played soccer, football, and ice hockey.

> *"I learned that I didn't have the skill set—like stickhandling—for hockey, but I loved the ice and challenging myself . . ."*

"I learned that I didn't have the skill set—like stickhandling—for hockey, but I loved the ice and challenging myself," comments Mark. It led to a switch in skates, from ice hockey to figure, and joining Erin for lessons at the Red River Figure Skating Club.

Dawn Frisch-Franklin became Mark's first figure skating coach and is full of praise for her star pupil. "Mark was very athletic and coordinated, flexible, had a lot of natural ability—always wanting to do more. He had a gung-ho personality." While few boys were in the club, Mark enjoyed the sport and earned badges quickly as he passed tests in rapid succession. Coach Frisch-Franklin then made a suggestion that he view a sectional figure pairs meet that would initiate an Olympic quest. "Kelsey Sollom and Mark came to it and decided they'd like to give it a try. He tried all disciplines of figure skating: dance, single, and pair skating. I think it was a plus for him."

Far from limiting his pursuits to figure skating, Mark's mother and father tick off his other high school endeavors: "Mark was a nighttime DJ at a radio station [with the handle "Moss Quito" at "Froggy" 99.9 KVOX-FM] his junior and senior years and served as a lifeguard; he and Todd both received Eagle Scout awards [Erin achieved the Gold Award in Girl Scouts], he pole-vaulted in track, was in high school plays, and took summer classes at the University of Minnesota in topology and architectural math." Of course, Mark dedicated lots of time to skating too, but he remained well-rounded. A final Moorhead High School memory happened in 1999, the year Mark graduated. With Erin present to support him, Mark asked Janet Beverley to prom. His proposal was met with uncomfortable—perhaps stunned—silence. He belatedly added, "As friends." The dance invitation was accepted, as was his marriage proposal seven years later.

"The experience made me curious. It solidified my belief that I wanted to be part of the Olympic movement . . ."

While Mark's parents were hoping that he would enroll in college, Mark was determined to pursue figure skating. Two weeks after graduation, Mark was headed to Delaware, where he worked in restaurants to support his living and skating expenses. It was there that he obtained the nickname "Fargo" when asked where he was from and he mentioned Moorhead's neighbor as a reference point.

In 2002 Mark headed west to volunteer at the Olympic Winter Games in Salt

Lake City. He gave directions to venues and witnessed sixteen-year-old Sarah Hughes surpass Michelle Kwan to win the women's singles gold medal in figure skating. "The experience made me curious. It solidified my belief that I wanted to be part of the Olympic movement," says Mark thoughtfully. After volunteering outside the barrier at the Olympics, Mark wanted more than anything to return and be inside the barrier.

Having been paired with Keri Blakinger for much of the time before the 2002 Olympics, a coach and a 1960 bronze medalist named Ron Ludington then connected Mark with Amanda Evora following a lengthy search for a new partner. "I received a message to call Kerry Leitch—'I've found a girl!'" smiles Mark.

MARK LADWIG AND AMANDA EVORA COMPETED IN FIGURE SKATING PAIRS TOGETHER FOR TEN YEARS
Photo credit: David Carmichael Photography

Amanda, four years Mark's junior, is the daughter of Filipino immigrants. She remembers their tryout in Florida vividly. "I always had strong faith in my coaches' opinion. At that time, my primary coach was Kerry Leitch, as well as Jim Peterson. Mark was already an experienced pair skater, having three other partners before me. Therefore he had his basic pair skating skills so we could advance into the senior level. He was open-minded to the skating technique in Florida and [had a] willingness to try new things. With our common goals, these qualities were good to have to start off a partnership." The pair would skate together for more than a decade—unusual longevity in pairs figure skating.

"In the 2003 United States Figure Skating Championships, our goal was to finish in the top half," states Mark. "We got twelfth of twenty-four pairs." Mission accomplished.

Then began a steady ascent developed through rigorous and dedicated training. At 5 feet 10 inches tall and weighing between 165 and 180 pounds, Mark has a long wingspan that makes him optically more aesthetic in the lifts and movements required in pairs figure skating. Amanda was just shy of 5 feet tall and weighed 100 pounds. The lithe bodies of figure skaters disguise their incredible strength, required for lifts and jumps. A training schedule would include short programs and free skates,

MARK LADWIG AND AMANDA EVORA PLACED 10TH IN THE 2010 OLYMPICS AT VANCOUVER, BRITISH COLUMBIA
Photo credit: David Carmichael Photography

massages, military presses, tons of ballet, squats, and clean-and-jerk lifting. They also learned from nutrition experts and studied videos. The pair set performance goals, but they were realistic in knowing that there would be mistakes. In total, Mark and Amanda and their coaches had devised a comprehensive strategy for their competitive future.

Mark supported himself by working at the Ellenton Ice Complex in Florida, sharpening skates and driving the Zamboni to resurface the ice, among other tasks. In 2006 he and his senior prom date, Janet, married. Janet had been attending North Dakota State University in Fargo with the goal of getting a degree in interior design. She would later graduate summa cum laude with a bachelor of fine arts degree in her chosen major from the International Academy of Design and Technology in Tampa.

In 2005 Mark and Amanda had placed fifth at nationals and continued to place between fourth and seventh through 2009. They received a bye from qualifying for the 2010 national competition—an Olympic Winter Games year—due to placing in the top five pairs the previous year. The top two pairs generally qualified for the 2010 Olympics in Vancouver, British Columbia. A mere four months earlier, Janet and Mark had become proud parents of a son, Holden.

Following the short program, Mark and Amanda were in third place. That score would be combined with the longer free skate to determine the pairs that would form the American Olympic team. "We doubled down and made it by the narrowest of margins," Mark says with pride. They finished third in the free skate as well, but their combined scores for the two events placed them less than one point ahead of Rena Inoue and John Baldwin to claim the national silver medal and advance to the Olympics.

That set off a mad scramble in Moorhead, Minnesota! John and Carol Ladwig were not prepared for the joyous outcome of the trials and rushed to secure lodging near Vancouver. The extended Ladwig family was joined by the Evora family at a house they rented thirty miles from Pacific Coliseum, the site of the Olympic figure skating event. They would take a commuter train to cheer on the excited Olympians.

> *"It was a good skate, not a clean skate. You celebrate that you made the Olympics and skated well."*

Mark and Amanda performed and competed well at the Olympics and received international acclaim for their lifts. Their tenth-place finish in the short program was followed by a tenth-place finish in the free skate, which equated to tenth place overall, highest of the American pairs. The skaters are judged on twelve elements in the free skate, and Mark and Amanda received the highest score of any pair on any element with a 9.15 on a reverse-lasso lift. They were the only pair attempting the feat with its unique back entry by Amanda: Mark lifting Amanda high above him and holding her in a horizontal position with one hand while pirouetting. Backwards. In that single element, Mark Ladwig and Amanda Evora were the best of the Olympians. In reviewing the video of their free skate, Mark points out minor mistakes that go unnoticed by the casual observer. "It was a good skate, not a clean skate. You celebrate that you made the Olympics and skated well," concludes Mark.

"It was the pinnacle point to my competitive career," declares Amanda. "Our goal [of] making it to the Olympics was already made, and we were there to skate our hearts out and represent our country. Thankfully so, we earned our season's best scores while we were there. We were all smiles in the kiss and cry [the waiting area where skaters stay to hear their announced marks]. And what I chose to say is this: 'It's worth it!' And what I meant was all the hard work, the sacrifices, and that attitude of 'never give up' was right.

MARK LADWIG AND AMANDA EVORA PLACED 6TH AT THE 2011 FOUR CONTINENTS COMPETITION IN TAIPEI, TAIWAN
Photo credit: David Carmichael Photography

At that moment, all of that [was] worth it. Worth it to have that Olympic moment."

One month later, Mark and Amanda competed at the World Championships at the Palavela in Turin, Italy, and climbed one more spot, finishing in ninth place. They continued to skate as pairs until 2012, when Amanda expressed her preference to retire and experience other things in life. Their last performance together went back at Mark's roots: they were guest skaters for the Red River Figure Skating Club's annual show in Moorhead. Coach Frisch-Franklin said the duo was well received: "They would take extra time with kids at shows. Mark is a well-rounded person and just such a down-to-earth and friendly guy."

> *"They would take extra time with kids at shows. Mark is a well-rounded person and just such a down-to-earth and friendly guy."*

JANET (BEVERLEY), HOLDEN (STANDING), FELIX, AND MARK LADWIG, 2015
Photo courtesy of Mark and Janet Ladwig

Mark did pair with twenty-year-old Lindsay Davis for one more season before retiring from the sport of pairs skating. He uses a metaphor about gambling to describe his decision. "I compare it to being in Las Vegas. I never hit the jackpot, but I won enough that it was time to cash it in. I was fortunate to heal well and have no surgeries." He confesses to missing competitive skating, though. "I enjoyed training. I loved what I was doing."

Now a technical representative for Jackson Skate Company, Mark also serves as the athlete representative for figure skating on the United States Olympic Committee. The alternate is the 2002 gold medalist he met in Salt Lake City, Sarah Hughes. "We verify procedures and fairness to all athletes," says Mark. "I believe that the Olympic family does really reach out to athletes." Skating in ice shows did not appeal to Mark despite knowing the success that former Moorhead resident Matt Evers, winner of the junior pair title in 1998, has experienced performing with *Dancing on Ice* in the United Kingdom. "I'm not interested in shows. It is hard on family life."

The Ladwig family lives near Tampa, Florida. Janet does interior design work, and Mark hopes to be as supportive of her profession as she was in supporting his years in figure skating. Their son Holden was joined by a brother, Felix, in 2014. Again, good things have come in pairs.

**MANNY LAGOS WAS A FIRST TEAM ALL-AMERICAN
WHILE PLAYING FOR THE UNIVERSITY OF WISCONSIN–MILWAUKEE TEAM IN 1991**
Photo courtesy of UW Milwaukee Athletic Communications

MANNY LAGOS

Fathers & Sons

IT IS EVIDENT MANNY LAGOS HAS GREAT RESPECT FOR the history, evolution, skills, and tactics of soccer, but when his father, Manuel "Buzz" Lagos, is added to the conversation, the respect is amplified to another dimension. Born in New Jersey, Buzz Lagos moved to Minnesota to attend graduate school at the University of Minnesota, taking up soccer in his twenties. Buzz quickly became passionate about the sport and learned its many intricacies. "He absorbed every nuance of the game," Manny says with quiet pride. Manny credits the lessons that Buzz Lagos learned and passed on to his sons and others for helping him make the 1992 Olympic men's soccer team.

The youngest of eight children, Manny Lagos was born in St. Paul in 1971 and raised in the Macalester-Groveland neighborhood of the capital city. While all the children played soccer, it was the two youngest, Gerard and Manny, who developed their skills the most and eventually ascended to professional careers in the sport.

After three years of coursework toward a PhD, Buzz was hired as a math teacher and soccer coach at St. Paul Academy and Summit School (commonly referred to as SPA), a college-prep school formed by the 1969 merger of St. Paul Academy, an all-boys school, and Summit School, an all-girls school. Buzz was the first coach in Minnesota to earn a United States Soccer Federation "A" license and also became an assistant coach with the Minnesota Kicks, the first professional soccer team in Minnesota. The Kicks would compete in the North American Soccer League (NASL) for six seasons (1976–81), surprising sports observers by drawing an average of more than 23,000 fans each game to Metropolitan Stadium in Bloomington their first season. It also drew the love and attention of a young soccer aficionado, Manny Lagos. "The Minnesota Kicks were a huge influence to me—it showed what soccer could be," relates Manny.

The Lagos family also had an international experience when Buzz took a sabbatical from SPA for a semester and went to Uruguay. "It was wonderful to be im-

GERARD, BUZZ, AND MANNY LAGOS AFTER THE 1998 MLS CUP FINAL WHICH THE CHICAGO FIRE WON
Photo courtesy of Buzz and Sarah Lagos

mersed in the Uruguayan culture," says Buzz. Manny, a fifth grader, basked in the attention soccer received in the South American country where it is the number one sport, and he witnessed the people's passion for the game.

The Minnesota State High School League soccer tournament began in 1974, and SPA fielded stalwart teams under Buzz's direction. They won state championships in 1986, 1987, 1991, and 1994—all during years the tournament had only one class. Playing as forwards and midfielders on the first two state championship teams were Gerard and Manny Lagos. "Soccer was not a mainstream sport, but I had friends that gravitated toward it," Manny reports. Several of the teams' players eventually played professionally: Manny, Gerard, Tony Sanneh, Amos Magee, Eric Otto, Matt Holmes, Chris Gores, John Coughlin, Tod Herskovitz, and Leo Cullen.

A proud father, Buzz states, "Manny had a great touch with the ball—wonderful control. People always thought it was like there was a string tied to the ball. He had great vision and was a complete scorer." Manny was named Metro Soccer Player of the Year in 1988 and 1989, following in the footsteps of Gerard, who received the award in 1987.

Manny was also a starting 6-foot point guard for a competitive SPA boys' basketball team, but the right-footed soccer star was primarily recruited for his soccer talents by Division I schools when he graduated in 1990. More time with the sport occurred when he joined the amateur soccer team the Minnesota Thunder, where he saw a familiar face—his father was the coach. Manny decided to attend the University of Wisconsin–Milwaukee (UWM), going with high school friend and teammate Tony Sanneh and also reuniting with his brother Gerard. "UWM was one of the soccer meccas," states Manny. Another bonus was that the US national soccer team head coach, Bob Gansler, had been the head coach at UWM from 1984 to 1988. In 1991 Manny was named first team All-American, was a member of the Pan Am Games gold medal–winning soccer team, and set his sights on the next level: professional soccer.

Manny signed a contract in 1992 to play in Spain. "It was my ambition at the time. It was a rapid exposure to the difference between amateur and professional soccer," he confesses. But 1992 also provided another opportunity: the Olympic Games hosted by Barcelona, Spain. All the teams would be comprised of players under the age of twenty-three (U-23)—essentially the best young players who would be pursuing a future in professional soccer. The selection of the team was a long process that started in a state pool, advanced to a thirteen-state regional pool, and then consisted of a national team pool of thirty to fifty players. The selection of the final team hinged on many factors: the player's position, previous experience, and the coach's style of play. Manny kept surviving the cuts and was named to the 1992 US Olympic men's soccer team, still the only Minnesotan so honored. "We were still pretty much an amateur team. At that point, US soccer was growing up," says Manny.

"We were still pretty much an amateur team. At that point, US soccer was growing up . . ."

The 1992 Summer Games had numerous highlights, from the dramatic shooting of a flaming arrow over the Olympic cauldron in the opening ceremonies, to the reunification of East and West Germany as a single country, to an Israeli winning an Olympic medal for the first time since the tragic massacre in the 1972 Olympics of several Israeli athletes. Also featured and receiving expansive media coverage was the American men's basketball team. The "Dream Team" included professional stars Michael Jordan, Larry Bird, and Earvin "Magic" Johnson, and had a horde of admirers as they dominated all their opponents. Manny admits, "In my youthfulness, I loved being around big-time athletes. My affinity for basketball saw the Dream Team create a lot of energy."

Now twenty-one years old and weighing 165 pounds, Manny played forward for the US Olympic team. On the world stage, the developing American team lost 2–1 to Italy in the opening game. They defeated Kuwait 3–1 in the second game—only the team's third victory in 18 appearances at the Olympic Games. Manny scored the winning goal, a 79-foot shot. The third game against Poland, the eventual silver medalist, ended in a 2–2 tie. Despite their respectable performance, the American squad did not advance to the quarterfinals.

Manny returned to Minnesota, rejoining the Minnesota Thunder while playing with Sanneh and Gerard and reveling in the team's success. Sanneh, who made more than 40 appearances on the national team, remarks, "Manny was a lot faster than

MANNY LAGOS AND TONY SANNEH WERE
TEAMMATES ON THE SPARTAN RANDOLOPH
BLACKHAWKS (ST. PAUL, MINNESOTA), WHICH
WON THE MCGUIRE CUP AWARDED TO THE
UNDER-19 NATIONAL CHAMPIONS IN 1990
Photo courtesy of Buzz and Sarah Lagos

people suspected. He had a killer goal instinct. He had a knack for scoring—he was willing to take the responsibility to strike." With a long relationship at multiple levels with Manny, Sanneh adds, "He definitely is competitive but a caring and pretty humble guy. He was a friend, very inclusive." In 1994 the team was undefeated in 18 games, and Sanneh's words were proven true as Manny, scoring 18 goals, was named Most Valuable Player. The following season, the Thunder was elevated to the professional ranks, and Manny scored 20 goals for a 19–1 team. In Manny's words, these seasons spent playing with friends and family members passionate about the game were simply "really good years," but Major League Soccer (MLS) was calling.

Signed by the New York MetroStars, Manny suffered a ghastly knee injury in the sixth game of the 1996 season. While rehabilitating, Manny met Aimee Kindsfather, a student at New York University School of Law, an event that salvaged a frustrating time for the young professional athlete. Manny and Aimee married in 1999, the same year Manny showed signs of recovering from his debilitating injuries. In 1999 and 2000, Manny scored twelve goals for the Tampa Bay Rowdies over the course of the two seasons. A trade to the San Jose Earthquakes would later lead Manny to say, "From a winning standpoint, the 2001–03 seasons were the best of my professional career. We had a nice mixture of ages and players." The Earthquakes were MLS champions in 2001 when Manny tied for eleventh in scoring goals (eight) during the regular season and was a scoring sen-

MANNY LAGOS PLAYED FOR THE SAN JOSE EARTHQUAKES, THE 2001
AND 2003 MLS CHAMPIONS
Photo credit: Pam Whitesell/isiphotos

MANNY AND HIS SON, MANUEL JERRY (MJ)
Photo credit: Aimee (Kindsfather) Lagos

sation in the playoffs with three goals and two assists, and again in 2003. Those three years coincided with Manny playing on the senior national team for international competition.

In 2005, at the age of thirty-four, he ended his nine-year MLS career, having scored 27 goals and being credited with 36 assists. Lagos believes his best position may have been center midfielder. "I took pride in trying to make the teams I played on better," he says summarizing his playing years.

Again returning to his native state, Manny has had a series of positions with professional soccer teams in Minnesota. He has been involved in administration and coaching with the Minnesota Thunder, the Minnesota Stars, and the Minnesota United Football Club (FC) Loons. Twice Manny has received Coach of the Year accolades: in 2011 when the Stars captured the NASL championship and in 2014 when the Minnesota United team had the league's top overall record. Manny quickly distributes kudos to the team and assistant coaches Carl Craig, Donny Marks, and Paul O' Connor.

Passionate and enthusiastic, Manny is articulate in expressing his viewpoint on soccer in Minnesota. "It is growing exponentially. Locally the sport is so relevant." He is also excited that MLS is expanding to the state. "They see the Twin Cities as part of a global market. The future of American soccer is so bright."

Instead of practicing law, Aimee (Kindsfather) Lagos became an entrepreneur and senior manager in marketing for Target Corporation. Manny and Aimee are the parents of two sons, Manuel (an eighth-generation name) Jerry and Jackson Edward Lagos.

AIMEE (KINDSFATHER), MJ, JACKSON EDWARD, AND MANNY LAGOS, 2015
Photo credit: Aimee (Kindsfather) Lagos

**KARI ERICKSON RELEASING THE STONE AND STACEY LIAPIS
SWEEPING IN FRONT OF IT AT THE 2002 OLYMPIC TRIALS**
Photo courtesy of USA Curling

KARI (LIAPIS) ERICKSON AND STACEY LIAPIS

Curling's Full House

RATHER RELUCTANT AND RESTLESS SPECTATORS OF curling as youths, Kari and Stacey Liapis (a Greek name pronounced Lee-op-iss) grudgingly attended curling matches their parents, Mike and Suzanne, participated in at the Bemidji Curling Club. "We did not appreciate watching and waiting," admits Stacey.

Bemidji, a town of approximately 14,000 people, bills itself as "the First City on the Mississippi." A northern recreational area popular for its lakes and trails, it is also home to the gigantic statues of Paul Bunyan and Babe the Blue Ox, a famous roadside attraction unveiled in 1937 and prominent in the circles of curling. Someone from Bemidji was on a United States Olympic curling team for a duration of four consecutive Olympics: Stacey Liapis, 1998; Kari Erickson and Stacey Liapis, 2002; Pete Fenson, skip and bronze medalist, and Cassie and Jamie Johnson, 2006; and Natalie (Simonsen) Nicholson, 2010. Clearly, the sport has a committed cadre of players showcasing their skills at the Bemidji Curling Club.

Organized during the Great Depression, the original Sports Arena in Bemidji was a Works Progress Administration

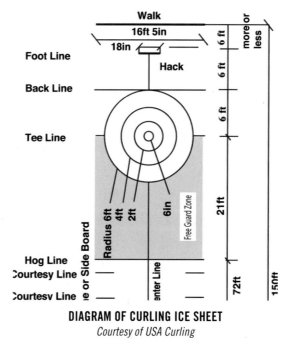

DIAGRAM OF CURLING ICE SHEET
Courtesy of USA Curling

MIKE LIAPIS, KARI ERICKSON, AND STACEY LIAPIS AT THE 2002 OLYMPIC OPENING CEREMONIES
Photo credit: Debbie McCormick

(WPA) project built in 1935. The arena was replaced by the current Bemidji Curling Club facility in 1967. It was in this building that Suzanne Liapis began a sport in 1972 that would lead husband, Mike, and—with a little coaxing—their daughters Kari and Stacey to join her. Eventually the foursome would have their own roles as an Olympic coach, a team manager, and two Olympian curlers in the 2002 Olympic Games in Salt Lake City, Utah.

Referred to as "chess on ice," curling is played on a narrow sheet of ice 150 feet in length by 16½ feet in width. The ice surface has three concentric circles surrounding a button, forming the house, a target area. Four players compose a team (rink) that competes against another rink, trying to get a 42-pound polished granite stone (rock) as close to the center of the house as possible at the conclusion of each end, often cited as similar to an inning in baseball. Only one team scores points in an end, based on how many of the eight stones the team has thrown that are closer to the center of the house than any stones by their opponent. A game consists of eight or ten ends, depending on the tournament. The four members on the team have detailed roles and play in a specific order: the lead throws the first two rocks, the second throws the third and fourth rocks, the third throws the fifth and sixth rocks, and the skip throws the final two rocks. The skip serves as captain of the rink, sometimes strategically directing the other team members on vigorous sweeping, a feature that captures the curiosity among casual observers of the sport. The purpose of the synchronized sweeping is to make the rock curl less and travel farther.

"Mom encouraged us to try curling, [saying] 'See if you like it,'" Stacey remembers. The year her change of heart occurred was the 1987–88 season. Kari was sixteen years old, and Stacey was fourteen years old. Kari had been competing on the Bemidji High School swimming team and playing in the school band, but she soon decided to dedicate her time to curling. Stacey made a similar resolution: "There was no wavering once we decided to pursue the sport." Their first endeavor was not auspicious—they finished tied for last in the state junior (up to age twenty-one) competition. Adding to the disappointment was Mike's seemingly harsh critique of their performance, which caused his daughters to cry. "Dad had a lot to learn about coaching girls," the sisters laugh in agreement.

"The turning point came when our rink won the junior state title in 1988–89 [the same year their mother was a member of the Minnesota Ladies State Championship team!] and then placed second in junior nationals," reports Kari. The four players and their positions on the team were Kari as skip, Heidi Rollheiser serving as second, Stacey as the third, and Bobbie Breyen as lead. The astounding turnaround was fueled by their devotion to the sport and being thrust into a higher tier of competition. "We greatly improved our skills competing in Canada due to their strong leagues," says Kari. "The travel and camaraderie with other teams was very positive." The rink improved on that performance by winning the national junior curling championship in 1990.

> *"We greatly improved our skills competing in Canada due to their strong leagues," says Kari. "The travel and camaraderie with other teams was very positive."*

With a shuffle of positions, the team continued building on their success. Kari changed to third, Stacey moved to second, Erika Brown was installed as skip, and Breyen remained as lead in claiming the 1992 national junior championship. Although Kari married Darren Erickson later that year, she continued to play, and the rink was still able to retain their championship in 1993 with Debbie Henry (later Debbie McCormick) now inserted as lead. That year Kari reached a personal summit when she was selected as the US Olympic Female Curler of the Year.

Meanwhile the International Olympic Committee named curling as a demonstration sport for the 1988 and 1992 Winter Olympics and an official sport for the 1998 Olympic Games in Nagano, Japan. Stacey and Kari continued their efforts to improve in the sport, training three hours per day by practicing, playing in leagues, and doing prescribed exercises. Their rink placed fourth in the 1992 Olympic Trials hosted in Duluth.

Mike was also on a high learning curve as he continued to coach curling through various levels. He was learning by doing and attending coaching clinics in Colorado Springs, Colorado. "You play the player, you play the ice, and you play the ends," he says, summarizing some of the strategy involved in curling. In 1998 he was selected as the women's coach for the World Championships, and he would serve in the role again in 2001—the same year he was named US Curling Coach of the Year. Another highlight for the family occurred when Kari's first child, Zachary, was born. But the honors continued when Stacey was named as an alternate on the 1998 Olympic team that competed in curling as a full-fledged Olympic sport. The

THE ERICKSON RINK TEAM REUNION IN 2012 (LEFT TO RIGHT) KARI, DEBBIE MCCORMICK, STACEY, AND ANN SWISSHELM
Photo credit: Debbie McCormick

team would be led by Lisa Schoeneberg, a skip whom Kari states she really respects. While the team finished out of medal contention with two wins in the eight-team round-robin tournament, the banner year ended with another high note when Stacey was named the US Olympic Committee Female Curler of the Year.

"When I returned home after the 1998 Games, I told Kari, 'I'm not going back to the Olympics without you. You're coming next time,'" vowed Stacey. She was referring to the 2002 Winter Olympics that would be held in their country—the curling event would be in Ogden, Utah. The trials were held at the site too. The Erickson rink (the team is generally named after the skip) won all their games with Stacey as second, Debbie McCormick in the role of third, and Ann Swisshelm as lead. Stacey's wish was not only granted, but the sisters' father was named the women's curling coach, and their mother was offered the position of team manager!

Kari recalls the wonderment preceding and during the Olympic Games: "Bemidji was very supportive. We received stacks of emails that were fun to read. The spectators at the opening ceremonies in a huge stadium just erupted when the United States was announced." Stacey Liapis was one of eight athletes chosen to carry a battered American flag that was rescued from the rubble of the World Trade Center collapse in 2001.

KARI ERICKSON, MIKE LIAPIS, AND STACEY LIAPIS ON THE SHORE
OF LAKE BEMIDJI, AUGUST 2012

The curling team's first draw in the ten-team round-robin tournament was Japan. They were trailing 6–1 after four ends when Kari successfully slid the rock expertly to gently nudge two of Japan's rocks out of the house and keep hers in play, leading the team to a narrow victory. "There was no room for error," her father and coach says. "The crowd really exploded after her throw. We were receiving a lot of attention and coverage because heavy snows were delaying some of the outdoors competitions."

After winning two of the first five draws, the American team won its final four draws, lifting it into the medal round, the first time an American team had achieved that level. In the semifinals, the American team was defeated by Switzerland 9–4 and suffered a final loss to Canada 9–5 in a quest for the bronze medal. The Erickson rink—with their staunch representation from Bemidji—ended the Olympic Games in fourth place.

Kari had graduated from Bemidji State University with a degree in geology in 1999. She returned to Bemidji after the Olympic Games and began teaching seventh-grade life science in the Bemidji Public School District. A second Female Curler of the Year award was presented to her in 2002. A second son, Walker, was born in 2004.

Stacey moved to Illinois and became interested in law enforcement. In 2010 she accepted a deputy sheriff position with Cook County. She is married to Tom Fuchsgruber, a Chicago firefighter, and they have two children, Samantha and Makayla.

The Liapis house in Bemidji is not full anymore, but Suzanne and Mike are still involved in curling—and there's always the next generation.

MARK LUTZ WINS THE 220-YARD DASH AT THE MINNESOTA STATE
HIGH SCHOOL LEAGUE TRACK AND FIELD CHAMPIONSHIPS ON
JUNE 5, 1970, IN RECORD TIME
Photo credit: St Paul Pioneer Press

MARK LUTZ

Sprinting to the Olympics

AN INTERNATIONAL STAR SPRINTER FROM MINNE-sota does not come to the forefront of a person's mind when thinking of people from the state who have competed in the Olympics. Ice hockey, skiing, and wrestling athletes, sure. But a speedster on land?

Meet Mark Lutz, a slight and speedy runner who was born in Minneapolis in 1951 and moved to Rochester, Minnesota, at age two. "I tried baseball, but I knew that I wasn't good. So I pursued track in eighth grade. I actually wanted to try pole-vaulting—but the coach knew better," Mark smiles. His speed and talent were evident, but he would not be running at the varsity level for the Rockets of Rochester High School, the only high school in existence in Rochester at the time.

Rochester Mayo High School opened for the 1966–67 academic year, and Mark became a Spartan. Track coach Dick Norman had him running varsity as a freshman. As a sophomore, Mark experienced early success by placing fourth in the 220-yard race and fifth in the 100-yard dash at the Minnesota State High School League Track & Field Championships in 1968. He would not lose another individual race throughout his high school career. In the 1969 state meet, he won the 220-yard sprint in 21.9 seconds, was part of the 880-yard relay team that placed third, and nipped rival Fred Merrill of Orono in the 100-yard dash, despite both of them being clocked with identical times of 9.9 seconds. Merrill would move to the state of Kansas for his senior year, but he and Mark would continue their rivalry at the collegiate level. As a senior in the spring of 1970, Mark repeated his triumphs in the 100- and 220-yard dashes and added a third crown with a victory in the 440-yard dash. His 220-yard time of 21.4 sec-

MARK LUTZ WON FIVE INDIVIDUAL MINNESOTA STATE HIGH SCHOOL LEAGUE TRACK CHAMPIONSHIPS
Photo credit: St Paul Pioneer Press

onds was a state record and nearly a full second ahead of the runner-up!

Coach Norman was in awe of the distance that separated Mark from other runners in the sprints. "I remember that he had such a commanding lead in a two hundred-and-twenty-yard straightaway race that the coaches recording splits had time to compare them before the other runners would hit the same midway point!" Norman has an Olympic footnote himself: he de-

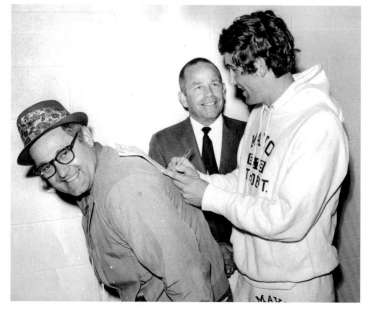

MARK LUTZ SIGNING A LETTER OF INTENT ON THE BACK OF HIS FATHER, ED, TO ATTEND KANSAS UNIVERSITY WITH USA TRACK & FIELD HALL OF FAME KU COACH BOB TIMMONS WATCHING, APRIL 1970
Photo courtesy of Mark Lutz, reprinted with permission of the Rochester Post-Bulletin

signed a ring reducer (a metal ring inserted inside the shot put and discus circle for the hammer throwers since the circle diameter for that event is 14½ inches smaller). To Norman's great personal satisfaction, it was used in the 1996 Summer Olympics in Atlanta.

At this time, Mark was clearly Minnesota's greatest sprinter ever. And he was daring to dream the dream of being an Olympian. The dream had been fueled by a family car trip to the 1968 Summer Olympics in Mexico City, Mexico. Traveling a distance of well over two thousand miles before the completion of the interstate system, Mark, his sister, and his parents, Ed and Velda, saw the long jump, sprints, and pole vault events. "It inspired me to excel in track," he recalls.

Mark's success and times brought attention from top-tiered track programs from across the nation. Assistant Mayo track coach Bob Robinson helped the family through the recruiting process as Mark prepared for graduation in 1970. "My parents wanted me to go to the University of Minnesota, I wanted to go to UCLA, so we compromised and I accepted a track scholarship to the University of Kansas," Mark chuckles. "They had great facilities, superior competition, and traveled to high-quality meets."

The University of Kansas Track & Field team, under the reins of legendary coach Bob Timmons, won the NCAA National Indoor Track & Field Championships in 1969 and 1970. They also were the NCAA National Outdoor Track & Field runner-up in 1969 and co-champion in 1970. It was a track power led by miler and Olympian Jim Ryun, a silver medalist in the 1,500-meter run at the tender age of twenty-one—in Mexico City. Mark sings Ryun's praises: "The amazing thing about Ryun is that he treated everyone the same. He was always polite and modest. He was a best friend to everyone. Despite being a world record holder, he continued to train at Kansas after he graduated. You had to respect him." With such laudatory remarks, it is unsurprising that Mark names Jim Ryun as his favorite athlete.

> *"The amazing thing about Ryun is that he treated everyone the same. He was always polite and modest. He was a best friend to everyone. Despite being a world record holder, he continued to train at Kansas after he graduated. You had to respect him."*

Mark contributed to the string of successes for the Kansas track team. Track was one of the few sports that freshmen were eligible to participate in at the time. He had received one of seven full-athletic scholarships, and by 1972 the faith put into Mark's sprinting ability came to fruition. He placed second in the 200-meter race at the NCAA outdoor championships in 20.5 seconds, the same time as champion Larry Burton of Purdue. He was excited about the upcoming Olympic Trials in Eugene, Oregon.

"I decided to concentrate on the two-hundred-meter dash because I wasn't quick enough for the hundred, and I lacked the endurance and mindset for the four-hundred-meter dash," Mark states candidly. "I got bumped out in the semifinals." Disappointed, but still a young sprinter at age twenty, Mark set his sights on 1976, when he'd be finished with his eligibility at Kansas.

In 1973 Mark ascended to the level of elite sprinter and was ranked fourth in the world at the 200-meter distance. He believes that he did not lose to any sprinter except those ranked ahead of him. The following year, he was an integral part of the national champion 440-yard relay team for Kansas. Mark was the Big 8 Conference

MARK LUTZ WAS A MEMBER OF THE 1974 NCAA DIVISION I TRACK AND FIELD 440-YARD RELAY TEAM
Photo credit: Kansas Athletics, Inc.

champion in the 100- and 220-yard dashes in 1973 and repeated the feat in 1974. Another honor was being named one of the captains during his junior and senior years.

Tom Scavuzzo, sprinter and lead leg on the championship relay team, remembers Mark as "full of energy. He was a lot of fun to be around. We all worked hard, but Mark did a little bit more. He always wanted to finish first—even in practice. He displayed a positive and winning attitude. And, man, could he run the curve! He could eat up any stagger."

Barry Schur, Mark's roommate for two years and the 1972 AAU outdoor high jump champion, adds, "He let his running do his talking. He had an extremely long stride for a guy his size." Schur then repeats what put teammates and track observers often in awe: "Mark would come catapulting off the curve."

To prepare for the 1976 Olympics, Mark joined the Pacific Coast (PC) Track Club in 1975 following the exhaustion of his collegiate eligibility. "There was no Olympic financial aid at the time, but I had the motivation to keep training," he says, remembering his dream. "The training was at UCLA with Jim Bush serving as coach. We had only one workout per day—minimal volume, but high quality. We trained fast to be fast. Most sprinters were lean [Mark was 5 feet 9 inches tall and 150 pounds at his peak]. Coaches did not realize the explosiveness of muscular, powerful sprinters." The training included runs between the distances of 220 to 660 yards, gentle downhill runs to stretch out strides, and extensive competition. It was at the PC Track Club that he became familiar with a favorite teammate, shot putter Al Feuerbach.

Mark had gained fame beyond Kansas for his ability to run the curve of the track, an important segment of the 200-meter dash. The stage was set for Mark to realize his dream. And he did. Mark placed third, behind Millard Hampton and Dwayne Evans, in the trials that were once again hosted at Hayward Track in Eugene, Oregon. For a time, the three American qualifiers in the 200-meter dash had the three fastest times in the world. The runners were hoping for a sweep.

His parents (who had faithfully attended his collegiate meets), his coaches, and his friends would be at the Olympic Games in Montreal, Canada, to watch a rarity: a Minnesota sprinter competing against the fastest humans in the world. But Mark was worried—and deservedly so—because he had injured his hamstring in the finals of the trials. Time was short—there were only six weeks to the Games. It did not fully heal, and Mark had what he calls "a totally bittersweet experience. I had achieved my lifelong dream of making the Olympics, but I could tell that I was in trouble and would not be healthy and be able to compete at my best." He finished fifth in his first qualifying heat and was bumped out of the competition. His time was 21.5 seconds, more than a full second slower than his personal best. Teammates Hampton and Evans won silver and bronze medals respectively.

MARK LUTZ'S 1976 OLYMPIC UNIFORM ON DISPLAY IN A ROCHESTER, MINNESOTA RESTAURANT

He retired from competitive running in 1977, a result of the disappointing Olympic performance and burnout. Mark had married Francie Larrieu (who became a five-time Olympian distance runner) in January of the Olympic year, but they divorced two years later. Mark then married a woman from Long Beach, California, and later divorced.

Mark has had a lengthy career in the trucking industry: first as an over-the-road driver for Atlas Van Lines from 1977 to 1987. He then returned to his hometown of Rochester and has been married to Rita Thompsen, a native of Ellendale, Minnesota, since 1987. His next job in the trucking industry was as a fuel transport driver for Greenway Co-op for a decade, then more than ten years at IBM's shipping/receiving department; he now continues to hit the road as a semi driver. In 1995 Mark was inducted into the Rochester Sports Hall of Fame.

Memories of the travel and competition excite Mark. He talks fondly of dual meets against Russia, being part of a Division I relay champion, participating in the World University Games, being a collegiate track All-American, and qualifying as the one and only Minnesotan sprinter for the Olympic Games.

Photo courtesy of USA Swimming

TOM MALCHOW

The Right Formula: World Record and Gold Medal

DIAGNOSED WITH ASTHMA AT AN EARLY AGE, TOM Malchow sometimes suffered asthmatic attacks that led to pneumonia and forced him to be admitted to the hospital multiple times. "I grew to understand the disease and better manage it," the three-time Olympian reports. While Tom, born in 1976, enjoyed the sports of baseball and basketball, the drier environments limited his playing time. Swimming soon became his primary physical outlet. "I started at a neighbor's pool and the St. Paul Athletic Club. I was exposed to water at an early age and [was] always comfortable in it." So comfortable that Tom Malchow became a world-record holder and Olympic gold medalist, achievements not duplicated by any other Minnesotan in an individual summer sport.

Tom's parents—Tim, an estate attorney, and Mary Jo, a social studies teacher at Bloomington Kennedy High School—lived in Lilydale, Minnesota, a tiny St. Paul suburb situated atop a bluff lying within the Mississippi National River and Recreation Area. They remember Tom as an energetic boy whose whole life was a growth spurt that resulted in their son rising to a height of 6 feet 6 inches and weighing 190 pounds before he graduated from high school. "His asthma never bothered him when he swam. It's a good sport for asthmatics," notes Mary Jo. A picture of Tom as a youngster holding a red ribbon that he won "could have been gold,"

TOM MALCHOW WITH RED RIBBON WON AT A COMPETITION AT THE UNIVERSITY CLUB IN ST. PAUL, 1982
Photo credit: Tim and Mary Jo Malchow

smiles Tim. "Tom just liked the water." According to Tim, it was Paul Schultz, a coach at the St. Paul Athletic Club, who first saw Tom's potential in swimming. "He said, 'Tom's a real talent. He's got a real feel for the water.'" The observation proved prophetic.

Starting with Betty Berreman instructing at the neighbor's pool, Tom's supportive parents rave about the excellent coaches Tom had the good fortune to have throughout his swimming career. At the age of seven, Tom joined the St. Paul and Roseville (STAR) Swim Club, headed by Paul and Sue Brings Lundsten. "Tom had a real good experience," notes Mary Jo. Paul Lundsten marveled at Tom's work ethic. "He was the hardest-working athlete we've ever worked with. He was driven to always do his very best. I don't recall him ever not giving one hundred percent."

> "He was the hardest-working athlete we've ever worked with. He was driven to always do his very best. I don't recall him ever not giving one hundred percent."

While leafing through a swimming magazine, twelve-year-old Tom discovered a picture of Michael "the Albatross" Gross, a three-time Olympic gold medalist from Germany, sitting on a Porsche. Approaching his father, Tom excitedly asked, "If I win a gold medal and set a world record, would you buy me one of these?" showing Tim Malchow the photograph. "No, but I will buy you the American equivalent, a Corvette," was the bemused response. While his father would nearly forget the promise, it would be a goal Tom would pursue with a vengeance. Seldom does a person thoroughly enjoy paying off such a large wager, but Tim Malchow would ultimately prove to be a prime example of one who did.

Tom enrolled at St. Thomas Academy (STA) High School, a Catholic college-preparatory, military/leadership school located in nearby Mendota Heights. He would rise to the rank of major at STA and propel the swim team to new heights by the time he graduated. It was a good fit. "I liked the culture at STA. I felt like I was a getting a good education," observes Tom. Minnesota State High School swimming rules stipulate an entrant be limited to a maximum of four events (two individual and two relay) at the state championships. Tom captured the 100-yard butterfly crown as a ninth grader and then won the 200-yard freestyle and 500-yard freestyle individual titles for three consecutive years (1993–1995). His 500-yard freestyle time of 4 minutes, 28 seconds (4:28.00) remained a boys' high school state record for eighteen years until it was broken in a dramatic 2013 state finals finish by winner Noah Lucas of Mounds View High School (runners-up Jonathan Lieberman of Eden Prairie and Erick Huft of Edina also clipped the record). The STA swim team had climbed the rankings too and captured the state team championship in 1995, Tom's senior year.

The high school swim teams Tom considered "especially tough" were Minnetonka and Bloomington Jefferson. Martin Zielinski, a 100-yard butterfly state champion from Jefferson whose time of 48.2 seconds has been an overall boys, high school state record since 1995, remembers Tom as a gangly swimmer who was most successful at nonsprint events. "Tom was very focused and determined. Nothing seemed to faze him. He was a very dedicated competitor," says Zielinski, who became an Academic All-American swimmer at the University of Minnesota and is now an associate professor of surgery at Rochester's Mayo Clinic.

"The level of training at Michigan was something I had never experienced," states Tom, who was quickly dubbed "Puppy Chow" by Urbanchek. "I had never worked so hard! I was getting my butt handed to me day in and day out."

Highly sought, Tom took official college visits to swimming powerhouses Stanford, Arizona, Auburn, Southern California, and Michigan. Jon Urbanchek, the successful University of Michigan and Olympic swim coach, vividly remembers the first time he saw Tom compete. "What impressed me the most was how aggressive he went out at the 1992 Nationals in Mission Viejo, California. I was watching the two-hundred-meter butterfly race, and he went like he was shot out of a cannon. He kept the lead through the hundred- and one-hundred-fifty-meter marks before he tired. And his range of motion was unbelievable!" So Urbanchek was elated when Tom opted to accept a scholarship to the 1995 NCAA champion. Tom joined the elite Michigan swim team with several future Olympians, including Andy Potts, a 2004 Olympic triathlete, and Tom Dolan, a future two-time Olympic gold medalist, who re-

TOM MALCHOW COMPETING IN THE 200-METER BUTTERFLY IN FULL STROKE
Photo credit: ©Rick Rickman/Corbis Images

ally pushed him with a weight training program and enhanced competition. Besides weight training, team members swam twice per day, usually two hours each session. "The level of training at Michigan was something I had never experienced," states Tom, who was quickly dubbed "Puppy Chow" by Urbanchek. "I had never worked so hard! I was getting my butt handed to me day in and day out."

Nevertheless, Tom discovered his forte in the middle-distances and was named Big 10 Freshman of the Year in 1996 and qualified for the 1996 Olympic Trials in Indianapolis, Indiana. Considering Tom's tall frame, one benefit at the Olympic Trials would be the pool length—50 meters instead of 25 yards, which would mean fewer turns. "A longer course is better for me because the turns were my weakest link of my racing," admits Tom. He was on track to realizing his goals. "My career was a natural progression. I set goals as I went: to make the national team, make the Olympic Trials, then to make the Olympics." He was at stage two and about to grasp his third goal. Puppy Chow would soon become the Big Dawg.

Only nineteen years old, Tom surprised the Indiana University Natatorium crowd by advancing to the finals by placing third overall in the heats with a time under 2:00 in the 200-meter butterfly, an event requiring a difficult, demanding stroke and exacting technique while synchronizing with a "dolphin" leg kick. The surprise was then elevated to a stunning victory in the finals with a time of 1:57.39, a half second ahead of American record holder and 1992 Olympic gold medalist Melvin Stewart, who placed third (in swimming only the top two finishers earn spots on the Olympic team). "After Tom won, we were all off the wall!" exclaims Tim Malchow. Onto the world stage: the 1996 Summer Olympic Games in Atlanta, Georgia.

Tom's race strategy in Atlanta seemed to mirror his swimming goals: improve and move up incrementally with a steady pace. "I had a huge contingent of family and friends there. The plan was to lay back. I was well prepared and raced the best race of my life." Qualifying for the finals in the 200-meter butterfly with the sixth-fastest time overall in 1:58.69, Tom was in last place at the start of the four-length (two laps) race. By 100 meters Tom had improved to fifth place, and at the turn of the final length he was in fourth place. With a furious finish, Tom raced to second place behind Denis Pankratov of Russia by beating Scott Goodman of Australia by 0.04 seconds with his final stroke! "He shocked us, himself, and everyone else by winning the silver medal," says a proud Tim Malchow.

> *"He shocked us, himself, and everyone else by winning the silver medal," says a proud Tim Malchow.*

Returning to Michigan, Tom was named Big 10 Swimmer of the Year his sophomore year and continued to perform well, though he wasn't dominant back in the shorter pools. Tom's sole NCAA title was in 1997 as a member of the 800-yard freestyle relay team with Chris Rumley, John Reich, and John Piersma. He graduated in 1999 with a business major. Meanwhile, Tom was swimming 5,000 to 8,000 meters daily, training for the 2000 Olympics in Sydney, Australia—back to the longer pools.

With a roaring crowd urging him on, Tom Malchow set a world record at the Charlotte (North Carolina) Ultraswim, an international Grand Prix meet, on June 17, 2000, in the 200-meter butterfly with a time of 1:55.18. The twenty-three-year-old shaved 0.04 seconds off the record previously held by Pankratov. With the world record now in hand, Tom reminded his dad of a promise made more than a decade before: a Corvette if Tom set a world record and won a gold medal. Two months later Tom was back in Indianapolis for the 2000 Olympic Trials, having decided to concentrate exclusively on the 200-meter butterfly, his specialty. Clearly a favorite now, Tom breezed through the heat in an Olympic Trials record time of 1:55.67, later winning the final handily over a fifteen-year-old phenom named Michael Phelps. The pair would be heading to the southern hemisphere for the Summer Olympics being hosted in mid-September.

The 2000 Olympics had an additional segment this time. Instead of the top eight swimmers advancing directly to the finals, the sixteen fastest would compete

TIM, TOM, AND MARY JO MALCHOW AT THE SYDNEY OLYMPIC SWIMMING COMPLEX, SEPT 20, 2000
Photo courtesy of Tim and Mary Jo Malchow

in a semifinals race. Tom had the fastest time as he moved to the semifinals and again for the finals. Repeating his 1996 race strategy in the finals, Tom went from fifth at the first wall, to third at the midway mark, to second on the final turn. Staying strong, pulling hard, and maintaining form, Tom Malchow won the gold medal in the 200-meter butterfly with an Olympic record time of 1:55.35. In a rare display of jubilation, the even-keeled "flyer" gave several fist pumps, exhibiting four years of emotion when he became aware he had won the gold medal.

When the family returned from Australia, "the mailbox was full of Corvette magazines from dealerships!" exclaims Tim Malchow. The gold medalist and his father went to Midway Chevrolet on University Avenue in St. Paul, ordered a silver Corvette, and had it shipped directly to Ann Arbor, Michigan. Tom would remain in Michigan and continue training.

Having generally remained injury-free, Tom tore a tendon in his right shoulder at a May 2004 meet in Santa Clara, California. While it still allowed full motion, the twenty-seven-year-old's strength was reduced, and he was concerned about competing at his best in his signature event, the 200-meter butterfly. Long Beach, California, hosted the 2004 US Olympic swimming trials with an outdoor venue using a temporary pool. Tom was able to advance to the finals with steady performances, but the star of the event was Michael Phelps, who had placed fifth in the 2000 Olympics and broken Tom's world record in March 2001 at the tender age of fifteen. Urbanchek found some consolation, saying, "Tom lost the world record to Michael Phelps—that's not a bad way to lose it." Tom did finish second to make the 2004 Olympic team, but three seconds separated him from Phelps. Tom, now a three-time Olympian, was honored to be named captain of the men's swim team heading off to Athens, Greece. Mary Jo Malchow appreciated the Olympic sites where Tom competed. "In Atlanta [1996], there was the home crowd; no one likes swimming like Australia [2000]; then to finish his Olympic career where the Olympics all started, Athens [2004]."

Using the same format as the 2000 Games, Tom qualified for the semifinals as he consistently raced in a time of 1:57 but barely squeaked into the finals with the eighth-fastest time. In the finals, Tom finished last of the eight finalists in a time of 1:57.48. Phelps set a new Olympic record time of 1:54.04 in winning the gold medal, one of his record number of eighteen Olympic gold medals and twenty-two medals overall.

Tom had surgery to repair the torn tendon in October 2004 and moved to the Pacific Northwest in 2005, where he became involved in orthopedic sales. He married Christie McMahon and they now live in suburban Seattle with their two daughters, Shannon and Marin. Tom immediately credits his parents for being supportive but never overbearing in his life. Tim Malchow happily relates, "We were just there to help him nurture his career." They struck the right formula.

TOM MALCHOW'S 200-METER BUTTERFLY GOLD MEDAL WON AT THE 2000 OLYMPIC GAMES IN SYDNEY, AUSTRALIA
Photo credit: Tim and Mary Jo Malchow

We were honored to have had a personal conversation with Tim Malchow. We regret to note that he died unexpectedly on July 8th, 2015. We appreciate his contributions to this profile about his son and offer our sincere condolences to his family.

SHANI MARKS IN FLIGHT AT THE 2008 US OLYMPIC TRIALS
Photo credit: Kirby Lee, Image of Sport

SHANI MARKS

Jumping as Part of the Journey

A CONVERSATION WITH SHANI MARKS CONFIRMS the accolades of coaches and fellow athletes: Shani (pronounced Shawn-ee) Marks is a first-class person in addition to being a world-class athlete.

Shani, one of four daughters of Curtis and Gloria, was born in Bloomington, Illinois, in 1980 but moved to Apple Valley, Minnesota, at a young age. She participated in softball through the Valley Athletic Association and was a spirited member of a year-round gymnastics club, TAGS Gymnastics. Shani firmly believes that the years she spent with the gymnastics team helped develop her strength and power, essential skills for a track athlete.

Initially Shani resisted joining the track team. "Originally I was not interested in track. My mother wanted me to broaden my horizons beyond gymnastics. She really influenced me. She was a great supporter and always stood by me, but at the same time she was never pushy." Shani was instrumental in the success of Apple Valley High School's championship relay teams as a ninth-grade student in 1995, her first season in track. The team won two relays and Shani added a fourth-place finish in the long jump (17 feet 2¼ inches) at the Minnesota State High School League Track & Field Championships.

Those immediate triumphs forced Shani to make the wrenching decision to leave the realm of gymnastics. "It was very difficult to leave the gymnastics club because it had a wonderful family feel," admits Shani.

Her sophomore year was injury plagued, but Shani rebounded strongly in eleventh grade, helping Apple Valley to three relay first-place finishes at the state meet. She was also crowned champion in the long jump with a leap 14 inches beyond her jump as a freshman (18 feet 4¼ inches). The 4 x 400 meter relay team, composed of Shani with identical twin teammates Maggie and Katie Curran and Tracy Frerk, set a state record with the breathtaking time of 3 minutes 52.13 seconds, which remained the top time until it was eclipsed by a Hopkins team in 2011. Apple Valley girls' track

SHANI MARKS COMPETED IN HURDLES, SPRINTS, RELAYS, AND THE LONG AND TRIPLE JUMPS AT THE U OF M
Photo courtesy of University of Minnesota Athletics

coach Geri Dirth fondly remembers Shani running the final leg of the championship relay. "It was a memorable race. We coaches watched a beautiful competitor simply put it in another gear." Those feats put Shani on the map, and she was recruited nationally by Division I college coaches.

More team and personal accomplishments followed her senior year with one more 4 x 400 meter relay championship and three third-place finishes, two in relays and one in the long jump. Summing up her high school athletic career, Dirth remembers, "Shani had the talent and natural leadership. She is absolutely a beautiful young woman inside and out." And about her cheerful disposition, Dirth adds this tribute: "Shani brightens up whatever place she is present [in]."

Despite the flattering attention from collegiate track powerhouses, Shani was pretty sure she wanted to stay local following graduation in 1998. "The appeal to the University of Minnesota [U of M] just seemed where I would be pushed to improve. It had the resources academically and athletically," she says of her decision.

Roy Griak, the legendary cross country and track and field coach at the U of M, recalls having Shani in a class. He encouraged her to try triple jumping, and it piqued her interest. "Shani had excellent motor skills, she was a quick learner, very strong and dedicated." Griak extolled other virtues: "She was diligent, intelligent, and a joy to be around."

At the U of M, Shani added triple jumping and hurdle races to her track repertoire, in addition to being a member on the 4 x 400 meter relay team and an occasional 400-meter individual runner. Shani often preferred the time spent on her high school and college relay teams because she enjoyed team events.

Shani did progress at the U of M, but it was her final year, 2002, that marked her coming of age as a world-class competitor. She qualified for the NCAA Division I nationals for both the indoor and outdoor track seasons. A leap of 43 feet 10 inches landed Shani sixth place in the indoor season competition in Arkansas and All-American status. It was the outdoor season, however, where Shani dazzled. Her jump at Sacramento State in the NCAA Division I Championship of 45 feet ½ inch held the lead until the final charge down the runway by Ineta Radevica of the University of Nebraska. Shani confesses, "It was a heartbreaking experience to lose on the last jump." Shani was the runner-up, second nationally at the collegiate level in the demanding triple jump.

While Shani credits U of M women's assistant track coach (currently head coach) Matt Bingle, who joined the coaching staff in 2002, for accelerating her improvement, Bingle says Shani's own athletic talents and dedication fueled her dramatic advancement in triple jumping. "Shani Marks was very driven, very coachable, very focused, and very committed," says Bingle, complimenting the student athlete. "A blind guy could have coached Shani. She pushed me as much as a coach as much as I pushed her as an athlete. She always wanted to know how she could do something better. When she realized her ability, she got the fire in her belly to be an Olympic-caliber triple jumper."

> *"A blind guy could have coached Shani. She pushed me as much as a coach as much as I pushed her as an athlete. She always wanted to know how she could do something better. When she realized her ability, she got the fire in her belly to be an Olympic-caliber triple jumper."*

Even Shani seemed somewhat stunned by her performances. "The Olympics had not been on my radar at all, and then suddenly I had a chance to hit the qualifying mark in Eugene, Oregon, in 2004," Shani says retrospectively. Shani did reach the required mark and with newfound confidence placed a surprising fourth in the Olympic Trials, also held at hallowed Hayward Field in Eugene—just missing a spot on the American Olympic team.

In the classroom, Shani completed her degree with a major in public relations

SHANI MARKS BY THE "BIRD'S NEST" AT THE 2008 OLYMPICS IN BEIJING, CHINA
Photo courtesy of Shani Marks

and then began a graduate program in applied kinesiology. She also started coaching as a volunteer at her college alma mater and working as a part-time professional trainer at Lifetime Fitness.

Shani's persevering spirit continued through four more years of training and conditioning as she prepared for the 2008 American Olympic Trials. She also found a friend and training partner to assist in the years-long process. Shani met Amanda Thieschafer of Melrose, Minnesota, at, of course, a track meet. Amanda had competed for North Dakota State University and was ranked nationally among triple jumpers. Shani was a four-time American champion in the event by 2007, but Amanda had her own successes too and had placed third in a national meet.

A wonderful friendship developed for the training partners. They created games to get through some grueling workouts. It was the daily dedication that Shani appreciated and that continued even though Thieschafer (now Smock) fell a few spots short of qualifying for the Olympic team.

Shani was now a favorite to land a spot on the 2008 Olympic team, and she did not disappoint herself or the crowd as she jumped a personal best of 47 feet 2¼ inches (14.38 meters), setting a Hayward Field record. "It came together at the right place at the right time," Shani smiles.

Beijing, China, hosted the summer Games of the XXIX

OLYMPIC HURDLER LOLO JONES AND SHANI MARKS AT THE 2008 OLYMPICS IN BEIJING, CHINA
Photo courtesy of Shani Marks

Olympiad in 2008. Shani was pleased that her entire family and close friend Jamie were able to be part of the grand festivities and mark her memories: "The opening ceremony was surreal. I was trying to take in every moment and enjoy the pageantry."

The lag time between the Olympic Trials and games proved troublesome. Although she went to China two weeks before the competition to acclimate to the time and geographical changes, Shani found it difficult to hold peak performances for the duration of the two months between the high-profile events. At Beijing she finished thirteenth in her flight and twenty-eighth overall.

Any disappointment soon evaporated for the sunny woman from Minnesota. She married Ron Johnson, another U of M student athlete who had played football, and became a mother in April

SHANI (MARKS) JOHNSON IS NOW AN INDEPENDENT TRAINER FOR HIGH SCHOOL ATHLETES SEEKING TO IMPROVE IN HURDLES, SPRINTS, AND JUMPS
Photo courtesy of University of Minnesota Athletics

2011. Their daughters, Kamryn and Quinn, are sometimes now found nearby when Shani is coaching the horizontal jumpers at Apple Valley High School; she also continues as an independent trainer of high school athletes in jumps, sprints, and hurdles through her own company, Johnson Jumps.

When reminiscing about her experience of a lifetime, Shani has this thought: "Jumping and the Olympics were great, but the biggest gift is about the journey."

JIM MASTRO THROWING THE DISCUS AT THE 1996 PARALYMPIC GAMES
Photo courtesy of Jim and Cheryl Mastro

JIM MASTRO

Having a Vision

BLIND IN HIS RIGHT EYE AT BIRTH DUE TO HYPOPLA-sia of the optic nerve, Jim Mastro (Mas-troh) has had a lifetime love affair with sports. Today he passes on that passion to blind kids through the Northern Plains Visions of Sport Camp that he started. The camp for visually impaired and blind children currently operates in Bemidji, Minnesota, for the purpose of introducing the campers to athletic involvement and educating coaches and counselors about blindness.

Born in Minneapolis in 1948, Jim and a twin brother, John, and a younger sister, Susan, are the children of Sam and Mary Mastro. Jim is appreciative of excellent physical education teachers and the opportunity to participate in gymnastics, wrestling, and track and field as a youth. A duel of sorts with a friend at age eleven led to Jim's complete blindness. Using curtain rods in the duel, Jim got hit in the left eye, which caused severe damage to his sight. After a series of surgeries he was able to see with thick eye glasses. However, doctors warned him that there was a chance he could be permanently blinded. Jim made the most of the time he had with diminished vision by wrestling and throwing the shot put on the track and field team for Minneapolis Edison High School. Powerful at 5 feet 8, Jim won the district championship and finished fourth in the region in wrestling. In track and field, he qualified for the state meet his junior year. "I was expecting to do very well my senior year, but then I went totally blind." At age eighteen, Jim had suffered a detached retina in his left eye during the summer. Instead of realizing his goal of being active at the elite level of high school sports, Jim would be tutored at home and attend vocational rehabilitation at the Minneapolis Society for the Blind to learn Braille and increase his mobility.

Jim enrolled at nearby Augsburg College and, restless, made a decision. "It was driving me crazy not to do anything physical, so I approached my parents and told them I was going to go out for the college wrestling team." Seeking approval

JIM MASTRO AFTER WINNING THE 1972 MIAC CONFERENCE TITLE IN WRESTLING
Photo courtesy of Jim Mastro

from a doctor, Jim received a negative response because of his blindness. At that point Jim decided no one was going to tell him what he could or could not do. The first year, he did not make the team. "I had to relearn how hard you had to work to become good," he says of the experience. Then he put forth the effort, with remarkable results: Jim was crowned as Minnesota Intercollegiate Athletic Conference (MIAC) champion at the 177-pound weight class in 1972 (his senior year).

In 1974, Jim married Cheryl Husmoe, who also attended Augsburg; he had first met Cheryl at a wedding.

Wanting to continue to compete in wrestling, an Augsburg teammate made a suggestion to Jim. "Pat Marcy knew that I was strong and had good balance, so he invited me to practice with these other guys at the University of Minnesota (U of M). Finding out about Greco-Roman wrestling really helped me out. It's the perfect style for someone who is blind." Since Greco-Roman uses only the upper body for holds, throws, and clinches, Jim did not have to worry about seeing his opponent's feet.

Suddenly, Jim was practicing with some of the country's most noted Greco-Roman wrestlers. "It was amazing to know who was in the wrestling room at Augsburg and the U [University of Minnesota]: Dan Chandler, Pat Marcy, Gary Pelcl, Ron Johnson, and Daryl and Dale Miller. Practicing with great wrestlers really helped. You are who you wrestle. They would give me rides to practices. Alan Rice, the 1972 Olympic coach, really helped me along." Marcy and Chandler would become Olympians, and Pelcl would land a spot on a World Team.

Jim's progress was astounding, and he made the 1973 World University Greco-Roman team. Unfortunately, he suffered an injury and was not able to compete. Jim had begun working on a master's degree at the College of St. Thomas in St. Paul (now the University of St. Thomas) in education and special education, and he would soon begin teaching at alternative learning programs. For some training periods, he devoted three hours to morning practice, did fifteen hundred push-ups, participated in another three-hour practice in the afternoon, and ran while Cheryl biked alongside him. In both 1974 and 1975, Jim placed third in the national Amateur Athletic Union (AAU) competition.

> *" It was an interesting match because I had never wrestled a blind person, and you must always stay in contact. I was obviously concerned because Mastro was a superstrong opponent. He was very powerful and very quick. He had good balance and knew his sport."*

There was a chance that Jim Mastro could qualify for the 1976 Olympics—as a blind person. Another Minnesotan, Evan Johnson of Orono, had won the NCAA championship in 1976 as a wrestler for the University of Minnesota. While never having wrestled Greco-Roman, Johnson thought his chances of making an Olympic team were better in that style due to his body build and fierce competition at his free-style weight. And the pair of Minnesotans did meet in the Olympic Trials as they kept defeating opponents. Johnson remembers, "It was an interesting match because I had never wrestled a blind person, and you must always stay in contact. I was obviously concerned because Mastro was a superstrong opponent. He was very powerful and very quick. He had good bal-

JIM MASTRO DEMONSTRATING A JUDO HOLD AT THE WISCONSIN ASSOCIATION OF BLIND ATHLETES SPORTS CAMP
Photo courtesy of Jim and Cheryl Mastro

JIM MASTRO AND COACH LARRY LEE CARRYING THE US FLAG AT THE 1996 PARALYMPIC GAMES
Photo courtesy of Jim and Cheryl Mastro

ance and knew his sport." Jim also has a vivid memory of the match, in which he was defeated. "I wrestled Evan really well, but he was an exceptional athlete. It was one of my best matches." Johnson wrestled one more match and qualified for the Olympic team; he would later place seventh in Montreal.

Despite placing third in the trials, Olympic Greco-Roman head coach Jim Peckham informed Jim that he would be an alternate to the team. That invitation coincided with the opening of the Paralympics to visually impaired athletes—and to being named to the first of seven United States Paralympic teams.

Jim qualified for Paralympic teams from 1976–2000, won ten medals in four different sports, and was the flag bearer for the US Paralympic team in Atlanta in 1996. He has been a gold medal winner in both wrestling and shot put. Wrestling was discontinued in 1984, but Jim found a new sport that shared some similarities. "I began judo in 1986. It was an easy transition due to years in wrestling." He is now a fourth-degree black belt in the sport and has won two bronze medals in it.

Jim won a silver medal in the shot put at the 1980 Paralympics (while the 1980 Olympics were boycotted by the United States, the Paralympics were hosted by the Netherlands and were not boycotted) with a splendid throw of 12.91 meters (42 feet 4¼ inches), which bested his gold medal throw in the 1984 Paralympics.

Equally impressive is what Jim has accomplished in his professional career. He was the first blind person in the United States to receive a PhD in physical education in 1985. In 1988, Jim received a position at the U of M, which forced him to miss that year's Paralympics. He worked for the Braille Sports Foundation for many years, an organization under the direction of John Ross. Ross was the sole Minnesota state wrestling champion who was blind. He wrestled for Marshall High School in Minneapolis and won the 120-pound weight division in 1953. Both Ross and Jim would be honored as recipients of the Medal of Courage Award from the National Wrestling Hall of Fame. Ross was also one of the founders of "beep baseball" while Jim was named the National Beep Baseball World Series Most Valuable Player (MVP) in 1978, 1979, and Co-MVP in 1980. Again sharing awards, both men have been inducted into the National Beep Baseball Association Hall of Fame.

JIM AND CHERYL (HUSMOE) MASTRO
Photo courtesy of Jim and Cheryl Mastro

Since 1998 Jim has been a professor at Bemidji State University. He teaches education foundations, special education, and physical education while also serving as coordinator of the Northern Plains Visions of Sport Camp that began in 1993. He and Cheryl have two children, Paul and Amber, and one granddaughter.

Visions can take many forms—as they have for Jim Mastro.

Photo courtesy of University of Minnesota Athletics

JOHN MAYASICH

First-Class Off the Ice Too

EARLY IN THE TWENTY-FIRST CENTURY, JOHN MAYAsich, the most acclaimed high school player in Minnesota hockey history, returned to his beloved hometown of Eveleth, Minnesota, after living for many years in Green Bay, Wisconsin, and the Twin Cities area. John speaks highly of the community of 3,700 people (its population peaked at 7,500 in 1930) known as "the Gateway to the Iron Range," which is rich in natural resources and his link to warm lifelong relationships. Asked whether he considers himself a true Minnesotan, he pauses and modifies the phrase slightly, saying, "a true *northern* Minnesotan." And the northern Minnesota city of Eveleth has embraced his return wholeheartedly.

One of twelve children (while it is widely reported that John is one of eleven children, a twelfth child died in infancy), John and his twin brother, Jim, were the youngest of the family and born in 1933. His father, Frank, an underground miner for forty years, and mother, Mary, were Croatian immigrants who met in Eveleth. Similar to many other large families in Iron Range communities, the Mayasich family eked out a frugal living through hard work, a large garden, and purchasing only the necessities. "We never had a car, but we had a cow!" laughs John.

Unlike many Iron Range families, John was the only Mayasich who played hockey. His unassuming explanation? "We only had one pair of skates. They were girls' skates—not hockey skates," reports John. "Later I got some used Tackaberry skates—I was probably in seventh grade. We taped and nailed broken sticks together that we found stashed behind the penalty box at Ranger [the local amateur hockey team] games. We'd play keep-away with the puck on streets or the rink. You learned stickhandling and deking. You were developing skills without realizing it. If you didn't touch the puck, you'd be trying out for the basketball team on Monday." The other Mayasich boys had gravitated toward basketball and swimming and were successful in those sports. Since there was no junior high school hockey team, John joined the swim team in seventh grade and cheered as his brother Bernard placed second in the Min-

THE EXTERIOR AND INTERIOR OF THE CENTERPIECE IN THE EVELETH HOCKEY COMMUNITY, THE EVELETH HIPPODROME WAS ORIGINALLY BUILT IN 1922
Photos courtesy of the City of Eveleth

nesota State High School swim meet. The next season John decided to try basketball as an athletic endeavor until he could try out for the high school hockey team.

Eveleth was the capital of Minnesota hockey in the forties and fifties, with evidence of its heritage downtown. A mammoth wooden structure, the Hippodrome, opened in Eveleth in 1922, allowing hockey to move indoors. The historic building is a few blocks north of the world's largest free standing hockey stick (110-feet long) and puck monument erected in 2002. It replaced an earlier version branded with the famous Christian hockey stick name emblazoned along the shaft and accompanied by a 700-pound puck which had originally been installed in 1995. The culmination of hockey treasures and history is located on Hat Trick Way: the United States Hockey Hall of Fame. It is incredible to discover eleven Eveleth players are enshrined: goalies Frank Brimsek, Oscar Almquist, Sam LoPresti, Mike Karakas, and Willard Ikola; and skaters John Mariucci, Serge Gambucci, Wally Grant, John Matchefts, John "Connie" Pleban, and John Mayasich.

The Eveleth High School Golden Bears' five state championships, twelve consecutive state hockey tournament appearances (1945–56), and John Mayasich's storied high school career still create a buzz among sports enthusiasts. The Golden Bears claimed the first Minnesota State High School League hockey trophy in 1945 at the St. Paul Auditorium and then added four more championships from 1948–51, the years John generally played center for the team, which won sixty-nine consecutive games. John appreciated his teammates and especially looked up to John Matchefts, a star two years his senior. Matchefts became captain of the hockey team at the University of Michigan, played on the 1956 US Olympic team, then started a long career as a high school and college hockey coach with tours at Colorado College and the US Air Force Academy. John also enjoyed having Ron Castellano and Dan Voce as linemates for two years. Voce, who became the high school hockey coach in Zimmerman, Minnesota, remembers growing up with John and their high school playing years this way: "Families were big then; we had to share a lot. John had vision on the ice, and he was a playmaker. He was kind and considerate to everyone." Castellano, a longtime hockey coach in Babbitt,

1950 ALL-STATE SELECTIONS

Richard Dougherty
International Falls

John McKinnon
Williams

Chester Lundstin
Williams

Ray Beauchamp
Williams

Ronald Castellano
Eveleth

Dan Voce
Eveleth

John Mayasich
Eveleth

Willard Ikola
Eveleth

Photo courtesy of Minnesota State High School League

Minnesota (who coached Buzz Schneider, a player on the 1980 Miracle on Ice team), echoes those attributes. "What made him great is the way he saw the ice and could anticipate. If you gave him the puck in the slot, you knew it was a goal! As a person, he was top-shelf. You'd never have known what a great athlete he was—he never said much about it."

John's phenomenal records at the state high school tournament, unsurpassed more than six decades later, include scoring 46 points (goals and assists), 36 goals, and seven hat tricks (three goals in a game), plus a single game record of scoring seven goals and being remembered for scoring all four goals in Eveleth's 4–1 victory over St. Paul Johnson in the 1951 title game to cap off his senior year. During his high school career, John never wore shoulder pads—a preference he would continue through his collegiate career. Still competing with inadequate equipment, John did own hockey skates—a single pair he wore throughout high school. "In ninth and

JOHN MAYASICH'S #8 JERSEY IS THE ONLY UNIFORM EVER RETIRED IN THE HISTORY OF THE U OF M'S MEN'S HOCKEY PROGRAM
Photo courtesy of University of Minnesota Athletics

tenth grade they were too big; in eleventh and twelfth grade they were too small," John laughs. He had grown to be 6 feet 1 and 180 pounds.

During his youth, John carefully observed other accomplished players in a variety of sports. In a way, he became his own coach as he tried to emulate the smooth skating style of Ben Swarthout of the Eveleth Rangers amateur hockey team or studied the throwing motion of a polished football quarterback or baseball pitcher. Although hockey is the sport with which John is clearly most identified, he was also Eveleth High School's starting quarterback, a heralded pitcher and infielder for the baseball team that played in the state tournament his sophomore year, qualified for the Minnesota State High School tennis tournament, and was recruited to high jump for the track and field team despite not practicing the event while playing full-time for the baseball team. Again, his studied approach to technique served him well as he won the regional title in the high jump, defeating Gino Cappelletti of Nashwauk High School (who later starred in professional football as a kicker and wide receiver for a decade with the Boston Patriots of the AFL). Then, at the 1951 state meet, John, using a straddle-style form, earned fourth place as he cleared 5 feet 10 inches! "I didn't have a favorite sport. I loved whatever the sport was for the season," he explains. "We were always in condition, though, because we went from one sport to the next."

John was a sought-after athlete upon graduating from high school in 1951. He entertained the idea of going to the University of Michigan to join Matchefts and best friend Willard Ikola, but the appeal of playing with an all-Minnesota group at a new hockey arena at the University of Minnesota (U of M; Williams Ice Arena opened in 1950) were deciding factors to stay in state. A girlfriend, Carol Doheny, remained in Minnesota too, and enrolled in St. Luke's nursing program in Duluth in 1952. John played immediately on the varsity team because of a roster depletion caused by the Korean War (otherwise freshmen were ineligible to play varsity in that era), centering a line with Dick Dougherty of International Falls on the right wing and Gene Campbell of Minneapolis on the left wing. The line clicked instantaneously. Dougherty, ranked among the greatest hockey players in the same era, shared a sentiment common in the state as he called John the greatest high school player he had competed against and a person he was thrilled to play alongside at the U of M. "John was a great player at handling the puck—very active, very talented."

JOHN MAYASICH HAD A LONG CAREER WITH HUBBARD BROADCASTING AND WAS INDUCTED INTO THE MINNESOTA BROADCASTING HALL OF FAME IN 2005
Photo courtesy of KSTP

John played for two coaches at the U of M, both of whom have been inducted into the US Hockey Hall of Fame. "Doc Romnes is a person at the U that I learned a lot from—he could show every phase of centering. He never really got credit for what he contributed," John says of his first collegiate head coach. Eveleth-native Mariucci, one of only a handful of Americans who played professionally in the NHL in the 1940s, became the head coach for John's final three years. Besides centering a prolific line, John played defense on power plays and the penalty-killing squad where he deftly maneuvered the puck around opponents. "I wasn't off the ice too much," he notes dryly. While Mariucci directed a more defense-minded team, John was still able to score 144 goals and contribute 154 assists for a total of 298 points in 111 games—still atop the U of M record charts—during his collegiate career, an average significantly over 2.5 points per game! John also holds single-game records of most goals in a game (six, in a game against Winnipeg) and most points (eight, against Michigan in 1955). He was an All-American for three years (1953–55) and led the Western Collegiate Hockey Association in scoring his junior and senior years. Attesting to the significance of John's achievements, his #8 jersey was retired from the U of M men's hockey program in 1998—the only one ever to receive the honor. John is also credited for being the first collegiate player to develop and use a slap shot. Friend Ikola described a new shot he had seen at the professional level. Again, John absorbed the information and practiced it until he refined it. The booming shot added to his potent scoring arsenal. Only a 5–4 overtime loss to Rensselaer Polytech Institute in the 1955 NCAA championship game at the Broadmoor Ice Palace in Colorado Springs, Colorado, still haunts John. Not being on a winning NCAA championship team appears to be the only title to elude his grasp.

John and his high school sweetheart, Carol, married after graduating in 1955. John had joined the Reserve Officers Training Corps (ROTC) while attending the U of M and became a commissioned army officer in the fall. He was fortunate to be assigned temporary duty with the US national hockey team, and in early 1956 it provided an opportunity to be in Cortina d'Ampezzo, Italy, for the Olympics. More than half of the team was from Minnesota, including Matchefts, Ikola, and John—all from Eveleth. College friends and teammates Dougherty, Campbell, Jack Petroske (Hibbing), Wendell Anderson (St. Paul Johnson), and Dick Meredith (Minneapolis Southwest) were also on the Mariucci-coached team. John thinks Mariucci had pretty well decided the members of the team. "The nucleus was hand-picked. There were very few open spots."

> *"After we beat Canada, I thought we had a shot at the gold medal," recounts John. "It was one of the best games I ever played. I scored a hat trick, but I got speared behind the knee . . ."*

At the 1956 Olympics, the two top teams from round-robin play of each of the three pools advanced. In the final round, the US upset Canada, a team that had been dominating international hockey for years, 4–1. John was the hero in the victory, but it came at a price. "After we beat Canada, I thought we had a shot at the gold medal," recounts John. "It was one of the best games I ever played. I scored a hat trick, but I got speared behind the knee. It was a tough injury. I couldn't do what I was used to doing." John had scored a total of six goals to this point, but would not score another, although he is credited with four assists as Dougherty banged in four goals in a 9–4 victory over Czechoslovakia. The Soviet Union team had ascended quickly in international competition and defeated the American squad 4–0. As a result, the US team earned a silver medal. Overall, it was a very positive experience for John and his hometown friends. "The exposure of hockey helped many in Eveleth," he says earnestly. "It also gave us the opportunity to travel."

> *"The exposure of hockey helped many in Eveleth," he says earnestly. "It also gave us the opportunity to travel."*

On completing his military service, John began working for Hubbard Broadcasting, a company he would remain with for the rest of his professional career—while still managing to play hockey. John and Carol relocated to Green Bay, Wisconsin, where he embarked on a twofold career, selling advertising and playing hockey as well as being the father of five children. John played and coached the Green Bay Bobcats hockey team and remembers drawing an average of four thousand fans to the Brown County Arena. He was also permitted to play on national teams and was once again invited to be on an American Olympic hockey team—this one would be played on native soil. The 1960 Winter Olympics were being hosted at Squaw Valley, California, and were the first Olympics to be televised. An electric-powered Zamboni ice resurfacer (the company was based in California) was also introduced at this Olympics. This time John, who had been guaranteed a spot, was the sole representative from Eveleth, and the contingent from Minnesota was slightly less. Jack McCartan of St. Paul (a renowned baseball and hockey player at the U of M), the starting goalie, Bill and Roger Christian from Warroad, and John, now playing defense, were instrumental in the success of the "Forgotten Miracle" team. Other Minnesotans on the team were Olympic veteran Meredith, Paul Johnson of West St. Paul, Bob Owen from St. Louis Park, and nineteen-year-old dynamo Tommy Williams of Duluth.

The American team once again made the medal round of six contenders, but they were not considered a threat to win a medal. The powerful Canadian and Soviet Union teams were expected to battle for the gold medal while Czechoslovakia or Sweden were favored to capture the bronze medal. Then began "the first miracle": victories over Sweden and Germany and a stunning 2–1 upset over Canada. They followed

A MURAL (JOHN MAYASICH APPEARS ON THE FAR RIGHT) AND A MONUMENT REFLECT EVELETH'S PRIDE IN THEIR HOCKEY HERITAGE

Photos courtesy of the City of Eveleth

that exhausting, but exhilarating, victory with another shocking win, toppling the Soviet Union by the score of 3–2 in a tightly contested game before a packed crowd. McCartan frustrated the Soviets with his spectacular play in the nets as Billy Christian hammered home both the tying and winning goals. One more victory and the undefeated American team would claim their first Olympic hockey gold medal in history. Playing early on Sunday morning, February 28, 1960, the determined young squad fell behind the respected Czechoslovakia team 4–3 after two periods of play. The final period was truly inspirational. The home team attacked furiously and scored six unanswered goals to win 9–4, with Roger Christian finding the net three times (and four for the game!). McCartan, a savior in goal, was named the best goalkeeper in the Olympic Games. John Mayasich scored seven goals and was credited with five assists, including two in the final game. "It was an experience I had that you don't expect," John discloses. "I joined the team only one day before the first game. The big memory was winning the gold medal. It was great since we thought we'd be lucky to win a bronze. Standing on the blue line, seeing the flag raised, hearing the anthem . . . There's nothing like it." On Monday, John Mayasich quietly says, he was back at work in Green Bay.

Continuing his work in Green Bay, John extended his playing with the Bobcats and US national teams including the 1969 team when, at age thirty-five, he was named player-coach of the team. On the team was rising young star Tim Sheehy of International Falls, who was playing for Boston College. Sheehy marveled at John's skills, but of equal or more importance are these words: "John is a first-class individual off the ice too."

Eventually John, Carol, and their family were able to return to Minnesota, where John advanced in his career with Hubbard Broadcasting. The two oldest children had graduated from Ashwaubenon High School (the city of Ashwaubenon borders Lambeau Field, the home of the Green Bay Packers) in Wisconsin and the youngest three children would graduate from Stillwater High School in Minnesota. Stanley S. Hubbard, a college teammate on the U of M hockey team who was now the president of Hubbard Broadcasting, valued John's abilities off the ice as well as on the ice surface, eventually naming John as general manager at KS95-FM and then president of the radio division when Hubbard was elevated to chairman, chief executive officer, and president of Hubbard Broadcasting in 1983. John had a twelve-year tenure in that position and later became head of the public affairs division before semiretiring in 1997 at sixty-four years old. Both Hubbard and John have been inducted into the Minnesota Broadcasting Hall of Fame.

In 2002, John and Carol returned to their northern Minnesota roots. Eveleth welcomed their return, and city leaders proudly note the couple's contributions to the community. Carol, a supportive spouse and loving mother who was a Girl Scout leader and religious education teacher, passed away in 2009, having suffered progressive supranuclear palsy, a rare brain disorder that affects balance, walking, and eye movement.

John remains active, playing golf and curling in a senior league with his twin brother, Jim, a retired Eveleth teacher and basketball coach. "Keep trying to be better than you are. That's how I approached sports and other parts of life," John says, summarizing his attitude and life. "I've had a good life."

Castellano, his high school linemate and lifetime friend, adds, "John Mayasich is one of a kind." That declaration is a tribute to a life on and off the ice.

ANGUS MORRISON NEARLY VERTICAL IN A CANOE
Photo courtesy of Angus Morrison

ANGUS "SANDY" MORRISON

Have Canoe, Will Travel

WHETHER IT BE CALM, SMOOTH-FLOWING WATER-ways or turbulent, roaring rapids, paddling and navigating rivers has become a way of life for Angus "Sandy" Morrison.

Angus, a name recognizing his Scottish heritage, was born in 1952 and known as Sandy during his childhood and athletic career at the Blake School in Hopkins, Minnesota. He excelled at ice hockey and the discus and shot put events in track and field at the private school, but it would be the sport of canoeing that captured his heart and became his ticket to becoming a three-time Olympian. Sandy was a two-time state champion discus thrower in the 1969 and 1970 Minnesota Independent School League track and field championships (private schools became part of the Minnesota State High School League in 1974), helping the team win one of nine state track and field championships in 1970 under the direction of inspirational coach Chub Bettels. Sandy's tosses were impressive: more than 162 feet in 1969 and 161 feet 4½ inches to capture his second crown in 1970. Forty years later, those throws would have still placed third in the large school (AA) state track and field meet.

It was a trip to the Boundary Waters Canoe Area led by Bill Fisher, a teacher at Blake, that sparked Sandy's interest in canoeing. He later became involved with the whitewater canoeing community and entered a citizens' race that included a stretch of rapids on the St. Croix River near Taylors Falls, Minnesota. And there was always a canoe at the family's cabin north of Grand Rapids.

Seeking a college that had a good academic reputation in a rural area that also offered an opportunity to pursue canoeing at a higher level, Sandy enrolled at Williams College in 1970. It is located in the extreme northwest corner of Massachusetts, near the Vermont border, and it offers access to many popular canoeing sites. The 6-feet-2-inch, 200-pound athlete played hockey for a talented freshman team that won eleven of thirteen games, but hockey became secondary in the spring of 1971 when he qualified to participate in the World Championships in Europe in a 13-feet-2-inch fiberglass canoe that he had constructed.

Whitewater slalom canoeing would be introduced at the 1972 Olympic Games in Germany, and Sandy was looking forward to being part of the inaugural competition. Competing all around the European continent, Sandy gained a preview of the proposed 660-meter artificial whitewater slalom course at Eiskanal, a diversion of the Lech River near the city of Augsburg. "When I first saw it, I thought that it was intimidating," Sandy comments. "It had tight turns and vertical walls that created surges and fluctuations."

Living on a shoestring budget, Sandy trained full-time during the 1971–72 academic year, a revolutionary concept for a canoeist. Sandy claims credit for coining the area in California called "Peanut Butter Park," the place a group of canoeists trained while eating cheap, basic foods and camping. The spot is along the Kern River, and it's still a popular space for canoe enthusiasts. A fellow paddler, Jamie McEwan, had a girlfriend named Sandy (Boynton) and believes that to lessen the confusion of whom they were speaking of, Sandy Morrison started being referred to by his birth name, Angus.

"The 1972 canoeing trials were on the Savage River in Maryland, an excellent

ANGUS MORRISON AND JAMIE MCEWAN
Photo courtesy of Jamie McEwan

river for competition," remarks Angus. He finished second behind Peanut Butter Park friend McEwan. Angus was a twenty-year-old Olympian.

McEwan, who later graduated from Yale with a degree in literature and became a noted children's book author, illustrates their training and how Angus rallied to his rescue when assistance was needed. "I had developed an allergy to epoxy, and so found it awkward to repair the epoxy slalom boat I had built for myself. Angus then undertook all repairs, free of charge, doing a much more meticulous job than I could ever have managed. That spring we traveled together to several races, just the two of us, and that is how we arrived at the Olympic Trials, whose results were anything but a sure thing. Luckily the young bucks stayed ahead of the guard, and there was room for both of us on the team."

"The 1972 Olympics was an overwhelming experience," Angus recollects. One strong memory is marching into the stadium during the opening ceremony. "I had never seen such a crowd. We were given a cornucopia of gifts: clothes, shoes, and luggage."

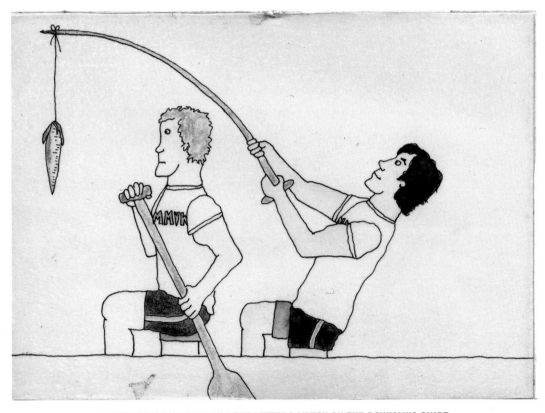

"CANOEISTS AND CARROT." THE LETTERS MMVW ON THE BOWMAN'S SHIRT
SIGNIFIED MORRISON AND MCEWAN VS. THE WORLD.
Art ©Sandra Boynton. Used by permission. All rights reserved.

In whitewater slalom canoe racing, there are gates that the canoeist must paddle through successfully in order as they follow a lengthy, rushing route to the finish. Penalty points are assigned if the paddler hits a gate, and a larger number of points are allocated for missing a gate. The competitor was awarded the best result of two runs (combined time and penalty points). Angus had an impressive first run and was sixth in the standings. The course was as challenging as he remembered it from his previous visit. "It was exciting and intense. The course paralleled the river and used a natural flow. It had cement-simulated boulders and over thirty gates." On the second run, he accumulated more penalty points and had a slower time. Based on the more successful first run, Angus finished in tenth place overall. McEwan startled the canoeing world, winning a bronze medal behind a pair of powerful Germans. Twenty years later McEwan proved his skill and longevity in the sport, placing an impressive fourth in the double canoe at the 1992 Olympics in Barcelona, Spain.

Angus returned to Williams College to complete his degree in psychology. Due to the cost of constructing the whitewater slalom course, the sport was dropped as an Olympic event for twenty years. The exhilarating feeling of competitive canoeing was still with him, though, and Angus switched to flatwater sprint racing. Unlike recreational canoeing, where a pair of people sit on seats, racers kneel in the Olympic style of competition and stroke the single-bladed paddle on only one side, steering with a rocking motion. "The United States was undeveloped in flatwater canoeing. It is dramatically different from whitewater slalom racing. It is extraordinarily difficult to master and technically challenging. It is a long, narrow boat—very tippy. You have a high center of gravity and take long, powerful, full-body strokes," Angus explains.

Photo courtesy of Angus Morrison

Placing third in the 1976 one-person canoe (C1) trials, Angus qualified for a second Olympic attempt in Montreal. He would be competing in the 500-meter C1 and 1,000-meter C1 events at a rowing basin on the artificial island, Île Notre-Dame in the St. Lawrence River. Paddling on the left side, Angus finished last in his heat in the 500-meter sprint and then failed to qualify for the semifinals through the repêchage, a competition where contestants have another chance to advance. He fared better in the 1,000-meter canoe race, qualifying for the semifinals through the repêchage with a vastly improved time of 4 minutes 18.11 seconds, more than 17 seconds better than his first heat. Angus did not make it out of the semifinals, however, ending his bid for a medal. He and his teammates were increasing attention to the sport, and a new crop of athletes would benefit from the experience and tutelage of Angus, McEwan, Bruce Barton, and others.

Pairing with right-handed paddler Rob Plankenhorn, Angus qualified for a third Olympic team in 1980 in the two-man canoe (C2) event. Again, Angus had to learn to adapt to a change. He summarizes his approach toward paddling this way: "Learn, analyze, and get technically perfect." Plankenhorn, a teammate whom Angus describes as "an extraordinary paddler," returns the praise. "Angus was a great athlete, very strong, and an exceptional sternsman. He was also lots of fun to be around." Due to the United States–led boycott, the C2 team never got to compete in Moscow, Russia, but Angus still has the cowboy hat and boots that the team was scheduled to wear for the opening ceremony.

Al Oerter, the four-time Olympic discus-throwing gold medalist, is Angus's favorite athlete. As a former discus thrower himself, Angus believes Oerter's performance in the 1964 Olympics is mindboggling. Competing with torn cartilage in his ribs, Oerter hurled an Olympic record toss despite the agonizing pain.

> *"Angus was a great athlete, very strong, and an exceptional sternsman. He was also lots of fun to be around."*

His passion for water sports led to a career for Angus. He became an instructor and guide, ultimately managing at Nantahala Outdoor Center, the largest rafting operation in the country, located on the edge of the Great Smoky Mountains in Bryson City, North Carolina. It is also where Angus met Lynn Brandon, whom he married in 1993. Several rivers near their home offer wild and scenic whitewater tours, and nearby hills and trails beckon people seeking outdoor adventure.

Today you can find Angus with a canoe strapped atop a van still searching for another river that brings a sense of exhilaration.

**GARY NEIST AFTER WINNING THE 112-POUND
MINNESOTA STATE HIGH SCHOOL LEAGUE WRESTLING TITLE IN 1964**
Photo courtesy of Gary Neist, used with the permission of Albert Lea High School

GARY NEIST

Albert Lea Tiger Became a Lion

BORN AND RAISED IN ALBERT LEA, MINNESOTA, A city of 18,000 surrounded by fertile farmland and once a thriving meatpacking center only eleven miles north of the Iowa border, Gary Neist participated in gymnastics, pole vaulting, football, and wrestling as a youth. While Gary gravitated toward the sport of wrestling, his three younger brothers, Roger, Earl, and Rollin, maintained their interest in gymnastics, with Roger claiming the all-around state high school title in 1966. Gary claimed his own state title during his junior year of high school in 1964 while wrestling for the Albert Lea Tigers at the 112-pound weight class. He had wrestled at the 95-pound division the two previous years, earning third place in 1963. His senior year he did not place at the state meet, blaming a drastic weight loss in attempting to qualify at a lower weight class.

Albert Lea has been known for the strength of its wrestling program for nearly the past half century. Gary was a part of the program on its upswing under the helm of Paul Ehrhard; the team won its first state wrestling championship in 1966, a year after Gary graduated. Another wrestler who helped the team reach new heights was Neal Skaar, a teammate a year older than Gary who continued in the sport at Luther College in Decorah, Iowa. The Neist parents pushed the value of education onto their four sons and daughter, Nancy, since the father, a regional Golden Gloves boxing champion, had only attended school for eight years and had worked hard, laboring as a meat locker plant owner and farmer. Gary chose to follow Skaar and attend Luther College.

Gary grew substantially and wrestled at 145 and 152 pounds at the collegiate level. His greatest individual success was in 1968, when he placed in the NCAA College Division and was invited to the more acclaimed Division I University-level wrestling championships at Penn State. Gary won his first match but was defeated handily in his second bout 9–0. His foe was Wayne Wells, a formidable opponent by any standard. A future gold medalist in freestyle wrestling, Wells not only went on to win

GARY NEIST AS A COACH AT THE US MILITARY ACADEMY IN WEST POINT, NEW YORK
Photo courtesy of Gary Neist

the NCAA University Wrestling Championship in 1968, but also qualified that same year for the US Olympic wrestling team.

Graduating from Luther in 1969 with a chemistry degree and the necessary education courses, Gary started his professional career as a science and math teacher and coached boys' gymnastics in Glencoe, Minnesota. After teaching one year, military service called, and Gary was trained as a fire direction specialist for artillery in the US Army. A high-ranking officer was aware of Gary's background as a wrestler and smilingly inquired about his interest in serving as an assistant wrestling coach at the US Military Academy in West Point, New York. Gary leapt at the opportunity to follow a passion and leave the risky position for which he'd trained.

It was at West Point that Gary met Vietnam veteran J Robinson (who also served as an assistant wrestling coach and later gained fame as the University of Minnesota head coach). Unknown to Gary was that he would learn a new style of wrestling at West Point and join Robinson and twin brothers Jim and Dave Hazewinkel of Coon Rapids, Minnesota, as members of the 1972 US Olympic Greco-Roman wrestling team.

Taking full advantage of the position at West Point, Gary was able to train after fulfilling his coaching duties and also learn from his colleagues, who had national and international experience in Greco-Roman wrestling—particularly benefiting from Robinson's tutelage. He says simply, "I learned that I loved Greco-Roman. It just was a better fit for my style since it emphasizes upper body strength."

Three-time Olympian (including the 1972 team) and head coach of the Air Force Academy for over two decades, Wayne Baughman offers this clinical assessment of Gary's wrestling prowess: "He was a powerful, flexible guy with explosive hip action and had a natural body for Greco-Roman wrestling. Gary was a smart guy who had the right mentality for the sport. It's a credit to Gary to make the Olympic team since he had the least amount of experience in the sport of any team member. He became one of our young lions."

Suddenly Gary was competing on the national and international stage himself. He competed in the All-Army and All-Military Games and then represented the United States at the 1971 World Games in Bulgaria, of which he remarks, "It was a wild experience. The Eastern bloc countries had very powerful teams. Later we had the chance to tour Germany as part of a ten-day bus tour. Wrestling is very popular there, and we would stop in tiny German towns that had wrestling teams to compete against them."

Qualifying for the US Olympic wrestling team at the 74-kilogram (163-pound) division would be no easy task. First, Gary participated in the freestyle competition and was the only wrestler that a rival from the NCAA tournament, Wayne Wells, did not pin. His showing at that event qualified Gary for the US Greco-Roman Olympic Trials.

Despite the intense instruction and workouts at West Point, Gary was still a newcomer to the Greco-Roman style of wrestling. To prepare for the Olympic Trials, Gary commuted three or four times per week during this training time from Albert Lea to the University of Minnesota, a journey of nearly two hundred miles round-trip, to practice with wrestlers under the direction of Alan Rice. On the days he did not commute, he faithfully adhered to a conditioning regimen. The trials were awarded to Anoka, Minnesota, probably since so many Olympic hopefuls trained there. Gary won the final at the Anoka High School venue, an exhausting marathon series of matches against 1968 NCAA champion Mike Gallego, a Fresno State graduate attending dental school. Gary cherishes the memory. "It was very exciting to make the team."

"The opening ceremonies at Munich were neat," recounts Gary. "We were rather formal. One odd thing was seeing Olympians pull out plastic sheets—I didn't know why—when the doves [pigeons] were released. After being cooped up, they were releasing too," he laughs.

The accommodations in the Olympic Village for the Greco-Roman team were far from luxurious. Ten wrestlers were packed into one apartment, which would be redesigned as a condominium after the conclusion of the Olympic Games. Gary slept with others in a room that was later destined to become the kitchen and dining room.

At 4:00 a.m. on the morning of September 5, 1972, Gary weighed in at the Administrative Building for his first match of the Olympics. He did not hear the terrorists' shooting that was later called the Munich Massacre. Instead, he prepared for his bout with Momir Kecman of Yugoslavia at an off-site location. After losing the match, he, head coach Alan Rice, and the other coaches at the wrestling setting were told that the second competition scheduled for the afternoon wouldn't be held. The reason for the postponement was not explained, and the athletes expressed a lot of confusion and frustration. The delay, they later learned, was due to the terrorist attack and hostage-taking of Israeli athletes and coaches. Gary believes he knew one of the wrestlers killed in the most tragic episode of Olympic Games history.

GARY NEIST CONTROLLING HIS SWEDISH OPPONENT IN 1972 OLYMPIC GRECO-ROMAN WRESTLING COMPETITION
Photo credit: J Robinson

A memorial service was held on September 6, and the Olympic Games resumed after a one-day suspension of competition. All the athletes were distracted by the brutality, and the 1972 Summer Olympics suddenly lost much of their luster. Gary did wrestle another match against Jan Karlsson, the welterweight from Sweden who would win the bronze medal. In each of his two matches, Gary surprised his opponents by putting them on their backs, but they fought back with a vengeance. "I went out aggressively with every intention to win," observes Gary. "I'm pleased with the work I did, but there's no question they beat me decisively."

Remembering the most illustrious American track star of the first half of the twentieth century, who later came to Albert Lea High School as an invited speaker, Gary lists Jesse Owens as a favorite athlete. Impressed by Wayne Baughman's unbelievable work ethic, Gary names him as an admired wrestler. He also classifies former teammate and colleague Neal Skaar, who later became the head coach of the Albert Lea Tigers' wrestling program, as a person he greatly respects.

GARY NEIST AND HIS OPPONENT FROM YUGOSLAVIA MEET IN THE 74-KILOGRAM WEIGHT CLASS OF THE 1972 OLYMPICS
Photo credit: J Robinson

Returning to Minnesota, Gary enrolled at Mankato State College (now Minnesota State University–Mankato) to obtain a degree in physical education. He then became a physical education teacher for twelve years at Albert Lea Public Schools while also coaching boys' and girls' gymnastics for ten years. Wanting to experience another career in a new environment, Gary moved to Colorado and began selling real estate for over a decade, eventually starting his own company. In 1999 he was accepted into the doctoral program for education at the University of Nebraska.

> *" I decided to pursue a professional career. I was not tempted to try out for any future Olympics because I needed to make a living and support myself. I feel very comfortable with both my successes and not-so-successful times. I just hope that I have helped others."*

Since 2004, Gary has been a college professor in physical education and methods classes, first at East Stroudsburg University in Pennsylvania, then at Minnesota State University–Mankato beginning in 2008.

The man called a young lion by Baughman decided not to undertake further training in wrestling after 1972, although he would have been in his prime four years later. "I decided to pursue a professional career. I was not tempted to try out for any future Olympics because I needed to make a living and support myself. I feel very comfortable with both my successes and not-so-successful times. I just hope that I have helped others."

Photo courtesy of SCSU Athletic Media Relations

VAN NELSON

Inspiration Is What Counts

AS A JUNIOR AT MINNEAPOLIS WASHBURN HIGH School in 1962, Van Nelson decided to give cross country running a try since he had performed fairly well in the 660-yard run in a physical education class. A mere six years later, he was competing against the greatest long-distance runners in the world in the Olympic Games in Mexico City, Mexico.

Born in 1945, Van (whose name is derived from the first part of his mother's Dutch surname, Van Scheick) was the oldest of four boys, all of whom found success in running. Other than playing some intramural basketball, Van had not participated in organized sports before entering the field of long-distance running.

Van quickly established himself as a force to be reckoned with as a first-year runner in the competitive City Conference, where Minneapolis Southwest High School reigned as the dominant running team in cross country and track and field not only in the city, but also in the state. His swift ascent to becoming a topflight runner in Minnesota was assured by the next fall following a summer of rigorous training of more than a thousand miles.

In the fall of 1963, Van was ready to make his mark in local running circles. Although Southwest again won the City Conference, Van placed second on the Lake Nokomis circuit of 1.8 miles with a time of 8 minutes, 40 seconds (8:40). "It was an out-and-back course," Van relates. "You ran about a mile and then curved around three big pine trees and returned to the starting point." The course also served as the site of the state cross country championship (won eight days later by Bob Wagner of St. Louis Park, a future University of Minnesota runner), where Van finished in an impressive seventh place, two slots behind his summer training partner from Southwest, Don Oliver.

Van won the Twin City Indoor one-mile event for high school runners at the University of Minnesota (U of M) Fieldhouse in early 1964 in 4:26. He was approached afterward by St. Cloud State coach Bob Tracy. The coach congratulated Van and asked about his interest in running at St. Cloud and becoming a national champion. Having experienced the sweetness of success, Van had even higher aspirations—he wanted to become an Olympian. Tracy was probably stunned when Van revealed his ambition. "'I'd like to have you be the nucleus of our team,'" Van recalls Tracy saying. "'We can become competitive at a national level.'" His words would become prophetic.

Later that season Van ran the fifth-fastest mile for high school students in the nation. The fastest time belonged to a junior from Kansas named Jim Ryun, who had run an incredible 3:59 mile, the first high school runner in history to run it in less than four minutes. Van went on to a runner-up finish at the state meet, less than two seconds behind Wagner, who remembers this about his foe: "Van had this huge up-and-down stride, but he was a tremendous runner. He had the desire and the heart, which allowed him to run blistering five-thousand- and ten-thousand-meter runs [or three- and six-mile runs] later that were collegiate records."

> *"Van had this huge up-and-down stride, but he was a tremendous runner. He had the desire and the heart, which allowed him to run blistering five-thousand- and ten-thousand-meter runs [or three- and six-mile runs] later that were collegiate records."*

Van was recruited by the U of M and the University of Wisconsin, but he decided to tour the St. Cloud State campus and determined "it had the right feel. At the time it was on the edge of town and had fifty-five hundred students. I liked Bob Tracy too—he was very personable. The University of Minnesota just seemed too big." Tracy not only continued to coach Van, but he became a lifelong friend to the industrious runner.

St. Cloud State, at the time a member of the National Association of Intercollegiate Athletics (NAIA), did not have the full complement of runners required to score in a cross country meet. Chuck Spoden (St. Cloud), Kenny Mitchell (Big Lake), and Van composed the entire inaugural team in the fall of 1964. Nevertheless, Van finished eighth in the national meet. It was the track season of 1965 that Van's meteoric rise captured the running world's attention. Van ran a three-mile race in 13:45, a national collegiate freshman record.

Over the following three years, the honors and titles Van accumulated were phenomenal. According to the NAIA sports archives, he captured nine NAIA track titles (six at outdoor tracks, three at indoor tracks) and achieved All-American honors four times in cross country and numerous more in track. A press release from the NAIA promoting the outdoor championships, to be held at the University of New Mexico in the spring of 1968, proclaims, "VAN NELSON OF ST. CLOUD STATE—BEST DISTANCE RUNNER IN U.S."

VAN NELSON WAS A THREE-TIME WINNER OF BOTH THE THREE AND SIX-MILE RUNS AT THE DRAKE RELAYS FROM 1966–68
Photo credit: SCSU Athletic Media Relations

A dedicated runner, Van usually ran ten miles in the morning—usually in a time around fifty-two to fifty-five minutes. Then, in the afternoon, he ran another ten miles doing 220-yard interval sprints followed by a 220-yard recovery jog. Such short intervals may seem strange to most serious runners, but the routine gave Van what he wanted. "The idea was to emphasize speed. I just know that it worked for me." Van estimates that his running mileage on weeks when there wasn't a race was 140 miles per week.

As Van prospered, the fortunes of the St. Cloud State cross country and track and field teams improved mightily. "For the 1965–67 cross country seasons, I placed third each year at the NAIA championships [with a best time of twenty minutes flat for the four-mile run] in Omaha, Nebraska. In 1967, we just missed winning the team championship by three points," Van laments. By now, the team had become formidable with the recruitment of more high-caliber runners from Minnesota: Bruce Johnson (Minnetonka), Earl Glauvitz (Belgrade), Chet Blasciek (Holdingford), Warren Slocum (White Bear Lake), and Lewis Johnson.

Track was Van's favorite platform for running, though. His preferred event was the three-mile race, which he ran in 13:29.7 in the 1967 NAIA Track & Field Championships and then lowered to 13:17.4 in the Drake Relays in 1968—averaging under 4 minutes, 26 seconds per mile. At the Drake Relays, he was a double-winner in the three- and six-mile runs for three consecutive years. Naturally, with such impressive victories, Van was sought to compete at the international level, where he also found success. He claimed two gold medals in the 1967 Pan Am games in the 5,000- and 10,000-meter runs at Winnipeg as he competed in cold, rainy weather. Out of twenty-five races in 1967 ranging from 1 mile to 10,000 meters at invitationals inside and outside the country, Van won nineteen of them and always finished in the top three places. He was ready for the Olympic Trials.

In a previous race, Van had the thrill of competing against Billy Mills, the Olympic gold medalist in the 10,000-meter run in 1964. Van had battled, staying close, and Mills told him afterward, "I can see we may be locking horns in the 1968 trials." Mills, unfortunately, was contending with an injury and just missed qualifying for the team. Van describes Mills as "not only personable, but one great individual. He was a tough, tough competitor."

VAN NELSON RUNNING SECOND (BEHIND LEADER TOM LARIS AND AHEAD OF 1964 OLYMPIC-GOLD MEDALIST BILLY MILLS AND TRACY SMITH) IN THE 10,000-METER RUN AT THE 1968 OLYMPIC TRIALS IN LAKE TAHOE, CALIFORNIA;
Photo courtesy of Van Nelson

> *Van describes Mills as "not only personable, but one great individual. He was a tough, tough competitor."*

A series of races in three locations determined the distance-running US Olympic team members: the first took place in the Coliseum in Los Angeles; the second race was in Eugene, Oregon; and the final race took place at Echo Summit in South Lake Tahoe, California. Van had trained well and felt confident. Coach Tracy and Van calculated the best opportunity to win a medal was in the 10,000-meter run and passed over his preferred race of 5,000 meters. Van qualified along with Tracy Smith and Tom Laris to go on to Mexico City.

Many team members trained at South Lake Tahoe to adapt to the altitude. What they didn't train for were the other conditions that hit them in Mexico City: heat, humidity, and smog. Van did not attend the opening ceremonies because his race was the next morning. He finished in twenty-ninth place, slightly over two minutes behind the gold medalist's time of 29:37.4, in the 10,000-meter run. Van was a proud Olympian and remembers the time and team camaraderie fondly. "It was the greatest track and field team ever assembled. We still have team reunions that I enjoy attending. It felt like you were at the state fair every day—except with an international flavor."

After the Olympics, Van returned to St. Cloud State University to complete his coursework for a biology degree and prepare to student teach. His running career remained successful until he ruptured the L-5 vertebra in his lower back when lifting wet sod in 1970 at a construction site where St. Cloud Apollo High School was being built. The injury resulted in his right leg being partially disabled. Van valiantly tried for a comeback, but he could not compete at the peak performance he was accustomed to and retired from international competition in 1971. Later Van was inducted into the Washburn, St. Cloud State University (SCSU gained university status in 1975), NAIA, and (as a charter member) Minnesota Track & Field halls of fame.

Van's younger brothers had their own triumphs in the running arena. Stephen Nelson ran at the U of M for two years. Greg also joined the U of M track team and set a family record with a time of 4:04 in the mile run. Youngest brother Rich was a state cross country champion and continued his athletic career at the U of M until an injury derailed his running during his sophomore year.

Following a one-year teaching stint at Maple Lake, Van started a long teaching and coaching career at Edina Public Schools. Beloved by students, Van taught a variety of science and health education classes at the middle school and high school levels. He married Linda, a teacher at Fridley High School. They are the proud parents of son Adam and daughter Katie and grandparents to Cole Nelson and Cora Messing. Both Van and Linda have now retired from the teaching profession, but Van has continued to keep his hand in the coaching field. "You don't have to be a super athlete to be a good coach. Inspiration is what counts," he concludes.

Van is still trying to inspire runners as he helps reinvigorate the program at St. Cloud State University by finding sponsors for awards at the Van Nelson Indoor Track & Field Open, established in 2012 as the only track or cross country meet that the college hosts. One of his own contributions is building a victory stand for the awards presentations for athletes to be recognized. Some of the SCSU award recipients may have been inspired by an Olympian, the most decorated track and field alumnus of their college.

Photo credit: Ann Marsden

LINDSAY NIELSEN

Embrace What You Have

ATHLETIC AND ADVENTUROUS, LINDSAY NIELSEN'S career in sports had a twenty-six-year gap. The lengthy interruption was caused by a dreadful accident at a railway yard that occurred when Lindsay was thirteen years old.

Born in 1955, Lindsay grew up in southeast Minneapolis and thoroughly enjoyed park board sports and running. The self-professed "tomboy" from a dysfunctional family was hopping and riding trains when a coupling between freight cars closed, trapping her left foot. The coupling opened, releasing her crushed foot, and the terrified eighth-grade girl yelled for help. After initially being yelled at by railroad employees for her actions, a short man wearing a polka-dotted hat came to her rescue. "He directed my care and said I'd be all right. 'You're going to be better than you were,' he told me. I never saw him again." She was eventually taken to Hennepin County General Hospital (now Hennepin County Medical Center) where she remained for four months, and after multiple surgeries and finally an amputation of her left foot, she was fit with a prosthesis.

The 1969 tragedy happened at a time when counseling and social work services were very limited. Her family didn't talk about the accident for many years. Lindsay got addicted to morphine during her protracted hospitalization. She admits that, along with a probable genetic predisposition, addiction and deep grief led to other substance addictions. Her school attendance was sporadic, although she did technically graduate from Marshall-University High School in Minneapolis. Lindsay became pregnant at eighteen. She stayed chemical-free during the pregnancy and gave birth to a son, Josh, in 1974. Josh was born with a rare heart condition that was diagnosed later.

A turning point in Lindsay's life occurred in 1976 when her boyfriend (and future husband) Jeffrey Hunsberger announced, "I am chemically dependent and so are you." Both gave up alcohol and drugs and went to treatment. Nearly forty years later, Jeffrey and Lindsay are still sober. Also in 1976, Lindsay began college and obtained a degree in social work at the University of Minnesota (U of M) in 1980, the same year another son, Miles, was born. Lindsay, now resolute and loving college, received a master's degree in 1982. After working at the Veterans Administration Hospital and other clinical settings, Lindsay began a private practice in 1983 and is now a licensed independent clinical social worker.

Tragedy struck in 1988 when Josh, who had become an active child, died from his heart condition on New Year's Eve. "Losing a foot paled in comparison to losing a child, but what was true during both crises is that I needed to lean on my community," says Lindsay of the profound grief she experienced. Fortunately, joy followed a few years later with the birth of a third son, Maliq, in 1992.

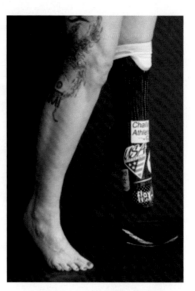

LINDSAY NIELSEN WEARING A PROSTHESIS ON HER LEFT LEG
Photo credit: Ann Marsden

A second turning point transpired in 1995, the year Lindsay turned forty years old. "I had a very significant midlife crisis. I realized if I wanted to run, I'd better do it now. I had never given up on running." Planning to run a three-mile loop, Lindsay's first attempt was quickly thwarted. "I ran less than one block," she laughs at the memory.

While finding a comfortable prosthetic was difficult, Lindsay doggedly continued to run—often joining a group of women who were older than herself. When a member of the running group disclosed that she was going to run in the Twin Cities Marathon in October, Lindsay was stunned. "I came home and said, 'If I can run three miles, why can't I run twenty-six miles? I'm a better athlete than others running it!' My husband said, 'I've been waiting for this.'" Increasing her mileage, Lindsay decided to enter and run the marathon too—the same year she began resuming the sport she'd cherished as a child. Using a new prosthetic, Lindsay says simply, "I finished, but it wasn't pretty."

Lindsay now became much more open about her artificial foot. She had been private, almost hiding her amputation, but now she began to connect with other amputees. In 1997, she connected with U of M track coach Roy Griak and learned some sprinting techniques that accelerated her improvement. When training for distance she ran up to sixty-five miles per week, which proved to be very hard on her body. Track training included weight training and running more for speed, but Lindsay would still run twenty miles per week.

3. LINDSAY NIELSEN PREPARING FOR THE 200-METER DASH AT THE 2000 PARALYMPICS IN SYDNEY, AUSTRALIA
Photo courtesy of Jeffrey Hunsberger

Her athleticism, dedicated training, and competitiveness propelled Lindsay rapidly to several awards. She won gold medals in five track events ranging in distance from 100 meters to 1500 meters at the Disabled National Track Championships in 1997 and was later named Disabled Female Athlete of the Year by the US Olympic Committee. In 1998 she won a gold medal in the 400-meter run at the Paralympic World Championships in England. The Northern Lights Running Club named Lindsay its Runner of the Year in 1999. Other amputees were aspiring to do what Lindsay had accomplished. "It's wonderful to know that there are people doing what you want to do," she says of both being a role model and having other role models. By 2000, she held multiple national and world records for the 400-, 800-, and 1500-meter runs along with World Bests in the half and full marathon.

The Paralympics followed the Olympics in Sydney, Australia, in 2000. Lindsay was one of only two American women amputees in the track and field events and finished fifth in the 200-meter finals. Teammate Shea Cowart was the gold medalist. The connection with other Paralympians proved inspirational to Lindsay. "You don't have better stories than those of Paralympians. There is never any whining. You don't see a more grateful group," she says of her experience.

While pleased to earn World Best for female amputees in the marathon in 1997 and regain the title in 1999, it is in the most grueling of all one-day sporting competitions that Lindsay takes the greatest pride—in 2004, at the Wisconsin Ironman Triathlon, she became the first female amputee in the world to complete an Ironman Triathlon. A 2.4-mile swim and 112-mile bike ride precede a full-fledged 26.2-mile marathon run in the rigorous competition, and she did the three demanding segments at forty-nine years old, a scant nine years after being unable to run one block.

Today Lindsay is a writer, psychotherapist, and public speaker. Her essays have appeared in *A Cup of Comfort for the Grieving Heart, Chicken Soup for the Soul (CSFS): Runners*, and *CSFS's Think Positive*, and an excerpt of her memoir was published in *Good Housekeeping*. She adores her husband, Jeffrey, and is a proud mother and grandmother.

Her thoughtful writings and speeches often touch on the topic of loss. She wisely states this on the subject: "The lesson of tragedy is to embrace what you have."

Photo courtesy of Washington Capitals Photography

BOB PARADISE

Life Is Now Paradise

AN OLYMPIC AND PROFESSIONAL ICE HOCKEY PLAY-er and cofounder of a successful property management company, Bob Paradise survived tough years as a youth, which just may be the most compelling part of his life story.

With seven boys and two girls, the Paradise family moved often within the city of St. Paul, particularly the West End. Bob, born in 1944, remembers attending at least four elementary schools and always living in rental housing as a child. Tragedy struck the Paradise family with the death of his father when Bob was ten years old. His mother struggled trying to cope with the overwhelming responsibility of providing for nine children. As a result, Bob and some of his siblings were enrolled at St. Joseph's Orphanage, located in St. Paul and operated by Benedictine nuns. The orphanage was a massive five-story, red-brick building located at the intersection of Randolph and Warwick in Highland Park adjacent to Cretin High School, an all-boys school. St. Joseph's Orphanage was razed in the early 1960s and became the site of Derham High School, an all-girls school, which had formerly been located on the College of St. Catherine (now St. Catherine University) campus. The two high schools eventually merged in 1987 to form Cretin-Derham Hall.

Bob lived at the orphanage for approximately two years and rates it as a positive experience. He credits Mike Scott as a person who took an interest in the Paradise family and became a lifelong friend for helping the family through the struggling times. Bob was then able to return home and live with his siblings and mother, who had now recovered from the trauma of her husband's death and trying to raise nine children as a single parent.

Throughout the family's many moves, Bob was always able to meet neighborhood kids and play baseball, football, and ice hockey games. Many ice hockey games were played at St. Clair Playground's outdoor rink. Wally Wescott, the playground's coordinator and a man Bob considers influential in his life, remembers seeing Bob and his brother Dick skating and shooting at the rink at eight o'clock on Sunday mornings. "You can't coach that," Wescott asserts. "It's called passion."

Bob's interest in sports continued when he entered Cretin High School and excelled at football, ice hockey, and baseball. Bob was named all-state (private schools in Minnesota had their own conferences and state tournaments at the time) in both football and ice hockey, helping lead the hockey team to a consolation championship in 1962 with his aggressive play.

Upon graduation, Bob opted to attend St. Mary's College (now St. Mary's University) in Winona, Minnesota, instead of accepting an offer to walk-on for the University of Minnesota (U of M) ice hockey team, then headed by coach John Mariucci. Bob explains, "The University often thought that they had the athletes in the Twin Cities sewn up, so they didn't offer guys like me scholarships. Through the assistance of Cretin teacher Keith Hanzel, I received a scholarship to St. Mary's. Sometimes it was cheaper to go elsewhere." Hanzel was a graduate of St. Mary's College who prevailed on the St. Mary's president to provide substantial financial aid to Bob. Hanzel later joined Bob at St. Mary's, where the alumnus became a history instructor and an assistant hockey coach.

At St. Mary's College, Bob achieved all-conference honors four consecutive years in ice hockey. While he played the center position briefly, he served primarily as a physical defenseman. St. Mary's, a Division III school, played at an outdoor rink. They did not field a football team, so Bob was unable to pursue that sport. However, he also found success in baseball as an outfielder and pitcher and in 1965 was offered a $500 signing bonus and $500 per month by the Boston Red Sox. It was not a difficult decision for Bob to turn down the offer since hockey was his first love and "I said that I wanted to graduate from college." He not only graduated the following spring and began teaching English at Hill High School in St. Paul, but he also married Maggie Dill, a girl who had attended St. Joseph's Academy and then St. Catherine.

His love for ice hockey continued unabated as he played for various teams while teaching. As an unheralded player, Bob had survived the cuts for the 1966–67 national team the previous year that had been coached by Murray Williamson. During his second year at Hill High School, 1967–68 (before its consolidation in 1971 with Archbishop Murray Memorial High School in Maplewood), Bob tried out for the United States Olympic ice hockey team, again under the direction of Williamson.

Being a Division III ice hockey player was a rarity on a US Olympic ice hockey team. Bob candidly says that part of the reason he may have made the team was because it was difficult for some of the best players to take two months or more away from their jobs, while he was able to obtain a leave from his teaching position to train and travel as they played exhibition games around the country. Nevertheless, Bob takes pride in being a member of a team that he evaluated as "not a star-laden team, but we had good chemistry, and the guys were great teammates."

The 1968 ice hockey team, cocaptained by Herb Brooks and Lou Nanne, placed sixth at the Olympic Games in Grenoble, France. Bob was one of eight Minnesotans on the roster and one of three players from St. Paul, joined by Jack Dale and Craig Falkman. He believes that was a fair placement for their ability and limited training time. "The Eastern European teams were so superior because of their year-round training, plus they just had better talent," he states matter-of-factly. The team lost their first four games (losing to Canada 3–2 in a heartbreaking game), bounced back to defeat both West Germany and East Germany, then ended the Olympics garnering a tie with Finland. Bob sums up his Olympic experience: "It was fun; I was proud to be a part of it, but now it's over."

BOB PARADISE BLOCKING A SHOT FOR GOALIE GARY INNESS VS MONTREAL CANADIENS
Photo courtesy of Pittsburgh Penguins

"It was fun; I was proud to be a part of it, but now it's over."

Bob continued in the sport as a member of the American team in 1969 that participated in the Ice Hockey World Championships. Afterward he was signed as a free agent by the Montreal Canadiens in 1970; he remembers being astonished by the number of roster candidates (110) in their training camp and being one of about 35 defensemen competing for a spot on the team! The Canadiens were a powerhouse with very limited turnover on their roster. To prove the point, Bob recalls with a sense of amazement, "They had the same three starting centers for thirteen years: Henri Richard, Jean Beliveau, and Ralph Backstrom (1958–71)."

Traded to the Minnesota North Stars along with the rights to Gary Gambucci in 1971, Bob was able to play in a handful of NHL games in his home state before becoming a member of the Atlanta Flames. Billed as a strong and physical defenseman willing to sacrifice his body, it was the start of an eight-year career in the NHL for the St. Paul native. Again honest, Bob thinks that the league's expansion in 1967 allowed him to become an NHL professional ice hockey player. Observers of the game constantly note that Bob was respected and played with lots of heart.

After playing one full season and part of another for the Flames, Bob played the first of two stints with the Pittsburgh Penguins. Sandwiched between the two tours with Pittsburgh was a stretch of two partial seasons with the Washington Capitals. The defense-minded defenseman ended his career with 8 goals and 54 assists with a best-scoring season of 3 goals and 15 assists in 1974–75 under coach Ken Schinkel (replaced midyear by Marc Boileau), who appreciated Bob's style of hard-hitting play. He also appeared in a total of twelve playoff games.

> *"The kids today are so much better. They have better venues, better equipment, better coaching, and better skills. The one thing that former players may have an edge in is being more rugged-minded."*

Ice hockey is tightly interwoven in his family. Bob's wife, Maggie, is the daughter of Bob Dill, who played both professional baseball and hockey. Dill spent two seasons with the NHL's New York Rangers during a fourteen-year hockey career (the first US high school player to play for the Rangers) and spent parts of three seasons with the Minneapolis Millers during a nine-year baseball career. Marc Paradise, son of Bob and Maggie, played for St. Thomas Academy and junior hockey before attending the University of St. Thomas. Marc is married to Kelly Brooks, daughter of Herb and Patti Brooks. Besides being a teammate of Bob's on the 1968 Olympic team, Brooks gained fame for coaching the U of M Gophers and 1980 Miracle on Ice Olympic ice hockey teams. Bob's younger brother Dick also played ice hockey professionally, including two years as a defenseman for the Minnesota Fighting Saints from 1972–74. In 1992, Dick Paradise shockingly died of a heart attack on an ice rink during a charity exhibition game in Medford, Wisconsin, at the age of forty-seven.

Of today's ice hockey players, Bob marvels, "The kids today are so much better. They have better venues, better equipment, better coaching, and better skills. The one thing that former players may have an edge in is being more rugged-minded."

Elected to the United States Ice Hockey Hall of Fame in Eveleth, Minnesota, in 1989, Bob was thrilled with the reception that he and fellow inductee Roger Christian received. "We were treated like royalty. The people of Eveleth were wonderful. It was great fun." With his induction, Bob joined his father-in-law, Bob Dill, in the Hall of Fame. Dill had been enshrined in 1979.

Bob quickly names Bobby Orr, the Boston Bruin great, as his favorite athlete. "He was simply the best. He was far ahead of anyone else in the era."

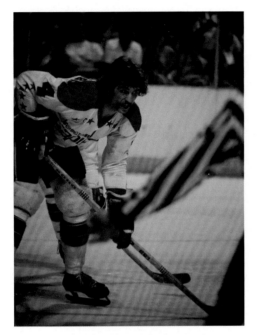

BOB PARADISE PLAYED IN 368 NHL GAMES FROM 1971–79
Photo courtesy of Washington Capitals Photography

John Mayasich, the remarkable ice hockey player who played for Eveleth, the U of M, and two American Olympic teams, is ranked number one on the Minneapolis *Star Tribune's* list of Minnesota's one hundred greatest high school hockey players. Bob applauds the choice. "He was the best. He had both the moxie and the skills." Bob Paradise was ranked number sixty-nine on the list.

While playing pro hockey, Bob and Maggie invested in some apartment buildings along with other business partners. That experience led them to cofound Paradise & Associates, a property management company, in 1980. They now manage more than ten thousand building units situated on more than one hundred properties with the valued help of sixty-five employees.

Bob Paradise does not dwell on the hardships of his youth. In fact, he says, "I have a great life. I have a wonderful and smart wife, two great kids [son Marc and daughter Danielle, who is married to Jeff Dobbelmann], and six wonderful grandchildren [Olivia, Joe, and Tom Paradise and Louis, Helen, and Henri Richard Dobbelmann]."

The name of the youngest grandchild, Henri Richard, was not only one Danielle and Jeff both liked, but also part of ice hockey lore—Henri Richard is a hockey legend who played on thirteen Montreal Canadien teams that won Stanley Cup championships and is also a member of the Hockey Hall of Fame. Even the grandchildren are part of the ice hockey fabric. Life is now Paradise.

JENNY POTTER PLAYED FOR THE UNIVERSITY OF MINNESOTA–DULUTH BULLDOGS AND LED THE NCAA IN SCORING FOR THE 1999–2000 SEASON
Photo courtesy of UMD Sports Information Department, photo by Brett Groehler

JENNY (SCHMIDGALL) POTTER

Playing at the Park

LEWIS PARK IS WHERE I REALLY LEARNED TO LOVE hockey," confirms Jenny (Schmidgall) Potter, a four-time Olympian. The twenty-one-acre park is tucked into the southwestern corner of Edina, Minnesota, less than one mile east of Braemar Golf Course. Featuring an outdoor ice skating rink still used by superb amateur and retired professional hockey players, Jenny has "great memories of times spent with family and seeing so many kids play outdoor hockey at the outdoor parks."

Jenny, born in 1979, and her older sisters, Stephanie and Amber, were part of an active family that "biked everywhere." The girls were competitive swimmers as youths, but Jenny liked physicality and joined a tackle football team in fifth grade. While she was a good swimmer and had early aspirations of becoming an Olympian in the sport, Jenny became convinced that she wouldn't reach the Olympics in the pool. Hearing an announcement when she was in eighth grade (1992) that women's hockey would debut in the 1998 Winter Olympics hosted by Nagano, Japan, the fierce competitor who loved contact thought that maybe a frozen water surface could be her route to an Olympic team.

Edina High School did not field a girls' varsity hockey team until 1995, so Jenny's path to become an elite hockey player may have appeared limited. She quit swimming and tackle football and quickly devoted her time to hockey, on and off the ice. "I would spend hours stickhandling, passing, and deking on tennis courts and an underground garage. I felt very fortunate; my biggest advocate was my dad," Jenny says appreciatively of the role Dwayne Schmidgall, a mechanic, has played as a self-taught skater and hockey player. Once again Jenny played on traditionally all-boys teams: the boys' bantam "B" team and the boys' junior varsity hockey team. It was not until her junior year that Jenny, a 5-foot-4 dynamo, joined a girls' hockey team, opting to play for the amateur Minnesota Thoroughbreds, an under-nineteen-year-old (U-19) team, instead of the newly launched Edina High School girls' hockey team.

Immediately after graduating from high school in 1997, Jenny joined the women's national team and soon met a young coach named Rob Potter from Anoka, Minnesota. She played as a forward and became a strong candidate for the 1998 US Olympic team. And Jenny did make the team (she was the second-youngest member at age nineteen), along with only one other Minnesotan, St. Paul Johnson graduate Alana Blahoski. Canada was the dominant team in previous World Championships and was favored to win the inaugural Olympic women's hockey gold medal. Down 4–1 against Canada in the final round-robin game, the American team battled back ferociously, with Jenny scoring the tying

JENNY SCHMIDGALL POTTER IS A FOUR-TIME OLYMPIAN
Photo courtesy of Cornelia Cannon Holden

goal of six unanswered tallies to defeat their rival 7–4. It gave the American squad confidence going into the final game—a repeat against their northern neighbor—for the gold medal. In a tight contest, the US team scored an empty-net goal with eight seconds left in the game to seal the title with a 3–1 win. "It was one of my most memorable hockey moments; you dream of winning gold and we won the gold medal, piling on [each other after the game], and defeating Canada," says Jenny of her Olympic experiences. Being so young at the time, she isn't sure that she fully comprehended the game's significance because her next three Olympic appearances would not have the same celebrated result.

Trained by Rob Potter after the 1998 Olympics, Jenny believes she got stronger, better, and faster; she eventually enrolled at the University of Minnesota–Twin Cities (U of M). Jenny was instrumental in the hockey team's success, scoring 33 goals in 32 games, but she decided to transfer to upstate foe, the University of Minnesota–Duluth (UMD). After transferring, Jenny erupted with 41 goals and 52 assists to lead the NCAA in scoring for the 1999–2000 season. The awards accumulated: the first of three Patty Kazmaier (outstanding women's collegiate hockey player) finalist nominations, first-team Western Collegiate Hockey Association (WCHA), and Most Valuable Player in the WCHA.

Jenny did not play for UMD during the 2000–01 and 2001–02 seasons because other events took priority—a daughter, Madison (Maddy), was born in 2001 to Jenny and Rob Potter, and in 2002 the Olympics were being held at Salt Lake City, Utah. Having been victorious in three consecutive World Championships, the American women's hockey team was favored to win the 2002 Olympics. Minnesotans Natalie Darwitz, of Eagan, and Krissy Wendell, of Brooklyn Park, joined Jenny on the powerful team riding a streak of thirty-one straight wins.

Sometimes referred to as "Mom" by teammates, Jenny worked diligently to get in shape after Maddy's birth and accounted for seven points (one goal, six assists) for the American team as it cruised through the preliminary round and semifinals. The gold medal game would be a rematch between the 1998 finalists, Canada and the United States. This time the US team lost the tense battle 3–2, claiming the silver medal. Jenny was sorely disappointed because she played ill and had a "helpless feeling" because she could not perform her best.

The UMD Bulldogs had won two NCAA championships during Jenny's absence. Her return and 88 points (an astounding 2.44 points per game) contributed to a third triumph. "The most memorable college game was at Duluth for the Frozen Four in 2003. It was a packed house. My husband and daughter, Maddy, were there," recalls Jenny. Yes, a record crowd of 5,167 people attending a women's college hockey game witnessed a 4–3 double overtime win for the home team over Harvard. The busy mother, student, and hockey player concluded her collegiate career in 2003–04 at the age of twenty-five with another stellar season, scoring 36 goals in 34 games; she also obtained a degree in business management. Five years later, Jenny would be named to the WCHA All-Decade team (2000–2009).

After years of coaching at various levels and as a long-time strength and conditioning coach, Rob accepted the position of head girls' hockey coach at Coon Rapids High School while Jenny also coached at the school and played professional hockey for the Minnesota Whitecaps of the fledgling Western Women's Hockey League (WWHL). In 2006 Rob was named Class AA Minnesota Girls Hockey Coach of the Year. Jenny admires her husband's all-around coaching ability, saying with conviction, "I never learned more about how to coach and train an athlete than I did from him." Her appreciation for Rob's support spills over to his parenting responsibilities during her absences from home to play on national and professional teams.

Only twenty-seven years old, Jenny, again with Darwitz and Wendell, easily clinched a spot on the 2006 US Olympic team, a clear contender for the gold medal. Ben Smith, head coach of the first three US Olympic women's hockey teams, has high praise for Jenny's skills and tenacity. "Jenny is probably the closest person to the Soviet

HILARY KNIGHT AND JENNY POTTER, TEAMMATES ON THE 2010 US OLYMPIC WOMEN'S HOCKEY TEAM
Photo courtesy of James Knight

Union men's dominant teams—an absolute hockey machine. She's a strong skater and strong stick handler who won practically every puck battle she was in." Playing in Turin (Torino), Italy, the United States team again breezed through the preliminary round but was tied by Sweden in the semifinal and lost in a shootout. The US team salvaged a bronze medal with a 4–0 shutout over Finland, but it was difficult to disguise their disappointment—they had come to the Alps of northern Italy to win the gold medal.

A son, Cullen, was born less than a year later, but Jenny quickly returned to the ice, playing on the gold medal–winning World Championship team in 2008. Still coaching at Coon Rapids and playing for the Minnesota Whitecaps, Jenny was named the WWHL's Most Valuable Player for the 2008–09 season. Playing as well or better than ever, Jenny was striving to make a fourth Olympic team, this one under the helm of Mark Johnson, and hoping to win a gold medal on an ice sheet in their archrival's domain, Vancouver, British Columbia, Canada. Jenny did make the team—now the oldest team member at thirty-one and the only mother on the squad—along with Darwitz and Gigi Marvin of Warroad, Minnesota. Sadly, personal tragedy struck the Schmidgall family as both Jenny's grandmother, Millicent, and mother, Terri, died less than three months before the 2010 Winter Olympic Games.

Canada and the United States each rolled to four consecutive victories, crushing the opposition with lopsided scores. Jenny recorded hat tricks (three goals in a game) in back-to-back games against China and Russia, the first to achieve the feat in Olympic ice hockey history. Jenny relates, "Hilary Knight [University of Wisconsin] and I were linemates who had an uncanny sense of connecting and playing well together." For a third time since the inception of women's hockey in the Olympics, a showdown for the gold medal would be between North American powerhouses, the United States and Canada. The climatic game was edgy and emotional from the time Jenny faced off with Canada's star player, Hayley Wickenheiser, whom Jenny respects despite the sometimes heated rivalry between the teams, until the horn sounded signaling the end of the game with Canada and a raucous home crowd celebrating a 2–0 victory. Maddy and Cullen Potter came on the ice to stand with their mother as she received her fourth Olympic medal, this one a silver.

Today Jenny and Rob Potter own and operate Potter's Pure Hockey (formed in 1998), training and high-performance camps for ice hockey players. Rob has been head coach of the Maple Grove girls' varsity hockey team since 2010, and Jenny— wanting to be the head coach of a college program—fulfilled that desire, albeit it at faraway Trinity College in Hartford, Connecticut. She returns to Minnesota often, but expresses appreciation to Rob and family members for making long-distance coaching workable. In April 2015, Ohio State University announced Jenny as their new head coach of the women's hockey team.

JENNY, MADDY, CULLEN, AND ROB POTTER
Photo courtesy of Jenny and Rob Potter

Jenny has coached Maddy's tackle football team, but like her mother, she has dropped the sport in favor of . . . swimming! A possible future Olympian, Maddy achieved the number-one national ranking in her age group in the 100-meter butterfly.

"The time my dad spent with me is where I really learned to love hockey—at the park, unstructured, and the freedom to figure it out on your own," Jenny says earnestly. Cullen, who loves being on the ice, may be found playing at Lewis Park.

**TRINA RADKE QUALIFYING IN THE 200-METER
BUTTERFLY FOR THE 1988 OLYMPICS**
Photo credit: Tim Morse

TRINA RADKE

Truth Seeker

IN THE DEMANDING SPORT OF SWIMMING, KATRINA "Trina" Radke found both success and stress. After three decades of experiencing the pair of intertwining emotions, she authored a book, *Be Your Best Without the Stress*, with the subtitle *It's Not About the Medal*. She collected her journals, memories, and thoughts to express ways to find what motivates a person to do their best while using a variety of tools and resources to simultaneously feel satisfied with their life. She describes herself as a "truth seeker." And it is obviously important to her as she enthusiastically continues to write, speak, advise (she is a certified family and marriage therapist), and instruct audiences about topics she views as essential to living.

Trina was born in 1970 and grew up in the west-central Minnesota city of Morris. The city, with a population of 5,000 people, is more known for agriculture and its respected branch of the University of Minnesota than for developing world-class swimmers. The land is what brought the Radke family to Morris—Trina's father was a soil scientist for the US Department of Agriculture. "Morris was a great town to grow up in. It was very safe, and I had the great fortune to have access to a beautiful eight-lane pool at the University," recalls Trina.

Participating in organized softball, gymnastics, and track and field, Trina also played the piano and followed her brothers, Greg and Earl, into swimming at age seven and soon joined the Morris Tiger Sharks Swim Club. It was the sport of swimming that she would soon devote hours to each day. "By nine years old, I was very focused on swimming. I was driven very early in life—although I was not pushed by my parents [Jerry and Barbara]." That determination was revealed in an essay that she wrote in third grade, which started with the provided phrase, "When I am 25 . . ." Trina did not shy away from her ambitions as she wrote, "When I am 25, I will be a swimmer. I am going to go to the Olympics and win lots of medals. After that I am going to be a swim coach for a couple years. Then after I am a swim coach I am going to get a boyfriend and then get married." While it might have easily been dismissed as a child's fantasy, most of the essay would eventually become a reality.

Jerry Radke was transferred to Adelaide, South Australia, for a one-year assignment when Trina was in fifth grade. The family accompanied him, and Trina joined a strong swim team that would later produce a 1984 Olympian. She was inspired by the performances of the top athletes on the swim team and longed to achieve their status.

The family returned to Morris the summer before Trina started sixth grade. Trina vividly remembers bursting out with a question to her mother and father about wanting to know where she could go swim so that she could go to the Olympics. The surprised parents made the commitment to make the lengthy three-hour commute to the Twin Cities on weekends so Trina could compete with a dedicated team. In 1983 she set a state record in the eleven-to-twelve girls' age group for the 50-yard freestyle event with a time of 23.71 seconds, a record still standing more than thirty years later.

In seventh grade she moved to the Twin Cities so she could devote more time with a dedicated swimming group, Team Foxjet based in Eden Prairie. She attended St. Paul Academy while living with the Bruce and Barbara Telander family (also involved in local swimming), who became a second family to Trina. It was during that year Jerry and Barbara separated and Jerry accepted a position in Allentown, Pennsylvania. The next school year Trina would again enroll in a new school, Germantown Academy in Fort Washington, Pennsylvania. The renowned Germantown Academy Aquatic Club was led by Dick Shoulberg, a nationally respected swim coach—in more than forty years of coaching, sixteen of his swimmers went on to compete in the Olympics—who later coached on US national, World Championship, and Olympic teams. It was here that Trina's intense training regimen was launched.

A demanding schedule of swimming up to five hours six days per week commenced. Trina began realizing her dream when she was named to the national team in 1985 at the tender age of fourteen. She credits Coach Shoulberg for being protective of her during the extensive traveling and also guiding her toward healthy decisions. The trip to the Pan-Pacific Games in Tokyo, Japan, also exposed her to teammates who had achieved international stardom. "I idolized Mary Meagher [a world record holder and three-time gold medalist]. She sat down on a bus next to me, and we had a normal conversation. She was a normal person too." This early success also raised expectations for young Trina Radke.

While feeling at peace in the water, the rigorous training, along with all the ancillary elements such as diet, nutrition, sleep-ing habits, and weight management, took a toll on Trina. Affectionately known by the nick-name "Rocky" for her extensive workouts, Trina and a teammate once completed a 16,000-meter butterfly marathon chal-lenge in three hours and fifty-six minutes! Trina continued to increase her speed in the butterfly and freestyle, her best event; at age seventeen, she qualified for the 1988 Olympic Trials in Austin, Texas. By now she had been swimming the 200-meter freestyle as a national team member several times. She was certainly marked as a contender to make the US Olympic team.

TRINA RADKE AT A RECEPTION WITH PRESIDENT REAGAN
Photo courtesy of Trina Radke

To her dismay, Trina did not make the finals in the 200-meter freestyle event, missing out by 0.27 of a second. Another opportunity for her to land a spot on the Olympic swim team would be the 200-me-ter butterfly. Trina won her heat and was ranked fourth of the qualifiers for the final. Despite a good start, she was in last place at the halfway point in the final. With 50 meters (one length) to go, she had only been able to move ahead to sixth place. With a furious finish, she propelled herself to the wall in second place and claimed the final place on the American Olympic team for the 200-meter butterfly event with a time of 2 minutes, 11.32 seconds (2:11.32). Trina Radke was eight years ahead of her self-im-posed prediction of being an Olympic swimmer.

The performance still awes longtime friend Jeff Prior (who would later become one of Trina's college teammates), causing him to remark on Trina's strengths as an athlete and as a person. "Trina has an undenying belief in herself and her abilities. Anything is possible. It was shown when she qualified in the two-hundred-meter butterfly, which was not her primary event. She could have crumbled with only one spot available since Mary T. Meagher was pretty much a lock for one, but she re-bounded to make the Olympic team. When you combine hard work, talent, and be-lief—that's a special package."

At Seoul, South Korea, the site of the 1988 Summer Olympic Games, Trina fin-ished second in her qualifying heat with a time of 2:12.93. In the finals she improved her time by more than one second, but Trina finished fifth with a time of 2:11.55. Trina's deeper understanding of racing and its benefits is reflected in her summary of time spent competing. "I treasure my days on the national team. I was always blessed with good coaches. The deep relationships I developed with many swimmers are very powerful." As with most Olympians, she found the opening and closing ceremonies the most memorable.

Heavily recruited by colleges with renowned swimming programs, Trina opted to enroll in 1988 at the University of California for its academics and the appeal of having a woman coach, Karen Moe Thornton. Trina had a successful collegiate career at the Berkeley school, in the classroom and in the pool. Trina was named to the Pac-10 All-Academic team in 1991 and achieved NCAA All-America status in 1990 and 1991. She then trained with Coach Shoulberg in preparation for the 1992 Olympic Trials. This time she fell short in her effort. She did not feel the natural energy. Nevertheless, Trina traveled to Russia after the trials—she's fluent in Russian—where she was part of a joint venture that helped establish the second radio station in Moscow.

With a year of eligibility remaining, Trina returned to Berkeley and to form, with another Pac-10 All-Academic award and a final NCAA All-American honor. Still perplexed by her state of exhaustion, Trina sought medical help. "The years 1991 to 1993 were a journey," she admits. Searching to explain her immune system issues and sense of fatigue, Trina consulted many doctors before it was determined that she had

Chronic Fatigue Immune Dysfunction Syndrome. It actually got to the point where Trina, a recent All-American and Olympic athlete, was issued a handicapped parking permit. "I was in denial, acceptance, and then began to appreciate my career."

Steeped in the corporate life for the next ten years, Trina was involved in pharmaceutical sales

TRINA RADKE SWIMMING FOR THE UNIVERSITY OF CALIFORNIA–BERKELEY
Photo courtesy of U Cal Sports Information, photo by Ethan Janson

TRINA RADKE AND HER HUSBAND, ROSS GERRY, NOW OWN AND OPERATE WECOACH4U
Photo credit: Venture Photography

and Internet companies related to health care. Some very positive and personally rewarding events occurred during this time, however. In 1996 Trina was proud to be asked to run the Olympic torch one mile. Interested in relationships, being a truth seeker, and wanting to help others as much as possible, it was during this time Trina received her master's degree in marriage and family therapy from Southern Connecticut State University. Part of her internship was through the Yale University School of Medicine.

Another highlight that occurred in the nineties was meeting Ross Gerry, a swimming coach at Stanford University who was later named a swimming coach for the 2000 US Olympic team. Ross and Trina married in 2004. That year, a rejuvenated Trina Radke Gerry, with a better understanding of what constituted a balanced lifestyle, qualified for the Olympic Trials in the 50-meter freestyle. Now thirty-three years old and more than a decade older than most of the competition, Trina finished a respectable nineteenth out of nearly fifty competitors.

Trina and Ross are now parents of two children, Shanti (Sanskrit for "peace") and Sanjay (Sanskrit for "victorious"), and live in Excelsior, Minnesota. "I wanted our children to have the same kind of safe, friendly environment like I had in my childhood, but with cultural and athletic resources more available," says Katrina. The husband-wife team owns and operates wecoach4u, programs designed to help people looking for positive changes in their lives. Oh, and swimming instruction is certainly available.

Photo courtesy of University of Minnesota Athletics

ALAN RICE

Minnesota Greco-Roman Wrestling Starts Here

THE NAME OF ALAN RICE IS SYNONYMOUS WITH GRE-co-Roman wrestling in Minnesota. Alan and his late wife, Gloria, devoted much of their married lives to growing the sport, forming the Minnesota Wrestling Club in 1966 and helping it become a nationally recognized powerhouse now known as the Minnesota Storm.

Alan, born in 1928, grew up in St. Paul and enrolled at the University High School on the campus of the University of Minnesota (U of M) in Minneapolis. University High School later combined with Marshall High School in 1967 to become Marshall-University High School (the school closed its doors in 1982). During Alan's enrollment at University High, tuition payment was required for those students attending the school, and he remembers it costing $15 per quarter and paying the fees by working at school. He graduated with approximately sixty classmates in 1946, but not before becoming a two-time Minnesota State High School wrestling champion at 135 pounds and then at the 138-pound weight class. The small school struggled to furnish a full wrestling team, yet one year they had two state champions and a runner-up.

Alan believes his father had some influence on his interest in wrestling because the two would "wrestle around" at home. His only sibling, a brother, did not pursue the sport, though.

Following high school, Alan entered the U of M. He majored in finance and eventually went into the investment profession. His passion for the sport of wrestling was fierce, however, and he was a two-time Big Ten Champion in 1949 and 1950 in the 128-pound weight class, and he placed fourth in the NCAA wrestling championships in 1949. At the time, only the top four individuals received All-American status. The most famous name of local wrestling, Verne Gagne, was a teammate.

ALAN RICE (LOWER ROW, FAR RIGHT) AND USA TEAMMATES
Photo credit: Alan Rice

Upon graduating in 1950, Alan went to New York, where he completed military service and began his career in the investment industry. He worked for eight years with Bear Stearns before the firm's rapid growth.

Alan was determined to continue his training as a wrestler, and he joined the famed New York Athletic Club. The many athletic highlights he achieved include: a silver medal in the 1955 Pan Am games in freestyle wrestling; winning the national Amateur Athletic Union (AAU) freestyle and Greco-Roman wrestling titles in 1956; and competing in the 1956 US Olympic wrestling trials in California.

Only Dan Hodge, the legendary wrestler from Oklahoma, whom the collegiate wrestling trophy (akin to football's Heisman Trophy) is named for, can claim a similar achievement—also in 1956. Hodge was undefeated in his collegiate career and pinned an incredible 78 percent of his opponents. Wrestling fans marveled at his strength, and he was famous for being able to squeeze pliers and snap them with his amazing grip. At over eighty years of age, he still crushes apples with one hand for awestruck crowds.

In a telephone interview, Hodge states this about Alan: "Alan Rice was a competitor. He trained very, very hard. He was a tremendous athlete and also a great person." Alan returns the compliment, saying this about Hodge's incredible strength: "He wasn't as strong as an ox—he was stronger."

To Alan's great personal disappointment, he placed second at the 1956 US Olympic freestyle wrestling trials in the 62-kilogram featherweight division (136 pounds) to Myron Roderick, a three-time NCAA champion from Oklahoma State, based on a point system despite defeating Roderick in the round-robin competition. However, Alan did recover to win the Greco-Roman trials—requiring wrestling another exhausting seven matches. The loss to Roderick (later Oklahoma State's wrestling and tennis coach at the tender age of twenty-three) may have been a gain for American Greco-Roman wrestling. Alan discovered that he loved the new style, which does not allow holds below the waist. The strength and technique required for Greco-Roman wrestling fascinated him, and he studied and practiced the sport for the next six months.

The 1956 team was the first contingent to represent the country in Greco-Roman wrestling. While Alan did not medal in the 1956 Olympics, he considers it a wonderful experience, and it did not diminish his enthusiasm for wrestling. In fact, he came to have a greater love and appreciation of the Greco-Roman style.

In 1960 he ended his investment tenure in New York City and returned to St. Paul for personal and family reasons. One reason for returning to Minnesota was to continue the family investment business that his father had started. Soon Alan began to serve as a mentor to wrestlers seeking advice for improved conditioning and training techniques.

The formal establishment of the Minnesota Amateur Wrestling Club occurred in 1966. Mike Houck, the first American Greco-Roman World Champion, considers Alan "a pioneer catalyst" at the forefront of the sport. The members initially practiced at the University of Minnesota–Twin Cities campus but eventually moved to nearby Augsburg College. With Alan's tutoring, the program not only became strong, it became dominant. The team claimed the Greco-Roman national championship sixteen out of twenty years. One year the team split into "A" and "B" teams and came out of the competition with the top two team spots! The club's achievement Alan takes the greatest pride in is that at least one team member has been on every US Olympic wrestling team since 1968. The 2012 team member was Chas Betts from St. Michael, Minnesota.

Alan's wife, Gloria, had been instrumental in his success. Their marriage was deemed a true partnership in every sense of the word. Born Gloria Marra, she was a very active community and church volunteer in addition to being a great support to Alan in his attempt to develop amateur wrestling. She was a very intelligent woman, graduating as the 1945 valedictorian of Washburn High School (more than three hundred graduating students) and then obtaining a degree from the U of M in 1950. She and Alan married in 1957.

Gloria is credited for mastering the intricacies of the complex pairing system used in international wrestling matches. Don Behm, a silver medalist in both the 1968 Olympics and 1969 World Championships, recalls that it was Gloria who spotted the probable pairings that would have required Behm to wrestle three matches in one day. When the situation was brought to the attention of the stunned officials, he was offered the choice to wrestle one more match that same day and two matches the following day. He accepted the opportunity and proceeded to defeat the Russian

ALAN RICE (COACH) IN HUMOROUS POSE AS HE LECTURES 401-POUND GRECO-ROMAN HEAVYWEIGHT CHRIS TAYLOR BEFORE 1972 OLYMPICS
Photo courtesy of Alan Rice

competitor that evening and upset an Olympic medalist from Iran the next day. By then the fatigued Behm was gassed and defeated by a wrestler from Japan.

Behm appreciates Gloria and Alan Rice advocating on his behalf. He exclaimed, "The two were inseparable. They worked great as a team." He also extols the skillful coaching of Alan Rice: "He had an answer if you had a question. Alan Rice is right up there among the best wrestling coaches the United States has ever had."

Returning to the business side of Alan's life, his investment firm later merged with a New York company. His specialty became options writing, and in 1970 Wheelock Whitney hired him to work at Dain Bosworth, a leading Twin Cities brokerage and investments firm. Alan recalls asking for time away from his new position to perform his next venture in the wrestling arena: coaching the 1972 US Olympic Greco-Roman team. Whitney, a well-known supporter of sports, quickly agreed to the request.

The US Greco-Roman team was participating in only its fifth Olympiad in 1972. While the freestyle team experienced great success capturing six medals, the Greco-Roman team had no medal winners. Sadly, a lasting image of the 1972 Olympics is the terrorist attack that killed many Israeli athletes from the wrestling team. Alan says that the wrestling teams did not really know what had happened at first, but they were informed that the competition was being halted. It did resume after a twenty-four-hour delay, but the team struggled to recover from the tragic and tense situation despite a news blackout in areas of the Olympic Village.

One member of the 1972 US Olympic freestyle wrestling team became a favorite of Alan's to watch. Dan Gable, the renowned wrestling warrior from Iowa, was considered a fanatical wrestler by wrestlers dubbed fanatics. "He was always training," marvels Rice. "Every movement he made was some form of conditioning or training."

Other wrestlers Alan most enjoyed witnessing compete were Shozo Sasahara, a Japanese wrestler who became the 1956 freestyle gold medal winner; Bill Koll, the

1948 Olympian from Iowa State Teachers College (now called University of Northern Iowa); and Alexander Karelin, the famed Russian three-time Greco-Roman gold medalist wrestler who was undefeated for thirteen years in international matches. Karelin in particular brings awe to Rice's voice: "The powerful heavyweight was always perfectly in control—even as he walked." Locally, he admires Brandon Paulson, who he says has "guts and dedication that are unequaled."

Throughout the next three decades, Rice continued to support amateur wrestling financially and as an advisor. In 2001, following the death of his beloved wife, Alan donated substantial sums of money to charity, particularly to the U of M wrestling program and Augsburg College. Augsburg, a Division III college, used the generous donation to build a state-of-the-art wrestling facility. The spacious Alan and Gloria Rice Wrestling Center permits three full-sized wrestling mats and two half-sized mats in one room.

Alan Rice is a member of several athletic Halls of Fame, including the National Wrestling Hall of Fame in Stillwater, Oklahoma (inducted in 2001); the M Club at the U of M (inducted in 1999); and the National Wrestling Hall of Fame Dan Gable Mu-

DAN GABLE PRESENTS ALAN RICE WITH THE 2011 LEADERSHIP AWARD FOR OUTSTANDING CONTRIBUTIONS TO GRECO-ROMAN WRESTLING
Photo credit: Larry Slater

seum, where Alan and Gloria are also the namesakes of the Greco-Roman Hall of Champions.

While Alan and Gloria Rice were certainly influential in spearheading the establishment, growth, and development of amateur wrestling in Minnesota, Alan has hopeful visions of creating much more. He would like to see the funding of scholarships for Greco-Roman wrestlers, who could receive a good education while performing in a sport that now has dedicated athletes with a passion for a wrestling style that was once secondary to him—a change of heart that led to winning many hearts.

KAYLIN RICHARDSON COMPETING IN THE 2007 FIS
WORLD CUP FINAL AT PAPAR-LENZERHEIDE, SWITZERLAND
Photo credit: ©Allesandro Della Valle/Corbis Images

KAYLIN RICHARDSON

Snow and Laughter Combined

ACTION PACKED, FAST, AND FULL OF LAUGHTER, A conversation with two-time Olympic alpine skier Kaylin Richardson resembles her skiing preferences on the slopes, emphasizing fun.

Born in 1984 as the youngest child of Steve and Linda Richardson, Kaylin started skiing at age four, and soon after starting elementary school, she joined a community program based in her hometown of Edina, Minnesota. She followed older brothers Chris and Tom into the Twin Cities Skijammers Ski and Snowboard School, where her father served as an instructor. A bus would take the members to ski nearby Minnesota ski hills: Welch Village (Welch), Buck Hill (Burnsville), and Afton Alps (near Hastings), along with Trollhaugen in Dresser, Wisconsin. Kaylin continued to follow her brothers into ski racing (both later captained the Edina High School alpine team and skied at the collegiate level—Chris at Albertson College in Idaho and Tom at Colby College in Maine), joining Team Gilboa at age nine and competing at Hyland Hills in Bloomington, a twelve-minute drive from their suburban home west of Minneapolis. "We are really community based—especially in the Midwest. It's such a family endeavor because we don't have ski academies," Kaylin says, explaining her roots and how involved her family was in skiing. Those conventional beginnings would eventually lead Kaylin to the most famous ski runs of the world and competing against the world's greatest ski racers.

The "gregarious" Richardson family also participated in sailing and soccer, and—due to Steve and Linda wanting the children to develop a love of the arts—attended theater productions at the Chanhassen Dinner Theater and Children's Theater. In fact, Kaylin even attended a Children's Theater camp during her active youth.

Often skiing under lights due to Minnesota's brief winter daylight hours—something Kaylin believes benefited her later in competition—she would practice about two hours per day and enjoyed the competitive side of skiing. Tall (5 feet 10), strong, and athletic at age fifteen, Kaylin began to compete throughout the Mid-

THE RICHARDSON FAMILY AT KEYSTONE MOUNTAIN RESORT IN COLORADO, IN 1993: (FRONT) LINDA, STEVE, AND KAYLIN; (BACK) TOM AND CHRIS RICHARDSON

Photo courtesy of the Richardson family

west and won some Midwest American (Mid Am) races in the Federation of International Skiing (FIS) series. That success earned Kaylin the only invitation extended to a skier from the Midwest to a Newcomers Trip for promising young skiers. In 2000 she was named to the United States Development Team.

Aldo Radamus, a former US Ski Team and Development Team coach originally from Golden Valley, Minnesota, who is now executive director of Ski & Snowboard Club Vail in Colorado, remembers Kaylin's time on the development team well. "Kaylin, as you would expect, was an extraordinary athlete. What set her apart from other great athletes and eventually made her an Olympian was her attitude. There was never a day when she did not view the world positively. I have never met a person, never mind an athlete, who was more optimistic and prepared to do her best in meeting any challenge she faced. A tough and gritty competitor, she was always a great supporter of her teammates, positive role model to younger athletes, and a compassionate, caring human being."

" I have never met a person, never mind an athlete, who was more optimistic and prepared to do her best in meeting any challenge she faced. A tough and gritty competitor, she was always a great supporter of her teammates, positive role model to younger athletes, and a compassionate, caring human being."

While Kaylin took great pride in earning a spot on the US Development Team, it would require a big change in her routine since she would be traveling with the ski team from October through March. Working with Edina High School administrators and teachers, Kaylin is very grateful that she was allowed to continue as a student at the school despite being absent more than one hundred days during each of her sophomore, junior, and senior years. Kaylin communicated with teachers via email, took a bevy of tests when she returned home for the holidays, and

Photo courtesy of the Richardson family

tried to be a positive and hardworking student when she was present at school during the months she wasn't training or competing away from Edina. "She was diligent on completing her work independently, and then I would clarify any questions for her, but it was rare that she was confused. A very independent learner with great motivation and drive would be my description of Kaylin," confirms Aimee Noeske, a former math teacher at Edina High School.

Kaylin desperately wanted to come home, though, for homecoming her senior year. She had been surprised to be nominated for the homecoming court. Kaylin's European coaches, not understanding the culture and importance of a high school homecoming, were perplexed by her request to go home for the event. Meanwhile, Kaylin's parents were astounded to be able to find a round-trip flight using an affordable number of frequent-flyer miles to fulfill Kaylin's wish. The puzzled coaches did approve the request, and the flight was booked. "I was home for four or five days, then flew back to Austria. I had so much fun! I was in the parade and the dance . . . it was important for me to have that experience." On her return, Kaylin lost her voice. The coaches insisted that she miss one day of training, but Kaylin, fuming, was just as insistent that she train. Finally, forced by the coaches' decision to miss training, Kaylin slept and rested all day, and her voice and strength returned following the whirlwind visit home. She apologized to her coaches and—happy with her adventure home—

Kaylin proceeded to ski her best times of the season. "My biggest breakthrough year was my senior year of high school. I won one Europa Cup, and I had been doing well on the Europa Cup Circuit—what we call 'the trenches'—and I did my first World Cup race at eighteen," reports Kaylin.

Making the leap to the US "B" Ski Team, Kaylin realized that making the 2006 Olympic ski team was possible and made it a goal. She graduated from Edina High School in 2003 and decided to defer enrolling at Dartmouth College to pursue her passion: skiing the technical (slalom and giant slalom) and speed (downhill and super-giant slalom) disciplines of the sport. Kaylin would defer her entrance for three years as she literally raced around the globe. Winning the North American (Nor Am) slalom titles for three consecutive years (2003, 2004, cochampion in 2005) automatically qualified Kaylin for a spot on the team going to the World Cup. The travel, teammates, ski runs, and dinners are some of Kaylin's fondest memories of her time competing abroad. "I ate so much dessert when I was on the World Cup," she confesses.

"I ate so much dessert when I was on the World Cup."

Slalom racing has more gates—up to sixty—on the women's course spaced closer together than the giant slalom or super-G (super giant slalom) races, requiring quicker and sharper turns of the skiers as they pass between two poles forming the gate. Not claiming a favorite ski race discipline, Kaylin says, "I'm a jack-of-all-trades, master of none." So it comes as little surprise that the twenty-one-year-old accumulated enough points in World Cup events to be named to the group that would be skiing the combined—an event that combines slalom and downhill racing—for the 2006 Olympics in Torino (Turin), a city in the most northwestern area of Italy's Alps. Also named to the alpine Olympic team was a pair of Minnesotans: Kristina Koznick and Lindsey Kildow (later Vonn), both having received their first exposure to skiing at Buck Hill. Kaylin thoughtfully says about making the Olympic team, "There is serendipity and luck and hard work. People always say luck is where preparation meets opportunity—and I believe that. The cool thing about the Olympics is it's the pinnacle of athletics. It is never replicated, never imitated. The electricity is almost tangible."

Placement in the combined event of alpine skiing in 2006 was determined by calculating the collective time of two slalom runs and one downhill race. Kaylin's two slalom runs added up to 1 minute 25 seconds (1:25), a tie for fifteenth place,

LEFT TO RIGHT) STEVE, LINDA, KAYLIN, CHRIS AND TOM RICHARDSON AT THE US ALPINE NATIONAL CHAMPIONSHIPS IN MARCH, 2005, AT MAMMOTH MOUNTAIN SKI RESORT IN CALIFORNIA
Photo courtesy of the Richardson family

plus 1:31.83 for the downhill race (eighteenth overall), combined for a total of 2:56.83 and seventeenth place in the final standings. Throughout the training and competition, Kaylin enjoyed her teammates, vital but often overlooked ski technicians, and laughing during time skiing on snow. Some coaches struggled with the way Kaylin operated, but her success seems allied with her attitude. "For me, I needed to have fun," she affirms.

A string of national championships ensued, starting with combined and downhill titles in 2007 and another downhill crown in 2009. Kaylin found the speed exhilarating and has been clocked at 83 miles per hour, although she has raced faster in nontimed runs. Core and weight training were part of her summer regimen when Kaylin did four to five hours of conditioning per day. During the race season—and carrying up to twenty-two pairs of skis for competitions—ten to twelve runs plus course inspection and meetings with coaches and technicians was considered a big day.

"What's better than being an Olympian?" Being a two-time Olympian!

Kaylin repeats an oft-asked question: "What's better than being an Olympian?" Being a two-time Olympian! That's exactly what happened as Kaylin again qualified in the combined for the 2010 Olympics in Vancouver, British Columbia. The competition was at the massive Whistler Ski Resort complex about seventy-five miles north of Vancouver. Training runs were limited and shortened due to bad weather, and a change from two slalom runs to one in determining total time was initiated. The maritime effect also caused challenging, bumpy conditions on the course for the

Olympians. Believing that she performed better than she had four years earlier, Kaylin had a time of 1:27.64 in the downhill portion and 45.76 seconds on the slalom run for a combined time of 2:13.40 in repeating her seventeenth-place finish. American teammate Julia Mancuso secured a silver medal with a time of 2:10.08 while fellow Minnesotan Lindsey Vonn surged to the lead after the downhill run, but hooked a gate on the slalom run and did not finish.

When Kaylin decided to retire from World Cup competition in 2010 at the age of twenty-five, she was remarkably injury-free and excited to pursue other opportunities in the sport. Having only undergone thumb surgery as a result of skiing (she had ankle surgery from a soccer injury), she wanted to share her passion for skiing and landed a position as ambassador of skiing at Canyons Resort in Park City, Utah, for four years. Despite leaving that position, her schedule is still action packed, with photo shoots, mountain skiing, attending Westminster College periodically, serving as a skiing correspondent for the Weather Channel during the 2014 Winter Olympics at Sochi, Russia, and encouraging people to look into the topic of climate change.

Among Kaylin's favorite skiers are Kristina Koznick ("I looked up to her coming from Minnesota") and Daron Rahalves ("He skied so dynamically"). She greatly respects technician Aaron Haffey, alpine racer and gold medalist Picabo Street, Coach Trevor Wagner, her teammates, youth coaches, and her lively family.

" Kaylin is one of the happiest people I know. She is very hard working, talented, and extremely intelligent to boot! Win or lose, she is a person who will always find the positive in a situation and get the most out of it. It is because of this quality that I think she will be successful in her life no matter where the road goes."

Koznick (now married; she has the surname Landa), a three-time Olympian with six World Cup victories in slalom racing who retained Minnesota as her home base throughout her racing career, has high praise for her fellow Minnesotan: "Kaylin is one of the happiest people I know. She is very hard working, talented, and extremely intelligent to boot! Win or lose, she is a person who will always find the positive in a situation and get the most out of it. It is because of this quality that I think she will be successful in her life no matter where the road goes."

Alyeska, Alaska, where Kaylin won three titles, and Cortina d'Ampezzo, Italy, with its colorful dolomites, are memorable skiing destinations for Kaylin. While focusing on racing, Kaylin still made an intentional effort to also appreciate her surroundings. "I really tried to remind myself to look up for a second and take it all in."

Kaylin has been filmed and featured in segments of four Warren Miller films. The unique settings have included: the Canyons Resort in Park City, Utah; different locations in Norway; north of the Arctic Circle in the Lofoten Islands; and a future one that will feature camping and back-country ski touring outside of Cordova, Alaska. Now that Kaylin makes her livelihood in the sport of skiing, she hopes to share her passion and joy. "I really gauge how fun skiing is by how many people are smiling," she summarizes. Snow and laughter combined are her ideal setting and attitude.

Photo courtesy of Phil Rogosheske

PHIL ROGOSHESKE

Man of Many Pursuits

NAME A SPORT IN MINNESOTA, AND PHIL ROGOSHeske has probably pursued it—often to the elite level. A native of St. Cloud, Minnesota, Phil was born in 1944 and participated in organized youth baseball (he was on the same team as eventual MLB pitcher Tom Burgmeier), football, and basketball programs as a child. He was already developing an eye for technique when a man at a Sauk Rapids church taught him how to high jump straddle style, landing in a sand pit or bed of sawdust. Being a student of sports helped him immensely throughout his lengthy—and ongoing—career as an athlete and coach.

The 1962 St. Cloud Tech graduate completed his high school career as a 5-foot-10 multisport athlete: he was quarterback and punter on the football team that was undefeated his senior year; he was a guard in basketball; he played centerfield in baseball; and he high jumped for the track team (achieving a personal best of 6 feet 2½ inches), tying for second in state as a junior and placing fifth as a senior—with identical 5-feet-11-inch jumps.

Influenced by his basketball coach, Bob Erdman, Phil enrolled at Gustavus Adolphus College in St. Peter, Minnesota. Phil seemed to continue his avocation of sports at a frenetic pace, adding swimming to his list. He participated in football only a single year, but he was a three-year starter at guard in basketball, earning All-Conference honors his senior year. What drew the attention of players and fans was his ability to dunk two handed despite being less than 6 feet tall. He was named captain for both the basketball and track teams during his junior and senior years. In track he was a three-time conference champion in

PHIL ROGOSHESKE CLEARS 6 FEET 8 INCHES IN THE HIGH JUMP AT THE CONFERENCE MEET
Photo courtesy of Gustavus Adolphus College

high jump and set the Minnesota Inter-collegiate Athletic Conference (MIAC) record in that event in 1966 with a jump of 6 feet 8½ inches, only recently tied for the best in Gustavus track history. To top it off, Phil swam as a member of a relay team at a conference competition! He is also very proud to be the recipient of two Sponberg Awards, an honor for a Gustavus athlete who demonstrates scholarship, leadership, and character. In recognition of these successes as a student and what he pursued later, he was inducted into the college's Athletic Hall of Fame in 1993.

PHIL ROGOSHESKE AT THE OPENING DAY CEREMONIES IN MUNICH, GERMANY, IN 1972
Photo credit: Steve Prefontaine

Eager to extend his love of sports, Phil chose education as a profession since it allowed him to participate and coach. He admits he joined the military "for the expressed purpose of making the Olympics. I was stationed in Virginia and watched rowing. There was outrigging that needed greasing and the boats and oars were heavy. Then I saw a guy carrying a craft by himself with a light double-bladed paddle, and I said, 'That's for me!'" laughs Phil. He had just seen a kayak, a boat that he would be paddling only two years later in the 1972 Summer Olympics in Munich, Germany.

Phil received training as a combat engineer and began teaching full-time at a prep school while training in his newfound sport. He was invited to the Potomac Boat Club, where he was mentored by Rod Debozy and met two nationally ranked kayakers, Jerry Welbourn and John van Dyke—men Phil would later join as teammates. Adjusting to the narrow (17 inches wide), 17-feet-long kayak was not easy. Phil used a Tracer boat to practice balance and quickly learned to draft in the wake of competitors' boats along the polluted Potomac. Only one year later, he and Welbourn won nationals in kayak pairs (K2) and won a trip to Europe. "It really opened my eyes to the skill and technique of others. We picked the brains of a pair of Swedes—the world's best," Phil remembers of the international competition. "We were underfunded too. The other teams had coaches—we had none."

Welbourn, a Big 10 pole vault champion from Ohio State who made the US Olympic kayak team at age forty, remembers Phil's quick development. "He was very athletic and very eager. Phil worked hard and became a good paddler. But when he first stepped into the very light, very skinny Olympic racing boat, he turned it over a few times," Welbourn chuckles softly.

A few months before the Olympics, Phil and Val Chelgren married. Val played a historical role in distance running: she was one of only eight women (in a field of more than eleven thousand) to run in the inaugural Boston Marathon open to women as officially registered competitors in 1972. She ran a creditable 4 hours 29 minutes (4:29), quite an accomplishment considering that her longest training run had been thirteen miles and she did not walk or stop throughout the entire marathon.

VAL AND PHIL ROGOSHESKE, 2012

The next fall Val won the City of Lakes Marathon in Minneapolis with a dramatically improved time of 3:21:57. In 1974 she was back in Boston and ran a 3:09:28 marathon and was ranked in the top sixty of the world in the burgeoning event, in which women had once been declared physically unfit. At the fortieth anniversary of the inviting of women to the Boston Marathon, Val and other pioneering women runners were honored for their contributions.

Progressing at a torrid rate, Phil would try out for the 1972 Olympic kayak team. "Kayaking requires a power element, an endurance factor, and overcoming inertia from a standstill. I was determined to study the techniques required in addition to the demanding physical training," reports the student-turned-teacher. "I probably weighed one hundred-seventy pounds and was burning five thousand calories a day." It all helped. He paired with Steve Kelly from New York for the K2 event at Rock Cut State Park near Rockford, Illinois, and won. The victors then decided to give up the Olympic spot to join Welbourn and van Dyke in the four-man kayak (K4) team. Watching a K4 team in action is like seeing a whirling windmill as they paddle at a furious 120 strokes per minute. Staying in unison in the 36-feet-long, 75-pound kayak is key.

The Olympic regatta course was in Oberschleissheim, about twelve miles from

Munich. It was familiar to Phil since he had paddled there in the 1971 international competition. In the first heat, the foursome was overmatched and finished the 1,000-meter race in 3:32.94. In the repêchage, a second-chance qualifying heat, the K4 team was more impressive with a finishing time that was a full ten seconds faster, but they did not finish high enough to make the semifinals. Their bid in the Olympics had ended. A week before his competition, Phil fondly remembers being on the track with Steve Prefontaine, the elite distance runner from Oregon; Phil has a picture Prefontaine took of him at the opening ceremonies. Tragically, it was an Olympics that was memorable in more than one way.

"The security in Munich by design was relaxed. They were trying to shed the image of tight control that people remembered under Hitler. Val was easily able to enter the Olympic Village. On the fateful day, I remember seeing a masked man in a window after returning from training," says Phil, remembering the terrorist attack by the Palestinian group Black September that killed Israeli athletes.

> *" The security in Munich by design was relaxed. They were trying to shed the image of tight control that people remembered under Hitler. Val was easily able to enter the Olympic Village. On the fateful day, I remember seeing a masked man in a window after returning from training, "*

Phil, ever the sports enthusiast, threw himself into teaching and coaching at St. Cloud Tech. Another new lifetime sport emerged, cross country skiing. Again Phil has had remarkable success and participated in more than thirty American Birkebeiner races (the famed nordic ski race from Cable to Hayward, Wisconsin), often winning his age group. He was a member of the national kayak team and remained on it for six years. Phil practiced on the Mississippi River and attended training camps in Florida and New York. He was thinking about a return trip to the 1976 Olympics, to be hosted on North American soil: Montreal, Canada.

The Olympic experience, combined with more knowledge about kayak training and technique, helped Phil. He kept improving and had his best international finish in the K2 with Bruce Barton when they placed in the finals of the World Championships in 1974.

Shortly before the 1976 Olympic Trials, Phil pulled a rib cage muscle when sprinting with Steve Kelly. Three weeks before the trials it had not fully healed, which severely limited his training. He made the K1 finals but lost by one second. Phil admits to being sad that he did not qualify, but he also recognizes that he did participate in one Olympics, which softened the blow.

Kelly, a former New York City firefighter who again made the K4 team for the 1976 Olympics, respects his friend and teammate, particularly for his spirited effort after his injury. "Phil's endurance was excellent. He was always one to do negative splits [each segment was faster than the previous one] and pass people toward the end. His positive attitude and good sense of humor showed as a fellow competitor."

Phil and Val, who earned a doctorate in exercise physiology, are the parents of two athletic daughters, Allie and Abby. Allie became a Division I soccer player and captain at the University of Wisconsin; she now coaches and teaches at the high school level in Dallas, Texas. Abby attended Northwestern University and is employed by an agriculture and policy organization in Minneapolis after working in Africa and Asia. Both daughters were ranked in the top ten of Minnesota high school cross country skiers when Phil was coaching the team.

Val, who loves her husband's "playful attitude toward sports" watched Phil try an array of sports during the thirty-three years he taught English (three years), health, and physical education classes at St. Cloud Tech and Apollo high schools and as a retiree. Advocating health and competition, he has coordinated and promoted various races throughout his adult life. Phil has been nationally ranked in the top five of five different sports at the master's division: nordic skiing, kayaking, swimming, race walking (starting at age sixty), and mountain biking time trials. Phil and Val have also hiked the full length of the mountainous 2,186-mile Appalachian Trail.

And don't think that he is about to stop his pursuit of more sport—not for a second.

Photo courtesy of Susan Sandvig Shobe

GENE SANDVIG

Speedskating a Family Affair

LIKE REAL ESTATE, SOMETIMES A FUTURE OLYMPI-an's success is determined by location, location, location. Gene Sandvig, a lifelong Minneapolis resident, was born in 1931 and lived near Sibley Field in south Minneapolis. A series of baseball and softball fields were flooded during the winter months to create a large ice skating rink, offering Depression-era children inexpensive recreation. As a preschooler, Gene towed behind older brother Gerald to skate at the rink. Less than two decades later, Eugene Myron Sandvig was an Olympian.

"When I was three years old, I pulled my brother's skates over my shoes," chuckles Gene as he lists the progression of skating equipment he tried. "Then I had a pair of Bob Skates, four blades buckled to my shoes. Next I had a tube skate, a soft shoe designed like a hockey skate. My first exposure to a pair of speedskates was from my aunt—I was between the ages of five to ten."

A Minneapolis newspaper sponsored a novice program in an effort to improve and promote the sport of speedskating in the city. In 1941, Gene, Gerald, and a friend attended the age-group tryout at Powderhorn Park. They approached a coach named Ted Brandt and asked if they could receive coaching. Brandt paired ten-year-old Gene against a twelve-year-old girl who was considered to be fast. Gene won the race and was invited onto the team. By the end of the season, Gene had increased his speed and endurance to the point where he defeated the national champion in his midget age group. The next season he was undefeated.

Gene's mother viewed speedskating as a healthy outlet for Gene, Gerald, and their sister, Connie. Their father, who was working more than seventy hours a week as a machinist for a defense contractor as the United States geared up for its role in World War II, also welcomed speedskating as a supervised activity for the children.

Though small and light at 5 feet 10 and 150 pounds, Gene also played football for Minneapolis Roosevelt High School. The running back did not see much

GENE SANDVIG RACING ON A LOCAL LAKE IN 1950
Photo courtesy of Susan Sandvig Shobe

action due to his size, but he performed well when given the opportunity. However, he experienced greater success in the pack-style racing (not racing against the clock) at the juvenile (ages twelve and thirteen), junior (ages fourteen and fifteen), and intermediate (ages sixteen and seventeen) levels of speedskating on the oval at Powderhorn Park. He raced as a member of the Bearcat Speedskating Club, an organization sponsored by a local American Legion post. It was only in 1947, when the Olympic team was selected—a year early due to a lack of speedskating facilities at the time—that Gene became aware that it was an Olympic sport! Not surprisingly to local fans, half of the eight-member 1948 Olympic speedskating team was composed of Minnesotans: Bobby Fitzgerald, Ken Bartholomew, Art Seaman, and John Werket, also a Roosevelt alumnus.

With such a large number of national-caliber speedskaters from Minnesota, the competitive races drew tens of thousands of spectators to the tight one-sixth-mile (293 yards) Powderhorn Park outdoor oval. "We had more fans in attendance than the University of Minnesota basketball team did for games. A sportswriter for a Minneapolis paper covered us!" exclaims Gene. "In 1948 I beat Fitzgerald and Bartholomew, Olympic medalists."

Gene graduated from Roosevelt in January 1949, the last year of midterm graduations in Minneapolis. He worked on a wheat ranch in Montana and was an enrolled student at the University of Minnesota for one quarter and then quit, awaiting the military draft since participation in the Korean War was expected. A delay occurred, and Gene tried out for the Olympic team—again being selected a year early—in 1951. The regionals had been held in Wisconsin, and the finals were at Powderhorn Park. Gene made the eight-man team in all events: 500-meter sprint, 1,500 meters, 5,000 meters, and 10,000 meters. The trials simulated the Olympic Games, racing on long tracks against the clock rather than pack style. One year later, Gene thought, he would be competing in the 1952 Olympics in Oslo, Norway.

Photo courtesy of Susan Sandvig Shobe

And then Gene got his military draft notice in April of 1951. Three-fourths of the two hundred men in the artillery company he trained with at a base in Oklahoma were sent to Korea. Gene was fortunate and assigned to go to Germany. Wanting to stay in shape, Gene, now bulked up to more than 170 pounds, agreed to play on the camp's football team and played well as a running back against experienced collegiate players. When substituting in a defensive role due to injuries, Gene was clipped and broke his leg. He would be in a cast for more than four months. Being a spectator—much less participating in the Olympics—looked bleak. A helpful warrant officer did arrange for the heartbroken athlete to be in Oslo, Norway, for the training and watch the events he had yearned to participate in.

Gene was discharged from the army in 1953 and encouraged by neighborhood friends to attend Gustavus Adolphus College in St. Peter, Minnesota. He played football while majoring in math and physical education, receiving all-conference honors in 1956 for his durable and effective play as a running back. A more cautious Gene Sandvig did not play football in 1955, however. He had again qualified for the 1956 Olympics the previous year, and he did not want to miss this chance.

Cortina d'Ampezzo, Italy, a town in the southern Alps, was originally scheduled to be the site of the 1944 Winter Olympics, which were canceled due to World War II. Now the town was hosting the sports spectacular twelve years later. The unique outdoor track on Lago di Misurina was similar to an ice floe. "They cut a lane through the ice to prevent ice cracking on the track. So there was actually open water around the racers," Gene reports. The Soviet Union, which had bypassed the 1948 Winter Olympics, dominated speedskating in 1956. Gene placed thirtieth of fifty-four racers in the 1,500-meter race, one second behind Werket and thirty-first of forty-six Olympians in the 5,000-meter competition, second on the American team. "I may have missed my best opportunity in 1952," adds Gene. "The Soviets planned in five-year stages and planned to peak in 1956—and they did."

1956 US OLYMPIC SPEEDSKATING TEAM SELECTED IN WEEK-LONG TRIALS AT COMO PARK. LEFT TO RIGHT ARE (KNEELING) JOHN WERKET (MINNEAPOLIS), GENE SANDVIG (MINNEAPOLIS), BILL CAROW AND (STANDING) COACH DEL LAMB, ART LONGSJO, MATTHEW "PAT" MCNAMARA (MINNEAPOLIS), KEN HENRY, DON MCDERMOTT, CHUCK BURKE AND MANAGER HERB SCHWARZ

Staff Photo, Minneapolis Tribune, Feb 3, 1955. Republished with permission

Graduating from Gustavus in 1957, Gene became a teacher at Phillips Junior High, Henry High School, and Washburn High School in the Minneapolis Public School system for twelve years. He was an assistant coach in football, tennis, and track. He continued to race competitively, defeating fourteen-time national champion Bartholomew for the all-around national speedskating championship in 1958 and then claimed the North American Championship in 1959. That year he again made the Olympic speedskating squad, and the team trained together at a high-elevation site in Truckee, California, not far from Squaw Valley, the location for the 1960 Winter Olympics. Speedskating would experience a pair of firsts: women would compete, and it would be the first time the races would be held on an artificial ice surface. Gene was not chosen to participate in any of the races, but he did work as an usher and was a spectator. "I escorted Vice President Richard Nixon to his seat," he recalls.

Changing professional careers, Gene was recruited by a former coach to join Advance Machine Company, where he worked his way through the ranks of the company and was eventually named national service manager. He is grateful that the company "allowed me the flexibility to be involved in speedskating programs" as an international referee in the 1980 and 1984 Olympic Games, on the administrative side as a delegate to the United States Olympic Congress for ten years, and as the general manager for the Olympic speedskating team in 1976—all in a volunteer role. Remarkably, Gene has been at thirteen Winter Olympic Games in some capacity connected to speedskating.

Gene and his wife, Carolyn, a 1958 graduate of Gustavus, are the proud parents of two daughters, Sarah and Susan. Sarah is a pediatrician in Michigan, and Susan earned a doctorate at Marquette and also serves as an international speedskating referee. Speedskating has become a proud family affair; daughter Susan experienced success, and niece Amy Peterson was a five-time Olympian and three-time medalist.

Witnessing the many changes in equipment, training, coaching, and ice surfaces through his many years of observing the sport, Gene cites uniforms as one small change that has made a significant difference in improved speed. "In 1952 and '56, our uniforms were wool tights. Then in 1960, a Russian wore women's leotards made of a synthetic material and discovered it made a difference of one second per lap. We did not understand the importance of the concept of wearing a uniform that offered less air resistance."

In recognition of his ability and many contributions to speedskating, Gene was inducted to the National Speedskating Hall of Fame in 1971 and to the Gustavus Adolphus Athletic Hall of Fame in 1992.

Photo courtesy of Princeton University Athletics

SUSIE SCANLAN

En garde, Prêt, Allez!

THE COMMAND SEQUENCE FOR A FENCING BOUT CUStomarily uses the French words en garde ("on guard" or "prepare"), prêt ("ready"), and allez ("go"). That series of words may also serve as a fitting description of Susie Scanlan's road to the 2012 Olympics in the historical sport of fencing.

Born in 1990, the third oldest of four children, Susannah "Susie" Scanlan decided at an early age that she would prepare to be an Olympian as she grew up near the Rice Street Corridor in the North End neighborhood of St. Paul. "When I was six years old, I told my mom that I would go to the Olympics. I didn't know what sport, but I was going to go." Her interest in fencing was piqued because "I wanted to try sword fighting. I had seen it in movies and thought it looked like fun."

Starting at age nine, Susie then readied herself by taking classes specializing in épée, the weapons category that has the heaviest blade in the sport of fencing (the other two are foil and sabre). The blade is ninety centimeters long, and a point is scored when the tip touches the opponent. The entire body is a valid target, and scoring is now determined when a set amount of force from the tip touches the opponent, sending a signal to an electronic scoring device. She practiced three or four times per week under the direction of Roberto Sobalvarro at the Twin Cities Fencing Club in the basement of a nondescript apartment building at the intersection of Holly and Grotto Streets in St. Paul. Susie also played softball, basketball, and volleyball as a youth, helping her St. Paul basketball team to the state championship as a sixth grader. It was a hand injury that played an integral role in her progress. "My freshman year I shattered my knuckle in my weapon hand [Susie is left handed], which kept me from doing any actual bouting. I just did physical training for the four months that I was out. I believe that newfound strength is what really prepared me," states Susie. By this time she was practicing five times per week with sessions lasting between two to three hours, and the disruption from being able to use her hands cemented her

SUSIE SCANLAN IN ACTION VS UKRAINE'S OLENA KRYVYTSKA DURING INDIVIDUAL EPEE COMPETITION ON JULY 30, 2012
Photo credit: ©Sergei Ilnitsky/Corbis Images

footwork skills.

Sobalvarro, a 1976 Owatonna (Minnesota) High School graduate who took up fencing as a student at Macalester College in St. Paul, was named the women's national head fencing coach in 1996. He took a four-year hiatus from international coaching after the 2000 Summer Olympics (in Sydney, Australia) due to the birth of a son. After his return, he coached the 2008 Junior (age twenty and under) World team. As Susie's longtime coach, he quickly recites her skills: "She is dedicated and knows what she wants by having long-term goals. Susie is fast and can change speeds quickly. She generates lots of power and has an astonishing amount of explosivity. You also need to be balanced, be flexible, and have fine motor control to manipulate the weapon with your fingers. And Susie is fearless."

Then came the "go" stage as the slender 5-feet-8 athlete competed success-fully at the national and international level. A highlight was the team event at the 2008 Junior World Championships, Susie remembers. "We beat Italy to win the gold medal—an upset—and I had plus-eight indicator [touches scored minus touches received]. Three out of the four on that team would be on the team going to the 2012 Summer Olympics in London, England." Susie gave the gold medal to Sobalvarro, a very meaningful gift to the coach who has helped the local—and national—fencing program grow significantly.

Articulate and intelligent, Susie took advanced placement classes and partici-pated in the international baccalaureate program at St. Paul Central High School, a school she describes as being "rich in different cultures and the alma mater of cartoonist Charles Schulz." In addition to her demanding academic curriculum and rigorous fencing training regimen, she also worked at Christos Greek Restaurant to help pay for expenses related to épée and ran cross country for two years. Susie graduated in 2008 and was accepted for enrollment at Princeton University, an Ivy League school in New Jersey. "I was initially drawn to Princeton early in high school because of its academic reputation. I also worked with the head coach, Zoltan Dudas, over a few summer training camps while he was still an assistant at Notre Dame. I really enjoyed his coaching style, so when he became the head coach at Princeton, I was totally sold. It has great academics and great athletics."

Achieving All-American status by placing seventh at the NCAA in épée her freshman year, Susie again attained All-American ranking as she moved up two spots in her second season at Princeton. Important in Susie's developing athletic career was winning the US Fencing Nationals in 2009 and placing second in 2010. After completing the first semester of her junior year, Susie took the calculated risk of taking a leave from her studies for two years in an effort to realize her dream of becoming an Olympian at the 2012 Summer Games. She was not expected to make the select three-member épée team.

Susie explains her conditioning as she sought to make the team: "I trained five to seven hours per day six days a week when I was not in between World Cups.

SUSIE SCANLAN AT OPENING DAY CEREMONIES AT THE 2012 SUMMER OLYMPIC GAMES IN LONDON, ENGLAND
Photo courtesy of Susie Scanlan

The World Cup circuit was composed of eight tournaments that took place every other weekend in February, March, May, and June. My training during my time off consisted of footwork, drilling, fencing, sprints, yoga, and weight training." A lengthy and grueling process based on performance at more than a dozen World Cup events and national tournaments followed. It was a stressful time for the underdog as she slowly climbed to forty-first in world rankings. "I had my best World Cup season ever but one of my worst national seasons ever. I finished third at the end of the qualification, so I made the team . . . barely. It was a nail-biter!" relates Susie. It was a strong sixteenth-place showing, the best by an American, at the Budapest Grand Prix in February 2012 that vaulted her from seventh in team rankings to third place, which she maintained for the remainder of the trials. Susie had secured a spot on the 2012 Olympic women's épée team.

"The opening ceremonies were incredibly emotional," Susie recalls. Her mother, Ann; father, Jerome; older sisters, Josie and Kathleen; and younger brother, Sawyer, were among her supporters in London. She credits her mother for always keeping her grounded. "Having regular contact with someone who could always remind me that fencing is, after all, just a game was very good for my sanity. She was incredibly supportive and sacrificed a lot so that I could compete on the national and international circuits." Her teammates were Maya Lawrence, a Princeton graduate, and Courtney Hurley, the NCAA champion from Notre Dame. Hurley's sister, Kelley, a 2008 Olympian, was the team alternate. Sobalvarro, her local coach and another St. Paulite, was the Olympic women's fencing coach.

> "*Having regular contact with someone who could always remind me that fencing is, after all, just a game was very good for my sanity. She was incredibly supportive and sacrificed a lot so that I could compete on the national and international circuits.*"

Susie suffered a disappointing 15–13 loss to a Ukrainian in the first round of individual competition. Épée bouts go to a score of 15 points (successful touches on any part of the body) or three periods of three minutes each. The team event would have a more rewarding outcome.

Eight teams had qualified for the Olympics. "We were probably rated eighth in the world, but I think the team was on the upswing," Susie reflects. The team defeated Italy 45–35 in the quarterfinals. Susie won two of three bouts with a critical 5–3 victory to give the team a commanding 40–33 lead. The team then went flat in the semifinals against a spirited South Korea team they had consistently defeated in previous tournaments, losing 45–36.

Susie voluntarily offered to let the team alternate, Kelley Hurley, compete in the bronze medal match against Russia. While wanting to redeem herself from the three bouts she lost by one or two points each to the South Korean team, Susie thought her teammate had a better style against the Russian opponent in the medal match. Coach Sobalvarro agreed, and Hurley substituted for Susie, adding an unexpected wrinkle into the match-ups. Kelley Hurley won one of her three bouts and the team match ended up in a 30–30 tie. A sudden-death bout with Courtney Hurley representing the United States team ended abruptly with Hurley making an attack from the line and scoring quickly. The women's épée team had won its first Olympic medal ever.

SUSIE SCANLAN, COACH ROBERTO SOBALVARRO, AND MAYA LAWRENCE AT 2012 OLYMPIC GAMES CLOSING CEREMONIES IN LONDON, ENGLAND
Photo courtesy of Roberto Sobalvarro

Having earned a bronze medal, Susie returned to Princeton in 2013 for the spring semester. She enjoyed being a key fencer on the Princeton team that edged Notre Dame for first at the NCAA Fencing Championships in San Antonio, Texas. In individual competition, she was awarded her third All-American honor as the runner-up to Olympic teammate Courtney Hurley.

An economics major, Susie now works in the White House; she is a macro/international research assistant at the Council of Economic Advisers. Once again she followed the path of en garde, prêt, and allez—this time for a career and profession in life.

Photo courtesy of University of Minnesota Athletics

BUZZ SCHNEIDER

Connecting in Hockey

WILLIAM "BUZZ" SCHNEIDER HAS PLAYED ICE hockey with so many people in so many leagues that he is connected with people involved in the sport not only nationally but also internationally. In any collegiate or professional hockey arena in the country, chances are Buzz will meet someone he knows. Born in Grand Rapids, Minnesota, in 1954, he received his nickname "Buzz" from his grandmother, who called him by the Croatian word for "brother." The pronunciation became altered and sounded similar to "Buzz," and the name stuck. The Schneider family had two girls and two boys and lived in the small Minnesota town of Coleraine until Buzz completed second grade, when they moved to Babbitt, where his father took a position as an industrial engineer with a mining company.

Babbitt, a growing town in the sixties on the eastern edge of the Mesabi Iron Mining Range in St. Louis County in northeastern Minnesota, is only seventeen driving miles south of Ely, a famed entry point to the Boundary Waters Canoe Area Wilderness, a recreational paradise, particularly for canoeists and fishermen. A new high school had been constructed in 1959 for the increasing student enrollment, and paired with the building was the start of a boys' ice hockey team under the direction of Ron Castellano. A former standout player who was a teammate of John Mayasich—often referred to as Minnesota's greatest high school hockey player—on Eveleth High School's dominating teams of the late forties and early fifties, Castellano was eager to bring the sport he loved to the mining community of Babbitt. The Schneider family had moved from towns known for their hockey prowess to one in its infancy. "There was not a lot of history or heritage in Babbitt," says Buzz.

While learning to skate in Coleraine, Buzz did not begin to play hockey until he participated in a city recreation program in Babbitt. Castellano remembers watching the talented, youthful skater: "He took to the ice like perpetual motion." The team played outdoors in some bitter cold. "It was so cold outdoors when the puck hit the steel pipes, it would break!" claims Buzz. In 1967 a welcome and beautiful indoor ice hockey arena was built with support from the community and the mining company. In fact, both Castellano and Buzz believe it was the first Minnesota high school hockey arena to have Plexiglas above the boards—and the second arena in the state (Metropolitan Sports Center in Bloomington was the first).

An exceptional athlete in high school, Buzz played quarterback, defensive back, and was the place kicker on the football team; played third base on the baseball team; and was playing on the varsity hockey team in ninth grade. The 5-feet-11-inch, 185-pound sports star was recruited by the University of Minnesota (U of M) baseball coach, Dick Siebert, and scouted by Gene Baker of the Pittsburgh Pirates of MLB. It was extremely rare for a professional baseball scout to make the trek to the remote Minnesota town of Babbitt. Buzz remembers Baker saying, "I know that up here you like shooting this little thing called a puck at a net, but I'd like you to consider playing for the Pirates if you don't go to college."

Hockey was Buzz's passion, though. "His big skill was acceleration. He could shoot really hard and had tons of energy," reports Castellano. Earning the additional nicknames of "Babbitt Rabbit" because of his speed and "Iron Lung" due to staying on the ice for nearly entire periods (and being from the Iron Range), Buzz was the stellar player on a team that struggled to compete in the powerful Iron Range Conference. Among the many outstanding Iron Range high school players that Buzz battled against, he names Pete LoPresti, the spectacular goaltender from Eveleth who later played professionally for the Minnesota North Stars; Doug Palazzari, another Eveleth star who played for Colorado College and was twice named Western Collegiate Hockey Association (WCHA) Player of the Year; the Carlson brothers (Jeff, Jack, and Steve) of Virginia; and Mike Antonovich of Greenway of Coleraine, a playmaker Buzz admired as a youth while living in that town, as favorites to watch. A longtime forward, Buzz was switched to defense for the 1971–72 season, his senior year, in an effort to give him even more ice time. Despite having fewer scoring opportunities because of being positioned farther from the net, Buzz still led the team in scoring. Buzz and Castellano both laugh when recalling a time when Buzz was exhausted and started to skate off the ice for a breather; he was ordered to "Stay on the ice!" by his coach.

Recruited by a few Division I hockey programs, Buzz was seriously considering attending the University of North Dakota or the University of Denver when a scholarship offer was tendered by the new coach of the U of M Gophers, a man named Herb Brooks who had played on several national and two Olympic hockey teams. Brooks had never seen Buzz play since he was hired only after Babbitt's playing season had

BUZZ SCHNEIDER PLAYED FOR THE GOPHERS' HOCKEY TEAM FROM 1972–75
Photo courtesy of University of Minnesota Athletics

ended, but he relied on reports from valued friends who had seen Buzz in action. The deciding factor for Buzz was that Brooks would also allow him to play baseball.

"I really liked Herbie. He treated me fairly," states Buzz about the U of M hockey coach known for his demanding practices and stern demeanor. One training device that Brooks introduced to the team was having a player wear a ten-pound weighted vest that was rotated among the players. After games on Friday and Saturday, a brief respite followed before grueling practices would resume on Monday. Buzz relives the days this way: "Sunday was an off day. Some guys would party, some would lay low. You died either way on Monday."

Playing left wing for the U of M from 1972–75, Buzz was named co-winner of the Frank Pond Rookie of the Year award with defenseman Dick Spannbauer in the award's inaugural year. He has fond memories and takes pride in playing for the 1974 NCAA championship team—Minnesota's first in hockey—which defeated Michigan Tech University (MTU) 4–2 at the Boston Garden. He loved having Hibbing, Minnesota, native Mike Polich, a 1975 first team All-American, as the center of his high-scoring line. The following year the results were reversed: MTU beat the Gophers 6–1 in the NCAA Championship finals.

Buzz did play right field on a skilled junior varsity U of M Gophers baseball team that lost 2–1 to the varsity in an intrasquad game. His coach was George Thomas of

Bloomington, Minnesota, who had played every position in the major leagues except for pitcher. "I really liked him. He was a great guy," notes Buzz. It is a tagline that Buzz uses about nearly every athlete he offers a comment on—he liked the people he knew on his sports teams. After one baseball season, however, Buzz decided to dedicate himself to hockey.

In 1974, Buzz was the youngest player (age nineteen) on the 1974 US national team under the guidance of Bob Johnson, coach at the University of Wisconsin, which won every game in Pool B of the World Championship tournament. Those victories would elevate the team to Pool A for 1975. The US squad lost every game in 1975, but Buzz achieved a remarkable feat in a game against the Soviet Union: he became only the second player to score a hat trick (three goals) against Vladislav Tretiak, the preeminent goalie in international hockey. "It put me on the map," Buzz says, summing up the extraordinary performance.

Still coached by Johnson, the 1976 Olympic hockey team roster of eighteen players was filled by eleven from Minnesota. Among them was Buzz Schneider—he and the team would be heading to Innsbruck, Austria. His linemates were two Minnesotans: Steve Sertich, a center from Virginia (Colorado College), and Robbie Harris, a right wing from Roseau (U of M). "We had a good team, but not enough depth," Buzz opines. The team had two victories (plus a win in the qualifying round) and three losses, but it was the final game that haunts Buzz. "We lost four to one to Germany, a team that we had previously beaten. If we had won, we would have won a bronze medal by tying for third. We played flat." Instead the team ended up in fifth place. Buzz tied for fourth in scoring on the team with two goals and one assist.

"If I had laid an egg, Herb would have cut me."

Drafted ninety-eighth by the Pittsburgh Penguins of the NHL and forty-fourth by the Minnesota Fighting Saints of the World Hockey Association (WHA), Buzz decided to leave the College of Liberal Arts at the U of M and pursue professional hockey after playing internationally in the Olympics and World Championships. For the next three years, Buzz played in an assortment of minor leagues—connecting with a host of players and coaches—and a four-game stint with the Birmingham Bulls of the WHA. Buzz then applied to regain his amateur status with the approaching 1980 Olympic Games, which would be hosted in Lake Placid, New York. And what a glorious decision that would prove to be.

Herb Brooks, still coaching at the U of M, was named the 1980 US Olympic hockey coach. While Buzz felt confident he would make the team after tryouts, he admits, "If I had laid an egg, Herb would have cut me." Buzz ended up being the sole return player from the 1976 Olympic team. Brooks introduced a new style of play to the team. "Herb never got outcoached. He was always prepared. He was innovative with training techniques. It took us a while to learn the weaving style. We outconditioned the other teams," says Buzz about Brooks's arduous practices. At the age of twenty-five, Buzz was shockingly the oldest player on the youthful squad, one month older than team captain Mike Eruzione. Buzz would happily again be on a line with two Minnesotans, Mark Pavelich of Eveleth and John "Bah" Harrington of Virginia, to form a trio of Iron Range players. Twelve of the twenty players on the 1980 US Olympic team roster were Minnesotans.

Americans still savor the 1980 Olympic hockey games. The determined young amateurs rolled to four victories and one tie in their group to qualify for the round-robin medal round. The Soviet Union, Sweden, Finland, and the United States would be contending for the gold medal. For the first game, the esteemed Soviet Union would be their foe. The Soviet Union had more wins than losses in games against NHL teams. They had crushed the American Olympic crew 10–3 only a week before the opening ceremonies, so little chance of victory was predicted by sportscasters. In the first period, Buzz fired a slap shot past Tretiak and—in a surprise move—the superb goalie was pulled after the period. "Pav [Pavelich] always told me, 'Just get in front of the net. I'll put it on your stick.' And he would!" Buzz exclaims. As most of America knows, Eruzione scored the winning goal midway through the final period, leading the United States to an incredible 4–3 win. Goalie Jim Craig then withstood an onslaught of shots on goal to preserve the victory.

The joy in Lake Placid and around the country was palpable, but the celebration by the team needed to be tempered because they had to win another game—this one against a formidable Finnish team—before they could claim the gold medal. History shows that the exuberant young American team prevailed with a 4–2 victory, coming back from a 2–1 deficit. At the medal ceremony, Eruzione waved wildly for his teammates to join him on the podium to receive their gold medal. If the 1980 Olympic hockey games, dubbed the Miracle on Ice, did not change history, it certainly changed the personal history of the twenty players and Coach Herb Brooks. And Buzz had played a major role in the memorable triumph with five goals and three assists, tying Rob McClanahan, a Mounds View High School (located in Arden Hills,

Minnesota) graduate, for second on the team in scoring.

Enjoying the international flavor of hockey and being offered more money, Buzz opted to play in Bern, Switzerland, for the next three years. He last played for the US national team in 1983. Soon afterward, Buzz suffered a herniated disk in his back and retired from playing hockey.

Connecting with an earlier Olympian (Mike Curran, the magnificent goalie on the 1972 team and now the general manager at Great Dane Trailers), Buzz became a successful sales executive at the semi trailer company until 2001. He then turned to commercial real estate ventures—except for time he spent in Turkey in the summer of 2009 as the Fulbright Grant recipient to coach youth hockey in Ankara and the 2009–10 season as general manager of the men's national team and head coach and general coordinator of the boys under-eighteen (U-18) team for the Turkish Ice Hockey Federation. "A very good high school team in Minnesota or a Division III college team could have beaten the [Turkish] national team," Buzz concedes.

Buzz and Gayle Warn of Eveleth married in 1977. Gayle is the treatment coordinator for an orthodontist in Maplewood, Minnesota. They have two sons, Billy and Neal.

Billy, born in Switzerland in 1980, was the Most Valuable Player on the Mounds View High School baseball team and batted leadoff and played second base for the Tri-City Red team, which won the American Legion World Series in 1999. He was recruited to play baseball at the U of M, but Billy suffered a back injury similar to his father's, and it ended his athletic career. However, he surprised himself and Disney movie director Gavin O' Connor when he landed a role in the 2004 movie Miracle playing . . . Buzz Schneider! Yes, O' Connor was not aware that Billy was Buzz's son until after Billy was cast in the role.

Neal played hockey at Roseville Area High School under coach Steve Sertich, a 1976 Olympian, originally from Virginia, Minnesota. Neal now works for Steve Schneider, Buzz's brother, a finance major at Notre Dame who also captained the hockey team.

One important moment—hour, actually—of Buzz's time on the Olympic team that the movie does not show is that Buzz was actually standing in street clothes next to assistant coach Craig Patrick when Brooks, upset with the team's play in an exhibition game against Norway, ordered the team back to the ice for almost another hour of conditioning. He escaped the brutal postgame drills because Brooks had ordered him to find out what teammate Les Auge was saying to a referee during the game. Auge was indicating that the referee was blind, and the irate man ejected Auge and then

BUZZ, GAYLE, SARAH AHLQUIST, BILLY, AND NEAL SCHNEIDER ON SARAH AND BILLY'S WEDDING DAY, JULY 26, 2014
Photo courtesy of the Buzz and Gayle Schneider family

tossed Buzz for coming into the conversation. Feeling guilty as he watched his teammates suffer on the ice, Buzz asked Patrick whether he should get back in uniform and join the team. Patrick discouraged him, thinking it would end soon. It did not, but a relieved Buzz Schneider was not nearly as spent as his teammates for the game the next day. They proceeded to defeat the same Norway team 8–2.

Palazarri, the Eveleth playmaker Buzz knew from high school and now the executive director of the United States Hockey Hall of Fame, knows Buzz from a pair of perspectives. As a player, he remembers Buzz as "incredibly fast" and adds, "I have had the good fortune to know him better now because he has been helpful by serving on our board. He has always been a cordial, humble, and wonderful person."

Buzz obviously considers himself a lucky man. He enjoyed his formative years but sadly notes the population of Babbitt is now only half the size it was when his family moved to the town. He is happily married, very proud of his sons, speaks warmly of his siblings, calls his 1980 Olympic teammates "an extended family," is amazed at the volume of Olympic-related mail that he still receives thirty-five years after the celebrated event, and is healthy and trim. "No serious injuries. I broke my nose a couple of times," he says of his many years playing hockey.

But listen to Castellano marvel at Buzz's hockey connections: "I was introduced to I don't know how many people when Buzz and I were at the 2014 state hockey tournament. Everyone knows him."

GOALKEEPER BRIANA SCURRY COMPETING IN WORLD CUP
FINALS VS CHINA IN LOS ANGELES, CALIFORNIA, ON JULY 10, 1999

Photo credit: J. Brett Whitesell/isiphotos

BRIANA SCURRY

Inspiring a Whole New Generation of Little Girls

EXPECTING A BABY BOY, ERNIE AND ROBBIE SCURRY had picked the name Brian for their newborn. To their astonishment, they had a baby girl! They decided to retain the name and simply add an a to the end of it and called their daughter Briana (pronounced Brī-an-a). It was September 7, 1971, and it would be the first of many surprises that their youngest of nine children would spring on them.

Raised in Dayton, Minnesota (population 4,500), a community on the northern boundary of Hennepin County that promotes itself as "Two Rivers, One Community" since it is located at the confluence of the Crow and Mississippi rivers, Briana recalls having "had a fantastic childhood." Her father, Ernie, was a foreman for International Telephone & Telegraph, and her athletic mother, Robbie, worked for Network Systems after the children got older. "Both of them were there, both of them were supportive. I would bring home a flyer to play soccer, and they said yes. I'd bring home a flyer for tackle football, and they'd say yes. They said yes for two years, then they said no." Briana laughs about her short-lived football experience. "Throughout all of my childhood, my parents never thought I was crazy."

Briana wanted to try every sport. She played floor hockey, softball, basketball, and ran track in addition to playing soccer and tackle football. While attending schools in Anoka-Hennepin, Minnesota's largest school district, Briana became all-state in soccer and basketball and competed at the Minnesota High School track and field championships in long jump, the 200-meter dash, and on two relay teams.

While Briana loved basketball, her soccer skills as goalkeeper were catching the attention of nationally ranked college teams. It was a goalie in another sport—ice hockey—that inspired her to try the position. She watched Jim Craig of the 1980 Miracle on Ice Olympic hockey team make acrobatic saves and realized the position's significance in keeping the squad in the game. Her teachers, coaches, and teammates have fond memories of the exceptional student athlete who won the 1990 Anoka High School Athena Award, an honor given to a female senior for her athletic achievements.

At an emotional homecoming of sorts, Briana was the speaker at the school district's Leadership Group meeting on August 14, 2014. Her first-grade teacher, Barb Swanson, introduced her. "Briana was a good student and had a quiet confidence. Her athletic ability was obvious. She was always striving to do her best. In 1978–79 she was a six-year-old who told me that she wanted to go to the Olympics."

In attendance was Denise (Swenson) Collins, an assistant principal at Jackson Middle School of the Anoka-Hennepin School District, who was a soccer teammate with Briana on the Brooklyn Park Kickers. Collins was a star forward at Osseo

High School who became a second-team collegiate All-American at the University of Connecticut. The guest speaker was a surprise to Collins, and the friends and former teammates had a joyful—and tearful—reunion. Collins expressed her warm memories of Briana and the

PAST TEAMMATES ON THE BROOKLYN PARK KICKERS, DENISE SWENSON COLLINS AND BRIANA SCURRY, AUGUST 14, 2014
Photo credit: Derrick Williams, Anoka-Hennepin School District

team. "You had your team, and you played where you lived. We had fun and liked each other. And we knew we weren't going to be scored on [with Briana as goalkeeper], so we thought we could win. Briana had a sense of humor but was intense at games. She could turn it on and off—a mindset shift like I've never seen in anyone."

Pete Swenson, Collins's father and longtime coach of the Brooklyn Park Kickers, excitedly recalls Briana's many varied contributions to the team. "She was so coachable. Her leaping ability was so amazing that she hit the top bar with her head. Bri [what her teammates and friends called her] worked hard and was so focused. She was energetic and a leader. I told her that she had the ability to be goalkeeper on the national team [soccer did not become an Olympic sport until 1996]. She looked at me in shock! She had the eye of a tiger. Yet she had a great sense of humor—she could imitate Kermit the Frog better than anyone—she was hysterical!" In 1986 the Under-16 Kickers team won the Minnesota State Cup under Swenson's guidance with Denise Swenson and Briana leading the team.

The Anoka High School Tornadoes (the team nickname originated in 1935 after a tornado destroyed much of Anoka's main street) girls' soccer team won the state title in 1989 with Briana, now a senior, completing her fourth year as the starting varsity goalkeeper. The 5-foot-8 athlete was recruited by many colleges in the Upper Midwest, including the University of Minnesota, to play basketball as a forward. Swenson tried to use his connections through coaching to help obtain a soccer scholarship. Jim Rudy, the coach at University of Massachusetts–Amherst, had tried to recruit Swenson's daughter when he was at the University of Central Florida and had stayed in contact. At Swenson's urging, Rudy came to Minnesota and watched Briana perform well in a soccer tournament in Apple Valley. Rudy was impressed and was willing to offer a half scholarship. Other tempting scholarships were tendered by Duke and the University of California–Santa Barbara. Later Rudy extended a full scholarship, a rarity for a first-year goalkeeper. Briana Scurry would be heading east for an education; she hoped to earn a degree in political science and then enter law school. She would also begin to face stiff competition and learn about the intricacies and demanding role of being a collegiate goalie and whether her dream of being an Olympic goalie would be possible.

The University of Massachusetts–Amherst thrived with Briana in goal. She had 37 shutouts in 65 starts for the women's soccer team. During her senior year in 1993, Briana allowed a meager average of 0.48 goals scored against her per game, the third-lowest in the nation. Named a

AS GOALIE FOR THE UNIVERSITY OF MASSACHUSETTS–AMHERST, BRIANA HAD 37 SHUTOUTS IN 65 STARTS
Photo courtesy of UMass Athletics

BRIANA SCURRY PLAYING IN THE 2009 OPENING GAME AS A MEMBER OF THE WASHINGTON FREEDOM

Photo credit: Michael Janosz/ isiphotos

second team All-American, Briana had 15 shutouts in 23 games in her final year of collegiate eligibility. Briana made the national team in 1993, fulfilling her youth coach's prediction and becoming the only African American starter on the team. She played on the national team for about fifteen years and was one of the first soccer players to receive an endorsement contract from Nike. Briana believes the trademarks that helped her get selected to the team were her "spectacular balance, quickness, rarely being injured, mental focus, and intensity." Tony DiCicco, the national women's soccer team coach from 1994–99, explains her skill set this way: "I look for two things in a women's soccer goalkeeper: one, athletic ability; two, mental skills. Bri made some really tough saves in the 1999 World Cup quarterfinals against Germany. She was able to slow things down and have a calming effect when we had only a one-goal lead and things can get chaotic." DiCicco also admires her personal attributes, saying, "Bri is a very compassionate and intelligent person. She is a deep thinker. When she spoke, you listened."

"The beautiful thing about American women's soccer is that once people watch it, they're hooked . . ."

In 1995 the US women's national soccer team took third in the World Cup with Briana, now twenty-three years old, starting in goal. The team was ascending and gaining popularity across the country with each victory. "The beautiful thing about American women's soccer is that once people watch it, they're hooked," points out Briana. Approaching the 1996 Olympic Games, the optimism and spirits of the team were high.

The US team rolled to five consecutive victories in the single-elimination tournament, winning the first gold medal in women's soccer in Olympic history. They won the gold medal at Sanford Stadium in Athens, Georgia, with a 2–1 victory over a talented Chinese squad. Briana played every minute of every game, permitting only three goals during the five games. While an Olympic dream had come true, Briana's most shining moment still lay ahead.

The World Cup in soccer is sometimes considered an even bigger stage than the Olympics. In the 1999 women's finals, China and the United States were scoreless at the end of regulation time and overtime, so a shootout ensued. In a shootout, five players from each team are selected to shoot—one at a time—with only the goalkeeper defending. In her most visible moment, Briana was able to block the shot of the third shootout kicker, Liu Ying, with a dramatic diving save in front of ninety thousand screaming fans at the Rose Bowl in Pasadena, California. Due to the clutch save, the US won the shootout 5–4 and first place in the World Cup.

More national teams and two more Olympic Games followed. The 2000 Olympic Games were less fulfilling for Briana since Siri Mullinex was named the starting goalie. The US team won the silver medal, losing 3–2 to Norway in the finals. Two months before the 2004 Olympic Games in Athens, Greece, Briana's father passed away. "He always said, 'Keep your eye on the ball,'" Briana says softly. Both the team and Briana rebounded with a gold medal in a 2–1 overtime victory against Brazil. "After a goal was scored on me, my mentality was I'll make it harder for them to score on me next time," related Briana. She had been on three Olympic teams, each team earning a medal, twice claiming gold and once collecting silver.

" *After a goal was scored on me, my mentality was I'll make it harder for them to score on me next time . . .* "

Between the 2000 and 2004 Olympics, Briana was a founding member of the professional Women's United Soccer Association (WUSA), starting as the Atlanta Best

BRIANA SCURRY HOLDING ONE OF HER TWO OLYMPIC GOLD MEDALS AS SHE SPEAKS TO THE ANOKA-HENNEPIN SCHOOL DISTRICT LEADERSHIP GROUP, AUGUST 14, 2014
Photo credit: Derrick Williams, Anoka-Hennepin School District

goalkeeper for three seasons. In 2003 she was named Goalkeeper of the Year. The WUSA folded after the 2003 season, and Briana later emerged playing for the Washington Freedom of the Women's Professional Soccer League.

In 2010 Briana got hit in the head and suffered a concussion when she was hit by the knee of a player from the Philadelphia Independence as she was storming toward the goal. Briana retired after the season-ending injury. Over the course of three lethargic years of battling constant headaches, memory loss, and struggles with the balance she describes as "spectacular" at the peak of her playing years, Briana had occipital nerve release surgery at MedStar Georgetown University Hospital in October 2013. She feels good and is hopeful about her long-term health. Briana also speaks out forcefully about the subject of concussions and traumatic brain injuries (TBI). In March 2014 she testified before Congress on TBI in sports.

Briana is now a preeminent motivational speaker, relating her experiences on the pitch and in life to the audience in an inspiring and memorable way. She encourages young people to have fun in soccer and live their dreams. Appearing in 173 international games, the most of any American goalkeeper, Briana has been nominated or inducted into many athletic halls of fame, including the inaugural class at her alma mater, Anoka High School, in 2011. Among the impressive list of twenty-four inductees were three other Olympians—John Bauer (1992, 1998, and 2002, nordic skiing), Brandon Paulson (1996, silver medalist in Greco-Roman wrestling), and Dan Chandler (1976, 1980, and 1984, Greco-Roman wrestling)—and 1989 Miss America and Fox News anchor Gretchen Carlson.

"Little did we know we were being inspirational to a whole new generation of little girls. It is the single most amazing thing about my athletic career."

Among the thoughts and words she shared in the poignant speaking engagement to the Anoka-Hennepin Leadership Group, Briana said of her playing career on the Olympic and World Cup teams, "Little did we know we were being inspirational to a whole new generation of little girls. It is the single most amazing thing about my athletic career."

STEVE SERTICH, CIRCA 1965
Photo courtesy of Steve Sertich

STEVE SERTICH

Iron Range Pride

LOCATED IN THE CENTER OF ST. LOUIS COUNTY IN northeastern Minnesota, the city of Virginia is a vital part of the Mesabi Iron Range and the state's logging and mining history. The Laurentian Divide, a continental divide separating water flowing into the Atlantic Ocean from water moving into Hudson Bay and leading to the Arctic Ocean, lies north of the city of 9,000 citizens. The area is a recreational wonderland of fishing, hunting, and water and winter sports for people who appreciate its natural resources.

Steve Sertich, a 1976 ice hockey Olympian from Virginia, Minnesota, speaks proudly of the people and communities of the Iron Range. "Growing up on the Range was a special and unique experience with the different ethnic groups, mines, and work ethic. I felt very supported by my parents." Steve's parents, Mark "Pa" Sertich, a welder, and Mary McTaminey, a Scottish woman Pa met during World War II, demonstrated their support for Steve throughout their lives. Early in Steve's life, born in 1952, and the lives of his older siblings, Mike and Paddy, Pa spearheaded the effort to build a full-sized ice hockey rink on mining land. Pa and community volunteers contributed hundreds of hours to create what locals referred to as Northside Rink—complete with lights—symbolizing their work ethic and pride. "I had a place to play," says Steve gratefully.

Originally showing an interest in ski jumping, Steve idolized his older brother and soon followed Mike into hockey. As Steve remembers, he began playing the sport when he was in third grade and received tremendous instruction from the wealth of Iron Range hockey players coaching in Virginia. Steve also witnessed the superb talent and play not only of high school hockey teams on the Iron Range, but also of men's senior teams still thriving in the area. "Eveleth was the mecca of hockey in the fifties and sixties," he says respectfully of the nearby Iron Range city's prowess in the sport.

One vivid memory Steve has is of watching a game as a youth that featured Tim

MIKE SERTICH, HEAD MEN'S HOCKEY COACH AT UNIVERSITY OF MINNESOTA–DULUTH, 1982–2000
Photo courtesy of UMD Athletics Communications

Sheehy, a marvelous player (later a 1972 Olympian) at International Falls High. "He could score from the red line," Steve says in wonder. After the game, Steve asked Sheehy if he could have his stick—not an uncommon request for young fans to make of high school players they admired. Sheehy asked his name and said that he'd send it to him after the state tournament. Sheehy won an everlasting devotee when he honored the request weeks later.

While Steve did play the middle infield positions in baseball for a successful Little League team that participated in a Midwest Regional Tournament, hockey was his passion and focus. When Steve entered Roosevelt High School in Virginia, Mike was already starring for the University of Minnesota–Duluth (UMD) Bulldogs as a defenseman. Steve did not play much for the varsity team until his junior year, but he appreciated the superior play of opponents Bob Collyard of Hibbing, Mike Antonovich of Greenway of Coleraine, and Henry Boucha of Warroad, "an incredible player to watch." The Virginia squad never qualified for the legendary Minnesota State High School Hockey Tournament because of the dominant teams fielded by the region. Nevertheless, high school coach Dave Hendrickson remembers Steve as a special player. "He had great hands, was so fast, and had a lot of courage. He knew what the game was all about. I would have loved to have more players like him. He's also a great human being, and that's more important than anything else."

At 5 feet 7 and 160 pounds, Steve was not a highly recruited hockey player when he graduated from high school in 1970. Herb Brooks, then an assistant coach at the University of Minnesota, did make contact with Steve, but it was the connection that one of his youth coaches, Pat Finnegan, had with Colorado College (CC) coach John Matchefts that enabled Steve to pursue hockey at the Division I level. Steve enjoyed his first airplane flight when he went on his one and only official college visit. It was at the college's Colorado Springs campus that Matchefts, a native of Eveleth and a member of the 1956 Olympic hockey team, offered Steve a full athletic scholarship.

Steve played little his first year at CC, but his fortunes skyrocketed when Jeff Sauer replaced Matchefts the next year. "Sauer gave us a chance to play: penalty killing, regular shifts, and power plays," Steve says appreciatively. He also felt fortunate to be able to play all three forward positions (left wing, center, and right wing) and often play on a line with Eveleth-native Doug Palazzari, a play-making wizard, at his center position.

Thriving under Sauer's guidance and Mike's tutelage, when he got together with his brother, Steve scored 75 goals and contributed 87 assists while playing in 125 games for CC from 1970–74. The team was never a championship contender, though. "We didn't have the depth the other teams had," Steve admits.

Sauer considered Steve a gamer. "He was not the biggest or strongest guy, but [he was] very skilled. He could score the timely goal in nearly every situation. Steve was a quiet leader, a hockey player who played his heart out in every game. And later, his sons picked up on that."

In 1973 Steve also made the US men's national hockey team, coached by Bob Johnson. "It was an absolute honor," Steve says with a mix of pride and modesty. It also fulfilled a goal that Steve had

STEVE SERTICH SCORED 75 GOALS WHILE PLAYING FOR COLORADO COLLEGE FROM 1970–74
Photo courtesy of Colorado College Sports Information

as a youth when he watched players in the men's amateur senior leagues playing in their national team jerseys and dreamed of someday wearing his own national jersey. Again paired with Palazzari, Steve played on the national team when it was playing in the lower level "B" group in 1973 and when it took the championship in 1974 to elevate the team to the "A" group in 1975.

Following graduation in 1974 with a degree in elementary education and humanities, Steve married Patty Frasca of Colorado Springs. Patty was the daughter of Tony and Evey Lou Frasca, a couple who began a restaurant in the city and would eventually expand the family business, Panino's, into Minnesota (North Oaks). In addition, Tony, an All-American hockey player at Colorado College, was the college's hockey coach from 1958–63 as well as its longtime baseball coach.

Steve was invited to the tryouts in Madison, Wisconsin, that would compose the 1976 Olympic men's hockey team. He had stayed in Colorado Springs to work and train and felt confident in his conditioning. Although he found it helpful to have been a member on past national teams and had Johnson as the coach, Steve states,

"It was very competitive and challenging." On the 1975 national team, Steve was the fifth-leading scorer on the team—most of whom would be going to Innsbruck, Austria, as part of the US Olympic hockey team.

More than half of the 1976 US Olympic hockey team was from Minnesota, and Steve would be playing center between two of them: wings Robbie Harris of Roseau (teammates Blaine Comstock and Gary Ross were also from Roseau) and Buzz Schneider from Babbitt. The youthful squad had to win a qualifying game versus Yugoslavia to advance to the "A" pool to be in medal contention. The game would be memorable for Steve. He scored three of the team's eight goals in an 8–4 victory. His excited father went to throw a hat onto the rink (a tradition when a player scores a "hat trick," or three goals) when security guards grabbed his arms as he reached back to make the throw. This action can be explained as a result of the terrorist attacks that occurred during the 1972 Summer Games. Security was heightened and tightened, and personnel quickly responded to what they thought could be a dangerous situation.

> *"You know you're part of something special, yet you have to focus on your work," Steve says, summarizing his Olympic experience.*

Losses to the powerful Soviet Union and Czechoslovakia teams followed, but the American team rebounded with a superb effort to defeat Finland 5–4 (with Steve scoring one goal). After a 7–2 win over Poland, a final game against West Germany would determine which team would claim the bronze medal. Steve brought a bronze medal won by ice dancer Jim Millns into the locker room before the game, hoping it would inspire the team to a third straight victory. Unfortunately, the American team played flat, and West Germany played very well as they earned a place on the podium with a 4–1 win. "You know you're part of something special, yet you have to focus on your work," Steve says, summarizing his Olympic experience.

Embarking on a career in teaching and coaching, Steve's first position was in Northfield, Minnesota. Northfield High School's inaugural boys' hockey season coincided with the recent Olympian taking the coaching reins in 1976. Scott Cloud, a member of the team, says, "He was awesome. He was a great coach. He'd jump

MARTY, STEVE, AND MIKE SERTICH ON THE 2000-01 ROSEVILLE HIGH SCHOOL HOCKEY TEAM
Photo courtesy of Steve Sertich

into drills, and we were in awe of his ability." Except for playing two years professionally in Germany, Steve was an elementary teacher and hockey coach in Colorado, making stops in the Minnesota cities of Virginia, Blaine, and Richfield before landing a position at Edgerton Elementary in Maplewood and coaching hockey at Roseville Area High School from 1993–2006.

Steve and Patty, now the parents of Sara, Marty, and Mike, built their own small backyard ice rink complete with a tree in the middle of it! There it was—Iron Range pride at work in a St. Paul suburb. Sarah decided to participate in gymnastics and continued to compete at Gustavus Adolphus College in St. Peter, Minnesota, but Marty and Mike utilized the backyard rink heavily and became skilled hockey players. Mike scored the winning goal in overtime in a section final propelling Roseville Area High School to the Minnesota State High School League tournament in 2002, one of the most thrilling moments of Steve's career in hockey. The team took runner-up honors that season and placed third when they returned in 2003, with Steve being named Class AA Coach of the Year. Marty, a 2001 high school graduate, was now excelling at hockey at Colorado College, and Mike would later join him as a walk-on (nonscholarship) athlete. Steve switched to coaching girls' hockey for the 2003–06 seasons, receiving his fourth Section Coach of the Year award in 2004 and guiding the

(LEFT TO RIGHT) STEVE, MARTY, MIKE, SON-IN-LAW TRAVIS, AND (SITTING) PATTY AND SARA SERTICH, FALL 2004
Photo courtesy of Steve Sertich

MARK "PA" SERTICH IN THE GOLD ROOM AT THE ICE ARENA IN COLORADO SPRINGS IN 1986
Photo credit: Bob Jackson

team to a fourth-place finish in the 2006 state tournament.

Marty had a sensational junior year at Colorado College and was named the 2005 Hobey Baker Award recipient as the most outstanding collegiate hockey player in the nation. Sadly, it was a bittersweet time for the close-knit Sertich family: Patty had brain cancer and died one month after Marty received the honor. Like his father did as a young man, Marty now plays professional hockey in Germany.

In 2006, at the age of fifty-three, Steve took the leap to coaching women's hockey at Bemidji State University (BSU). The hockey program made strides in improvement and Steve received another accolade: Western Collegiate Hockey Association Coach of the Year for the 2009–10 season. Another major change in Steve's life occurred in 2008 when he married Sally Krause, a physical education instructor at BSU. In 2010, Steve was inducted into the Minnesota High School Hockey Coaches Hall of Fame.

In 1974, Steve's parents had moved to Colorado Springs, where "Pa" became a maintenance man and Zamboni driver at the city's ice arena. A beloved character and dedicated employee, the city later named the ice arena Mark "Pa" Sertich Ice Arena in his honor. Steve's brother Mike eventually became the head coach of UMD for

STEVE SERTICH ANNOUNCES HIS RETIREMENT AS HEAD WOMEN'S HOCKEY COACH AT BEMIDJI STATE UNIVERSITY IN 2014
Photo courtesy of BSU Photo Services

eighteen years and was named WCHA men's hockey Coach of the Year three consecutive years. Steve retired from BSU in 2014 in good humor, saying, "My time has passed [referring to George Harrison's song, "All Things Must Pass"]." Later he summed up his career by saying, "Coaching has been great. I've had great players and great kids." All accomplished and said with Iron Range Pride.

Photo courtesy of Boston College Athletics Communications

TIM SHEEHY

Bronco Goes to Boston

IT MAY COME AS A SHOCK TO AVID FANS OF MINNESO-
ta high school ice hockey to learn that in the mid-twentieth century, the northern Minnesota town of International Falls did not have a high school ice hockey
rink. This is a rather amazing fact considering the hockey-crazed town of 6,000 people has such a strong tradition in the sport, with seven state high school championships (out of nineteen appearances) at the renowned Minnesota State High School
League Hockey Tournament.

International Falls didn't have a rink or a modern hospital in 1948, but Fort
Frances, Ontario, directly across the Rainy River and Canadian border, had both. As a
result, Tim Sheehy was born in Fort Frances (he has dual citizenship) and would play
many memorable high school hockey games there, including the home games of a
fifty-nine consecutive victory streak from 1963–66.

The fourth oldest of nine children, Tim is proud that he and all his siblings are
college graduates. His father, Larry, worked in the real estate insurance business, and
his mother, Kathleen, was a county social worker. Finances were challenging for the
packed household, and the Sheehy children had humble beginnings. "Timmy grew
up next door to me," reports former high school teammate Jim Amidon. "He grew up
in a large family and didn't have a lot. A lot of the equipment he used was my old stuff.
When Timmy was in seventh grade or so, we laid out a sheet of hardboard over the
ground and shot at a net with a can swinging on a string. We'd shoot to try and hit the
moving target. On weekends in the winter, we'd play huge games at a place we called
the Bandshell Rink [in Smokey Bear Park]."

Practicing diligently on a neighborhood rink, Tim and classmate Dan Mahle led
their International Falls bantam team to the state title in 1962. The environment was
ideal for building a strong future for International Falls sports teams. "We all knew
each other growing up. We played baseball and football together too," recalls Tim. "It
was a very, very competitive environment—and everyone stayed there."

Larry Ross, the high school coach, observed the talent of the two players and wanted to elevate them to the varsity team in ninth grade—something prohibited by local school board policy. Ross petitioned the school board for freshmen to be eligible for varsity play, and his request was granted during the 1962–63 playing season as the International Falls Broncos made a run for the state high school tournament. The team nickname is actually in honor of Tim's uncle, Bronko Nagurski, the Hall of Fame football player and professional wrestler, who lived most of his life in International Falls. Tim's mother and Bronko's wife, Eileen, were sisters. When the high school wanted to change their unusual team nickname from the Men of Purple and Gold to the Bronkos in 1942, to honor their local legend, Nagurski demurred and only consented after the spelling was changed by replacing the letter k with a c. The alteration in spelling gave the team a more traditional moniker.

> *"It was an emotional time. Jim was going to Colorado College. I made a twenty-dollar wager that the team would win the state title the next three years. He paid!"*

Starring senior Jim Amidon, the Broncos were the surprise of the 1963 state tournament, but they faced stiff competition from St. Paul Johnson in the championship game. "Jim Amidon was the best player in the state," says Tim flatly. "He was a strong leader and had very good character. Dan Mahle and I sometimes played on his line." The Broncos suffered a heartbreaking 4–3 overtime loss to the perennial powerhouse from St. Paul. Amidon and Tim lingered afterward, trying to recover from the devastating loss. "We were the last ones to leave the locker room after the 1963 loss," remembers Tim. "It was an emotional time. Jim was going to Colorado College. I made a twenty-dollar wager that the team would win the state title the next three years. He paid!" Tim laughs.

Indeed, the Broncos not only won the single-class state high school hockey tournament in 1964, 1965, and 1966, but it was during these three years that the team reeled off their fifty-nine consecutive victories. Included in the streak was a sweet win of revenge over St. Paul Johnson in the 1964 state championship game. Smooth, swift, and agile at 6 feet 1 and 185 pounds, Tim was named to the all-tournament team each year. He had an astounding 54 goals and 42 assists in the 1965–66 season, his

TIM SHEEHY SCORED 185 POINTS IN 80 GAMES FROM 1966–70 FOR THE BOSTON COLLEGE EAGLES HOCKEY TEAM
Photo courtesy of Boston College Athletics Communications

senior year at International Falls. Tim was a starting end who also played some quarterback on the football team, but it was his hockey prowess that brought coaches from the nation's most celebrated college programs to Minnesota's Northland.

Although his mother was a University of Minnesota (U of M) graduate, Tim visited the campuses of Michigan Tech, Colorado College, the University of Denver, the University of Minnesota–Duluth, and Boston College (BC). Max Winter, an owner of the Minnesota Vikings and a friend of Tim's father from his boyhood, tried to interest Tim in attending the U of M. "Max Winter and his brothers, Henry and Harry, owned the 620 Club on Hennepin Avenue in Minneapolis. It was a real treat for us to go there and meet sports celebrities like George Mikan and Ernie Fliegel," Tim says of the visits. "Max would treat us to a turkey dinner." The 620 Club at one time served more turkey dinners than any other eatery in the country.

Despite calls from Winter and other people connected to Minnesota sports and businesses, Tim was not persuaded to attend the U of M nor did he sign to play professional hockey (there were only six NHL teams at the time, and very few Americans played in the league). "I was looking forward to something different. I wanted to be challenged, and it was important to stay motivated as I was still seventeen when entering Boston College. Boston was a young person's town." Tim sought advice from former teammate Amidon. "He said, 'BC is as good a spot as any if you're going east.' That was good to hear from someone I knew and respected." And go east is exactly what Tim did in 1966 to join the BC program led by longtime coach John "Snooks" Kelley. Wisely, Kelley had Tim hosted during his visit by St. Thomas Academy graduate and St. Paul resident Mike Robertson, the last known three-sport male athlete (football, hockey, baseball) at BC. Robertson was an instant fan of Tim's attributes on and off the ice. "Tim was a marvelous player. He was likable, coachable, and smart— all qualities you want in a player."

Boston College (and later, Olympic and New England Whaler) teammate Kev-

TIM SHEEHY WAS NAMED EASTERN COLLEGE ATHLETIC CONFERENCE PLAYER OF THE YEAR FOR THE 1969–70 SEASON
Photo courtesy of Boston College Athletics Communications

in Ahearn reports, "Tim was one of the most highly touted high school players in the nation. He lived up to all of the billing. His skill set was very advanced for his age. He was big, strong, and very smooth. He seemed to move effortlessly. When Tim arrived, he was pretty shy. After time, he made the adjustment and seemed comfortable at BC and in Boston. He spent quite a bit of time with my family."

While college freshmen were not eligible for varsity play in 1966–67, Tim became a prolific scorer; he set the school's freshmen team scoring record. His sophomore year, BC qualified for the Frozen Four hosted by Duluth, a bonus allowing Tim and his family to visit together in March 1968. "We had good teams my junior and senior years, but we didn't make the Frozen Four. We had to compete against Ken Dryden at Cornell. He was great," Tim says respectfully. A modest man who deflects questions about his abilities and awards, Tim speaks of his teams' strengths. Scoring data, though, shows that when he graduated with a degree in finance in 1970, Tim had registered 185 points (goals and assists) in 80 games—an amazing 2.31 points per game, a BC record. Those phenomenal statistics led him to be named Eastern College Athletic Conference (ECAC) Player of the Year for the 1969–70 season.

As early as 1969, Tim had already earned a spot on the US national hockey team, which would be competing in the World Championships in Stockholm, Sweden. Minnesota legend John Mayasich was on the team as its player–coach. "I didn't really miss school because it was during a break," notes Tim. "I saw all these great Soviet and Czech players. It was during a tense time because Russian tanks had been in Prague. I saw Vaclav Nedomansky and Valeri Kharlamov, the greatest players in the world." Nedomansky, the large and powerful Czech legend, would defect to Canada in 1974 and become a linemate with Tim and Toronto Maple Leaf great Frank Mahovlich in the World Hockey Association (WHA).

In 1970 Tim was drafted—by the US Army. US national hockey team coach Murray Williamson was confident that Tim would make the national team and be on American ice rather than in Vietnam jungles. Tim continued to play for the national team and had Herb Brooks, Olympian and future Minnesota Gophers and 1980 Olympic team coach, as a roommate.

An accident during an exhibition game at the Olympia Stadium (nicknamed "the Old Red Barn," it was the home of the Detroit Red Wings until 1979) almost derailed Tim's hopes of making the upcoming Olympic Games in Sapporo, Japan. He hooked skates with young Mark Howe, son of hockey legend Gordie Howe, and suffered a serious ankle sprain. He recovered only one week before the opening of the 1972 Olympics. The small city of International Falls had a prodigious representation on the Olympic squad: three standout players including Tim and playmaking center Keith "Huffer" Christiansen serving as co-captains and starting goalie Mike "Lefty" Curran. The US team had faltered since their "Forgotten Miracle" gold medal in 1960. This Olympics was expected to be no different, with experts predicting a sixth-place finish for the team, which did not impress coaches during their exhibition games. "We had a good team—a lot of them are in the US Hockey Hall of Fame [Tim was inducted in 1997]," Tim testifies. "We had very good defense and goaltending plus strong forwards." Christiansen centered a line with Tim on right wing and Mark Howe on the left side.

"We had very good defense and goaltending plus strong forwards."

"We had two tough games [Switzerland and Poland] to get into the final round," Tim mentions. Tim scored two goals in the tight 5–3 victory over Switzerland. The final round started with a 5–3 loss to a strong Swedish team. The upset of the tournament occurred when the US team won convincingly over the powerful Czechoslovakian team, 5–1! Tim smiles at the memory. "Mike Curran played so well against the Czechs. He stood on his head! We needed a big game from Lefty, and he gave it to us." Tangling with the vaunted Soviet Union team was next, and although they lost 7–2

(Tim had one assist), it was a dramatic improvement over their 17–2 loss in 1969. Tim smiles as he relates, "We softened them up for Brooks and [Mike] Eruzione in 1980." The American squad then battled back and surprised Finland before a final 6–1 win against Poland, with Tim making two of the tallies. The American team had tied with Czechoslovakia behind the Soviet Union in overall standings, and by virtue of their victory over the Czechs, they won the silver medal.

> *"It was so cold in Sapporo! International Falls seemed warm to me." In fact, the Rocky and Bullwinkle cartoon show setting of Frostbite Falls is a spoof of Tim's hometown.*

Tim has an Olympic memory that would surprise most people who know that International Falls broadcasts itself as the Icebox of the Nation. He says with a grin, "It was so cold in Sapporo! International Falls seemed warm to me." In fact, the Rocky and Bullwinkle cartoon show setting of Frostbite Falls is a spoof of Tim's hometown. About the team he says, "We had a real good group of guys that still keep in contact."

When Tim was twenty-four years old, he signed a contract with the New England Whalers (initially located in Boston for the 1972–73 season) of the fledgling WHA. He was the fourth-leading scorer on the team. Tim played in the WHA through 1978 except for a fifteen-game stint with the Detroit Red Wings of the NHL. Tim ended his professional hockey career in 1980 at age thirty-one playing for the Hartford Whalers (now an NHL team), playing on a line with Gordie Howe (amazingly, still playing at fifty-one years old) and Nick Fotiu. Occasionally, Gordie's sons, Marty and Mark, would be playing defense at the same time, a feat unlikely to be replicated again in the

TIM SHEEHY IN SOUTHBOROUGH, MASSACHUSETTS, JULY 17, 2014

NHL. Tim concluded his career with 351 points, 178 of them goals.

Tim married Massachusetts native Jane Trinque in 1988, and they live in South-borough, Massachusetts, a city of 10,000 people twenty-seven miles west of Boston. They are the proud parents of three children who attended Boston-area colleges. Tim, his younger brother Neil (a Harvard University graduate who played defense in the NHL for nine seasons), and another associate, Paul Ostby (a former U of M goalie and assistant coach), are members of the ICE (Influential, Committed, Experienced) Hockey Agency, serving as NHL Player Association certified agents and have been in the hockey business for more than twenty years. They offer a variety of services to their primary target market of college hockey players who are turning professional, including contract negotiation, marketing for product endorsements, and financial services. Tim is the main Boston and East Coast contact.

Photo credit: Kirby Lee, Image of Sport

AMANDA SMOCK

Perseverance Payoff Is London Flight

STEADY, INCREMENTAL PROGRESS ENCOURAGED Amanda (Thieschafer) Smock to persevere with her triple jumping career through three Olympic Trials and reap the sweet reward of qualifying for the 2012 Olympics in London, England.

Amanda's early interest was gymnastics, enhanced by watching the movie *Nadia*. "I knew all of the lines," she says, grinning. Born in Long Prairie, Minnesota, in 1982, Amanda and her older brother, Josh, attended Melrose High School in central Minnesota. The town of 3,500 in Stearns County is in the heart of Minnesota's dairyland. It is also the hometown of Mark Olberding, one of Minnesota's better-known professional basketball players (1975–87). Her father, Glen, was a housing contractor, and her mother, Beth, was an accountant; both parents served as gymnastics coaches for the school district. Melrose captured the Class A state gymnastics titles in both 1994 and 1995 under their guidance. "Being in the gym was a big part of our childhood," adds Amanda.

Combining her love for gymnastics with her dedication and athleticism, Amanda placed third in the all-around competition in the state meet and second in the vault in 2000. She actually had more success in track and field, but she disliked the sport. "In junior high I once hid while the team was preparing to go to a meet so I wouldn't have to go," she admits. Nevertheless, Amanda participated in pole vault, long jump, and triple jump for Melrose and won both jump events at the state track and field meet her junior and senior years. Her triple jump of 39 feet 4¼ inches in the 2000 state meet won by a convincing margin of more than 2½ feet ahead of the second-place finisher.

Amanda's opinion of track and field changed following her graduation from high school in 2000. She wanted to fill the void left from gymnastics and decided to continue long and triple jumping at the collegiate level. The prospect of going to a Division I school was intimidating, so Amanda checked out North Dakota State

AMANDA IN FLIGHT AT THE KANSAS RELAYS
Photo courtesy of NDSU Athletics Media Relations

University (NDSU) in Fargo, North Dakota. The school seemed to be a good fit in multiple ways. "I liked the size of the school, and things just clicked with Brent Parmer, the jumps coach. He was very knowledgeable in jumps and energetic. At the college there was a lot more excitement in the environment, and NDSU had a good team." Amanda now liked the challenge, technique, and focus required of triple jumping. Parmer remembers their introduction. "Amanda seemed shy and reserved, but you could tell—through her father—she was a very determined athlete. She always wanted to learn more."

A technical sport, triple jumping has been an athletic event in all the modern Olympiads, but it did not open to women until 1996. Also known as the "hop-step-jump," the triple jump demands acceleration, rhythm, speed, and strength while also maintaining control and using good body position. The athlete must take off and land on the same leg (the "hop"), then land on the other foot (the "step," sometimes referred to as the "bound"), and finally take flight (the "jump") and land in the sand pit.

As a first-year student with the NDSU Bison, Amanda gained technical skills, qualified for nationals, and also met Greg Smock, a middle-distance runner on the men's track team from Big Lake, Minnesota. They would marry eight years later. Coach Parmer noted Amanda's improvement and strengths. "Her biggest asset is her body and spatial awareness—and that made her easy to coach. She was a lot of fun and ready to go—so was the whole 'jump crew.' We had some other great athletes, and they helped each other become even better jumpers." Indeed, two Bison teammates from Minnesota—Cassandra Olson (Ogilvie) and Sara Skudlarek (Holdingford)—and a third teammate, Crystal Cummins (Fargo, North Dakota), also became All-Americans. Amanda became a three-time NCAA Division II national champion in the triple jump, twice at the indoor championships (2002 and 2004) and once at the outdoor championships (2003). She reached the 13 meter (42 feet 8¼ inches) mark in 2004 and earned an invitation to the Olympic Trials at venerable Hayward Field in Eugene, Oregon.

Nervous, Amanda finished seventeenth at the trials, but she met a fellow Minnesotan named Shani Marks (of Apple Valley, Minnesota), and a warm friendship developed. Amanda was also hooked on the sport and determined to improve although she had completed her collegiate eligibility and graduated with a degree in exercise physiology. "I knew I wasn't ready to stop competing. The solid progression made me think I could continue to get better. Going to the University of Minnesota [U of M] for graduate school made the transition seamless. I had a training partner [Shani, who had finished fourth at the trials], a training facility that was convenient, and a coach." Matt Bingle, the women's track and field coach at the U of M, was Amanda's new resource. And Amanda was a new resource to the young women on the team as a volunteer assistant coach.

> "I knew I wasn't ready to stop competing. The solid progression made me think I could continue to get better. Going to the University of Minnesota [U of M] for graduate school made the transition seamless. I had a training partner [Shani, who had finished fourth at the trials], a training facility that was convenient, and a coach."

While working on a doctorate in exercise physiology at the U of M, Amanda and Marks trained five to six days per week. They created games like "Champion of the Universe" to make the practices more fun and stimulating. The pair also critiqued each other's technique and did sprint drills, weightlifting, and event-specific com-

**THE CREDENTIALS OF GLEN THIESCHAFER WITH NEW DATE
INSCRIBED ON IT**
Photo courtesy of Amanda Smock

ponents of the triple jump such as approach and takeoff. Marks notes, "Amanda's technique and form were always constant." Amanda also spent her afternoons helping coach the women's track team.

Amanda was hopeful as she prepared for the 2008 Olympic Trials. "I felt ready and excited, but I would still have to jump farther than I had ever before." With her parents in attendance, Amanda placed fifth but found consolation in her good friend winning the competition. "I was excited for Shani," she says sincerely. Marks was realizing her dream and going to Beijing, China, as a member of the US Olympic team (she would finish twenty-eighth). Afterward, her father, Glen, rubbed off the marked "2008" year on his credential tags and replaced it with the number "2012." Clearly Amanda had her family's support to continue her efforts to realize her dream.

Glen Thieschafer, age fifty-two, had cancer. In 2009 Amanda experienced a year fraught with emotions. Amanda and Greg Smock, who had graduated from law school at the U of M and was now a patent attorney, married in February. On the opposite end of the spectrum, Glen's health worsened, and Amanda returned to Melrose for the last six weeks of his life. Shani would graciously meet Amanda on occasion at St. John's University (about twenty-five miles east of Melrose) so she could continue to practice. Glen died in June, two weeks before the United States Track and Field Championships. He and Beth had been inducted into the Minnesota Girls' Gymnastics Coaches Hall of Fame in 1999. Ten years later, the Minnesota State High School Coaches Association honored Glen by enshrining him into their hall of fame. For the next three years, Amanda would have Glen's rewritten "2012" credentials tag posted to inspire her to practice, compete, and win.

Following a doctoral degree in 2010, triumphs were gained. Amanda Smock was the 2011 national outdoor champion and the 2011 indoor runner-up. In the 2011 US Track and Field national championship, she won with a distance of 46 feet 2 inches, nearly a foot more than runner-up Toni Smith. Despite the national championships, Amanda had to scramble to qualify for the World Championships in 2011. She darted from one meet to another to try and hit the qualifying standard of 46 feet 3½ inches (14.1 meters) without success. In August of 2011, she entered a meet at Chula Vista, California, and soared to a personal best of 46 feet 6¼ inches (14.18 meters). An elated Amanda had not only qualified for the World Championships, but she had also hit the "B" qualifying standard for the 2012 Summer Olympic Games. The importance of that achievement is that if no athlete from a country meets the Olympic "A" qualifying mark for an event, one person (rather than three) can still qualify and represent their country if the "B" standard is met. At this time, Amanda was the only American triple jumper to attain the "B" standard.

Amanda had added a full meter to her triple jump distance since she had graduated from college. She was ready for her third Olympic Trials, and she was taking an extra set of credentials, the set her father had rewritten, to Oregon. Amanda won her flight (a group in the preliminary round of competition) to qualify for the finals and then duplicated that feat by winning not only the finals with a leap of 45 feet 9 inches (13.94 meters), but also a berth on the United States Olympic team. A bonus was four of Glen's sisters driving to Hayward Field to witness and celebrate the victory. Certainly Amanda felt her father's presence as she remembered his lifetime of encouragement. The credentials would now be taking an international flight—to London, England, for the 2012 Olympics. Her husband, Greg, and mother and brother, Beth and Josh, would also make the trip to London to cheer on Amanda.

GREG AND AMANDA SMOCK AT NDSU NIGHT AT A MINNESOTA TWINS GAME (AMANDA THREW OUT THE FIRST PITCH)
Photo courtesy of NDSU Athletics Media Relations

AMANDA SMOCK SPRINTING DOWN RUNWAY
Photo credit: Kirby Lee, Image of Sport

"I turned thirty on Opening Day of the Olympics. It was electrifying in the stadium. It was a thrill to stand shoulder to shoulder with the world's greatest athletes," Amanda says reflectively. She struck up a friendship with javelin thrower Rachel Yurkovich (now Buciarski) at the training camp in Birmingham, England, before the start of the Olympic Games. "We had a good time as we trained and hung out in the Village. It was everything you could imagine."

Rather than the customary six jumps of most competitions, the Olympics only permits three jumps in the qualifying round for an athlete to reach the finals. "It was about executing my jump and doing my best," states Amanda. She scratched (a foul, usually due to stepping beyond the starting line on the takeoff) on her first attempt and had a best jump of 44 feet 8 inches (13.61 meters), placing twenty-seventh of thirty-five Olympic triple jumpers. "I came away with so many positives that it was easier for the disappointment of my jumps to roll off," Amanda affirms.

"I came away with so many positives that it was easier for the disappointment of my jumps to roll off,"

Understandably, Amanda most respects people who have persevered and realized their dreams. Endurance swimmer Diana Nyad is a case in point. Nyad became the first person to successfully complete the 110-mile swim from Cuba to Florida without the aid of a shark cage—at sixty-four years old. Another inspirational athlete is Yamilé Aldama, a Cuban-born triple jumper who won the 2011 indoor World Championship five months shy of her fortieth birthday.

Meanwhile, Amanda and Greg Smock live in Minneapolis where she is an assistant track and field coach at Macalester College and continues with her triple jump training. She won the bronze medal at the 2013 national championships, won both the indoor and outdoor national championships in 2014 and the national indoor championship in 2015. She is still persevering toward another flight—Rio de Janeiro, Brazil, in 2016.

**DON TIMM LEADING PACK OVER WATER JUMP IN
1976 OLYMPIC TRIALS STEEPLECHASE PRELIMINARY**
Photo courtesy of Dave Griffith

DON TIMM

Minnesota Tough

A **MODEST MAN, DON TIMM WILL QUICKLY CORRECT** a visitor who refers to him as an Olympian. "I was an Olympic team alternate, but not an Olympian. I placed fourth [the top three make the Olympic team] by two hundredths of a second in the 1976 Olympic Trials in the steeplechase." It was a photo finish with heartbreaking results for the man from Burnsville, Minnesota, who had such a quiet high school running career that he "was not recruited at all."

Sandwiched between sisters Diane and Debra, Don was born in 1949 to Ervin and Elsie Timm. His father worked at Pillsbury Mills and later for the St. Paul Chamber of Commerce. His athletic mother was a homemaker who had been a star hitter on the Ford Motor baseball team when she was first employed. Don credits his mother for instilling a "never quit" attitude in him as he witnessed her overcome a debilitating stroke. It was that approach that propelled Don to the upper echelon of American runners in the sport of steeplechase.

It was a one-week unit on running in a physical education class that encouraged Don to compete in track. "I improved every day, and one day the instructor was still having coffee and did not give me my time because I got back earlier than expected," Don smiles. He performed well enough at the high school level to win the Missota Conference championship in cross country his senior year and also the mile in track with a personal best time of 4 minutes, 38 seconds (4:38). But he confesses, "I didn't know anything about training" because he ran when Burnsville High School still did not have a track.

Don enrolled at the University of Minnesota (U of M) following high school graduation in 1967 and decided that he would still like to compete in running for the Gopher team. "I remember very clearly trying to get enough nerve to call Coach [Roy] Griak to ask him about joining the team. It was the day before fall classes, and the cross country team had been doing two-a-day workouts for a month. Coach said,

'Come see me,' and I knocked on his door in Cooke Hall the day school started. He gave me shoes, a uniform, and welcomed me to the team," Don recalls. It was the start of a lifelong friendship. Griak has his own memories of Don's growth in running. "He developed from being a nondescript runner to an elite runner and still holds Minnesota records. Don Timm is one of the greatest people I've ever met. He still visits and comes to mow my lawn—for years!"

> ## "Don Timm is one of the greatest people I've ever met. He still visits and comes to mow my lawn—for years!"

Surviving the first practice was a challenge. Don admits that he did not complete the entire workout. Since freshmen were ineligible for the varsity team, he did have time to train and get acclimated to the intense workouts. He did not compete in track that spring because his father was seriously ill. Don then rejoined the cross country team his sophomore year, and his time improved nearly three minutes as he rose to become the eighth man on the team. The cross country team, led by Steve Hoag (Anoka, Minnesota), was peaking and finished fourth in the nation.

In the spring of 1969, Don was introduced to steeplechase, a grueling track event that combines speed, endurance, jumping, and hurdling over 3,000 meters on a track with hurdles and a water jump. Competitors jump over four hurdles each lap during the course of seven laps (a total of twenty-eight times) and a water jump pit (a total of seven times) during the event. An exhausted Don Timm finished with a time of 9:35 in his first attempt in the demanding sport. Showing steady improvement, he placed fourth in the Big 10 Championships with a time of 9:08.

Henry Marsh, a national champion and four-time Olympian, describes the steeplechase this way: "It is a demanding race, a cerebral race that involves strategy. The more efficient you are over the barriers, the better you race. To run at the level that Don did, you had to be efficient, technically sound, and strategic."

One of Don's favorite memories is from his junior year at Minnesota—the Big 10 Cross Country Championships, which were hosted by Indiana University. Hoag had graduated, but freshmen were now eligible for varsity, and newcomer Garry Bjorklund from Twig, Minnesota, had quickly ascended to become the top runner on the team. The weather conditions in Bloomington, Indiana, were miserable: it was cold and snowy, and the Gophers, while contenders, were not expected to win. Don beams, "Coach Griak told us, 'We are Minnesota tough,' and I only wore socks over my hands. We were all Minnesota runners. Garry won, I was second, Tom Page [Edina] was third, and Mike Hanley [Anoka] was eighth. Terry Thomas [Mounds View High School], Gene Daley [St. Cloud Tech], and Pat Kelly [St. Paul Monroe] all ran too." With such a dominating performance, "Minnesota tough" had indeed been successful, and the Gophers won the conference championship with a score of forty.

The Gophers went on to finish in seventh place in the NCAA Championships at Van Cortland Park in New York, with Don finishing twenty-ninth overall, defeating 1968 track Olympian Marty Liquori and future gold medalist Dave Wottle. His dra-

DON TIMM COMPLETING A CROSS COUNTRY RACE
Photo courtesy of University of Minnesota Athletics

matic improvement was due to sweat, hard work, and the arrival of Bjorklund.

Besides his mother and Coach Griak, Garry "BJ" Bjorkund is the third person Don credits as being influential in his running career. "BJ is a friend, teammate, and hero all rolled into one. It was a thrill to train with him and watch him compete. He was not afraid of anyone. He was the best Minnesota runner."

In 1970, Bjorklund and Don, now a senior, again paced the Big 10 Cross Country Championships with a 1–2 finish, but the team finished second (with a team score of sixty-six) to Michigan State (which had a team score of forty-two). Don finished sixty-first in the NCAA Championships at William & Mary College (in Williamsburg, Virginia) with a personal-best time of 29:30 in the six-mile run. The Gophers placed twelfth in the team standings. His steady improvement in the steeplechase was evident in 1971 when he won the event in the Big 10 Championships in a conference record time of 8:43.8; he then lowered his time to 8:39.0 in the NCAA Track and

ROY GRIAK, DON TIMM, AND GARRY BJORKLUND AT THE ROY GRIAK INVITATIONAL HOSTED AT THE UNIVERSITY OF MINNESOTA LES BOLSTAD GOLF COURSE
Photo courtesy of Don Timm

Field Championships and achieved All-American status. A team of just three Gophers vaulted the team to an eighth-place finish at the national meet—Bjorklund, who won the 6-mile competition handily (and broke the collegiate record previously set by Van Nelson of Minneapolis); Tim Heikkila (Superior, Wisconsin), who tied for second in the high jump; and Don, placing fourth in the steeplechase.

A history major, Don continued to train with the U of M team while he did his student teaching at St. Louis Park High School in the fall of 1971. He decided to prepare for the steeplechase at the 1972 Olympic Trials, in Eugene, Oregon, which invited the top twenty-four athletes in each track and field event. While not expecting to qualify for the team, Don told himself, "You've come a long way. You're not going to do less than your best." He finished a respectable sixth on a suffocating day when the air temperature was 94 degrees and the heat on the track reportedly reached 135 degrees. Steve Savage, who did qualify for the 1972 Olympic team, says, "Don was always in the race and very competitive."

Afterward, Don established residency in California to compete for Athletes in Action and roomed with 1968 Olympian distance runner Tracy Smith. Coon Rapids High School contacted him there and said they were seeking a social studies teacher who could also coach long-distance runners. Don returned to Minnesota in January 1973 and began a more than thirty-eight-year career in education, but his coaching career continued after retiring from the classroom. The job move was eventful in another way: Don met English teacher Bonnie Worrel, and they married in 1974. Their first of three children, Andrew, was born in 1975; daughters Elizabeth and Catherine were born later. Thanks to Bonnie's support and dedication to the family, Don was able to continue to train for the 1976 Olympic Trials, but because it was necessary to support his family, he refused to take an unpaid leave from his teaching and coaching positions to compete at the highest level.

Like many runners, Don has logs in notebooks detailing his runs. In one period of ten weeks he ran 1,001 miles. He was very appreciative of having elite runners Mike Slack (St. Paul Harding and North Dakota State) and Bjorklund as training partners two to three times per week. "We'd just hammer each other. We had some hellacious workouts. It made us tougher," he reports with pride. One hilly nineteen-mile loop the trio ran once a month was from Don's home in Anoka to Dayton and back.

Don did well in the 1976 steeplechase Olympic Trials preliminary and qualified for the final. "I took the lead with three hundred meters to go. I ran my lifetime best," says Don of the photo finish for the final qualifying spot. Doug Brown and Marsh, multiple-time Olympians, passed him and so did Mike Roche, but then Roche tripped on the final hurdle and Don passed him. To Roche's credit, he sprang back up (it was later discovered that he had severely injured his arm) and with a burst of speed caught Don at the finish line. The judges finally declared Roche's official time as 8:32.70 and Don's time at 8:32.72. "I ran the best race I could. My tongue was so thick, I couldn't even talk. I have no regrets," Don says, summing up what would weigh heavily on most athletes. Don competed one more year until a serious calf injury forced him to quit racing.

Don was inducted into the U of M Athletic Hall of Fame in 2004 and received a Breaking Barriers Award at the Minnesota Girls and Women in Sports Day in 2014 for his thirty-seven years of coaching girls' cross country at Coon Rapids High School. Until the fall of 2014, his final season as a coach, Don would run with the team at practices.

When asked to show his most important piece of sports memorabilia, Don hoists the trophy that the Coon Rapids High School girls' team won at the Griak Cross Country Meet, hosted by the U of M in 2007. It figures . . . Don Timm is a team guy.

Who says Don's not an Olympian? There are such things as Olympian heart and character too.

DON TIMM HOLDING THE 2007 GIRLS' HIGH SCHOOL MAROON DIVISION CHAMPIONSHIP TROPHY WON BY THE COON RAPIDS HIGH SCHOOL TEAM HE COACHED

Don Timm was one of four people who provided reflections at the celebration of life service of Roy Griak, who passed away on July 9, 2015.

**CARRIE TOLLEFSON WINS THE 3,000-METER
RUN AT THE 2006 USA INDOOR CHAMPIONSHIPS**
Photo credit: Kirby Lee, Image of Sport

CARRIE TOLLEFSON

A True Minnesotan

"**T**HE HIGHLIGHT OF MY CAREER IS THAT IT ALL began here in Minnesota," states a modest Carrie Tollefson, a stellar middle-distance runner and 2004 Olympian.

Born in 1977, the youngest of three daughters of John, a lawyer, and Ginger, a hairdresser, from Dawson, Minnesota, Carrie participated in many activities in the small (population 1,500) western town near the South Dakota border. Surrounded by vast farmland in Lac qui Parle County, Carrie played trumpet in band and violin in orchestra, sang in a choir—she cherishes a two-week summer Christian choir tour—and participated in basketball and running sports. "Family fitness was important to our family. Our father was a football player in college, and sports were a part of our lives," reports Carrie.

> *"Family fitness was important to our family. Our father was a football player in college, and sports were a part of our lives," reports Carrie.*

In her first cross country meet as a seventh grader running on the varsity team of Dawson-Boyd High School (Boyd, a town with a population of 175 people, and Dawson had a consolidated school district), Carrie surprisingly found herself running on her older sister's shoulder. Kammie, a gifted senior athlete who was later named a finalist for best girls' basketball player in Minnesota, insisted her younger sister move ahead and catch the leading runners. While uncertain about pacing at such a tender age, Carrie did pass her sister and finished third in the race! "I owe a lot to her," says Carrie. "She and Stacey [her other older sister] led the way for me." For the rest of her high school running career, it was other runners who were trying to catch Carrie.

Carrie placed ninth in the state cross country meet in 1989 at the University of Minnesota golf course as a twelve-year-old. She then established a national high school record as she rattled off five consecutive state cross country championships on three different courses at both the A and AA classes as Dawson-Boyd/Lac qui Parle's enrollment fluctuated enough to shift the school into different divisions. The 1991 championship was won at the Arrowhead Resort golf course in Alexandria, and the 1992 crown was achieved at St. Olaf College in Northfield due to snowstorms that hit the metropolitan area so severely that meet officials were forced to hurriedly make a change of venue.

The 1994 title at the Class AA level was the most memorable for Carrie. She and Kara Wheeler of Duluth East, another future Olympian, had pulled ahead of the competition to a sizable lead. Carrie surged ahead near the end of the race to edge Wheeler by a second in a state record–setting performance of 14 minutes 9.2 seconds (14:09.2) in the girls' 4,000-meter run. "We talked during the race," recalls Carrie. "We had the same things in common. We were rivals but friends also. It was huge for me to finish my high school career on top—a nice way to go out. People really seemed to respect Kara and me and the performance we had. We both teared up as we received a standing ovation at the awards ceremony."

"We had the same things in common. We were rivals but friends also . . ."

Carrie graduated from high school in the spring of 1995 with eight track state championships in the 1,600- and 3,200-meter runs in addition to the five cross country titles. She was the most heavily recruited female distance runner in the country. Carrie left her native state for the next few years to attend college at Villanova University. The appeal of the Philadelphia-area college was its academics, size, and athletics. "Villanova had won the last six cross country championships, was the home to many Olympians, and had a reputation for developing runners," asserts Carrie. "It was a twenty-six-hour drive, but it was a small college [undergraduate enrollment is 6,500], and it felt like an extended family. I loved it!"

Immediate success was in store for the star runner. Carrie placed seventh in the NCAA Cross Country Championships at Ames, Iowa, as a true freshman, but the team's winning streak had been snapped by Providence College. In 1996 Carmen Douma of Canada joined the Villanova team. "I looked up to Carrie and hoped to do some of the things she had accomplished in her first year," remembers Douma. "She had a fun rapport—

CARRIE TOLLEFSON WON THE 1997 NCAA DIVISION I CROSS COUNTRY CHAMPIONSHIP IN GREENVILLE, SOUTH CAROLINA
Photo courtesy of Villanova University Athletics Communications

can get along with anyone. Everything gives her joy." The team finished as runner-up to Stanford with Carrie moving up two places.

The 1997 season proved to be very rewarding personally for Carrie. The team failed to qualify for the NCAA Cross Country Championships in Greenville, South Carolina, but Carrie and Douma did qualify as individuals. Carrie won the championship by an impressive ten-second margin with a time of 16:29 on the 5-kilometer course. Making the event all the merrier were Carrie's South Carolina grandmother and her great aunts, cheering her on with their distinctive southern drawl! Friend and teammate Douma placed sixth. It was a very joy-filled day for the woman from Dawson.

Carrie's final cross country season in 1998 was memorable for its team achievement: Villanova returned to its path of championships. Carrie had battled heel injuries previous to the season and underwent surgery that caused her to miss the 1998 spring track season, but she recovered enough to lead the team with an eleventh-place finish and restore Villanova to its victorious ways.

The 1999 track season was one of triumph, with an indoor 3,000-meter NCAA championship and two outdoor championships—including a three-second win over Kara Wheeler, now running for the University of Colorado—in the 3,000-meter run (the other title was in the 5,000-meter run). She was the first woman to win both events the same year in NCAA track history.

With one year of eligibility still remaining in track, Carrie competed in 2000 and claimed a final national championship. Gina Procaccio, previously an assistant and now the head coach of Villanova's women's cross country and track programs, praises Carrie for her leadership and mental toughness. "The thing I remember about Carrie is that she was a tremendous leader and motivator for her teammates. She was also a gifted athlete who was a fierce competitor and mentally tough." To illustrate her point, Procaccio points to the indoor track championships in 2000. "Carrie got second in the five-thousand-meter run [15:51.39] and was beat up physically and down in spirit, but she came back in the three-thousand-meter run [9:13.68] and hammered away and won the race. You could never count her out!"

Graduating with a communications degree, Carrie was recognized as an elite runner on the national level in multiple events. The shoe company Adidas expressed interest in sponsoring Carrie and she signed a small contract and represented the company for a decade. It was also an Olympics Trials year and Carrie and Kara Wheeler (later taking her married name Goucher) had qualified as the only collegians in the 5,000-meter run. Another familiar face joined them—Coach Procaccio. The pair of Minnesota natives both qualified for the final at the stadium in Sacramento with Wheeler taking eighth (15:34.47) and easily outdistancing Carrie in fifteenth (16:02.28). Wheeler, a longtime rival and friend says of Carrie: "She is the definition of Minnesota Nice." A year later Carrie did return to Minnesota, a move that proved positive in multiple ways.

"The thing I remember about Carrie is that she was a tremendous leader and motivator for her teammates. She was also a gifted athlete who was a fierce competitor and mentally tough."

In 2003 she married architect Charlie Peterson, a man from Appleton, Minnesota, she met in 1993 and then got reacquainted with by chance on a run on the Stone Arch Bridge in 2000. She continued to train and compete and did a variety of jobs while also trying to take advantage of her education. "I had many part-time jobs: an after-school program, baby-sitting, and I always had a foot in the broadcast industry. I usually ran two times a day four to five days per week. I did strength workouts, did weightlifting two to three times per week, yoga, and ran seventy miles per

CARRIE TOLLEFSON OUTDUELING JEN TOOMEY FOR VICTORY IN THE 1500-METER RUN AT THE 2004 OLYMPIC TRIALS
Photo credit: Kirby Lee, Image of Sport

week, which is considered high for a fifteen-hundred- or five-thousand-meter runner." Carrie had high expectations for the 2004 Olympic Trials. She entered with the seventh-fastest time (15:04) in the history of the 5,000-meter run. She was confident and primed to make a return trip to Sacramento and then participate in the Olympics in Athens, Greece.

And then the unthinkable happened. "Everyone in my running career was at Sacramento to watch. I got sixth. I was devastated." A final opportunity to make the Olympic team in the 1,500-meter run awaited. Villanova teammate Douma—like Coach Procaccio—had witnessed such a scenario in college when Carrie had run two events. "Carrie had lost a tough race. She had the mindset that the race had been the day before, leave it behind—that's mentally tough. And then she won the next race." The memory of that win proved prophetic.

Carrie took an early lead in the 1,500-meter final and held it for nearly the entire race in torrid ninety-six-degree heat. When Jen Toomey edged ahead briefly on the final curve, Carrie fended off the challenge and won in 4:08.32. "I was a long-shot to make the team in the 1,500-meter run. I learned a life lesson about perseverance and defied all odds." Carrie Tollefson would be going to Athens—suffering from a stress fracture in her pubic bone—in a different event than she had expected.

Naturally, Carrie has her favorite Olympic memories. "'Welcome Back,'" greeted

CARRIE TOLLEFSON NOW SERVES AS A RUNNING ANALYST FOR REGIONAL AND NATIONAL NETWORKS
Photo credit: Kirby Lee, Image of Sport

Olympians at Athens [the original site of the Olympics] and walking into the arena. There was an amazing love shown to the United States. My parents, Charlie, both of my sisters, and their husbands were all there." Another person there was Carmen Douma, representing Canada in the 1,500-meter run.

Carrie placed sixth (4:06.46) in one of three preliminary heats at Athens's Spiros Louis Stadium (named after the first marathon winner of the modern Olympics), advancing to the next round. Running in the same semifinal heat as Carmen, Carrie finished a respectable ninth (4:08.55) despite the pain and other ailments she endured, but she failed to qualify for the finals. She was happy to watch her friend and former teammate take ninth in the finals.

Continuing to train and stay involved in broadcasting through a variety of gigs, Carrie once again made an effort to qualify for the Olympics in 2008. A case of pneumonia shortly before the trials stymied the quest, and she finished sixteenth in the 1,500-meter run.

Carrie now lives in St. Paul with Charlie, daughter Ruby (born in 2010), and son Everett (born in 2013). The busy mother has switched sponsorship allegiance and is now the Global Reebok Run Ambassador. She also works as a motivational speaker, runs

RUBY, EVERETT, CHARLIE PETERSON, AND CARRIE TOLLEFSON
Photo credit: Carlos Bravo Photography

a training camp at St. Catherine University, hosts a weekly running and fitness show online called C Tolle Run, and serves as an analyst for local (including the Twin Cities Marathon), regional, and national networks. "I am still involved in the running world but do not devote so much time to it."

Carrie summarizes her life and running career this way: "I am very thankful to call myself a true Minnesotan."

> *" I am very thankful to call myself a true Minnesotan."*

Photo credit: Ed Merrens

CAROLYN TREACY

Many Faces of Joy

THE WORD JOY IS AN OFT-USED WORD IN THE FAMI-ly of Kevin and Ann Treacy. Kevin describes his daughter Carolyn as "a joy of motion." The family refers to their mission trips to the island country of Saint Vincent and the Grenadines in the Caribbean Sea as a joyful opportunity to improve the lives of its inhabitants. And Olympian Carolyn Treacy believes the 2006 Olympic Games in Torino, Italy, was "a joyful time for sharing all the things we have in common with other peoples around the world."

Born in St. Paul, Minnesota, in 1982, Carolyn (the family calls her "Cair") has athletic roots: Grandmother Treacy was a basketball player and swimmer at the College of St. Catherine (now St. Catherine University) in St. Paul, and Kevin captained the men's golf team at the University of Minnesota (U of M) in 1977. The family moved to Duluth in 1988 when Kevin joined an ophthalmology practice in the port city.

Ambitious and intelligent, Carolyn moved from one activity to the next: swimming, playing piano, figure skating, participating in science fairs, soccer, caddying (including one stint for PGA star Tom Lehman in 1997), building snow forts, and golfing with younger brother John (who would continue the sport at the University of St. Thomas), volunteering at the Benedictine Health Center, and cross country skiing. "She is blessed with a positive attitude," reports Kevin. "At the local level, she was strong in a number of sports, but we just enjoyed watching her pursue and participate in them." Carolyn achieved success in multiple endeavors, including swimming at a National YMCA meet at age twelve and qualifying for three state high school meets. She also qualified for the state nordic ski meet three times (she was runner-up to Anna McLoon, later a teammate at the Maine Winter Sports Center, in the freestyle competition in 1999), and won the state junior PGA golf tournament at age thirteen, as well as the high school section tournament in golf in 2000. The only hiccup was when Carolyn had surgery at age sixteen for compartment syndrome, a condition that developed from the overuse of some muscles in nordic skiing. She was confined to bed for two weeks and a wheelchair for six more weeks, but the change was unmistakable: "The surgery made an amazing difference."

She goes on to say, "I only practiced nordic skiing a few times in the backyard in third grade until ninth grade. Then I practiced daily to keep in shape for swimming. Our Duluth East High School team won the state meet in 1998 and 1999." Dave Johnson, the nordic ski coach at Duluth Marshall High School, had a contagious enthusiasm and encouraged her to attend a weekend biathlon recruiting camp in Elk River. Afterward she was selected to participate in a training camp in Lake Placid, New York. Biathlon, introduced as a women's medal event in the 1992 Olympics, is a sport wildly popular in Europe that combines the power of skiing with the precision of shooting. Competitions include races of different lengths. Depending on the race, a biathlete will ski three or five loops of a two-kilometer to four-kilometer loop, returning to the shooting range for two or four shooting stages. The shooting stages alternate between the prone and standing positions. The biathlete attempts to hit five targets from a distance of fifty meters with the allotted five bullets (rounds) for each stage. Accuracy is vital because the fastest time wins, and for every target missed the skier does a two-hundred-meter penalty loop that increases the racer's time. The speed of shooting is also important as it affects the overall time for the race. In a relay, the biathlete is provided three extra bullets, but the racer does not want to need these extras because it takes an additional eleven seconds to shoot each relay round. If any targets are still up at the end of a shooting stage, the skier also does the two-hundred-meter penalty loop. Marksmanship with the .22 caliber straight-pull bolt-action model is obviously key, but as Carolyn explains, "It's difficult to go from the physical demands of skiing challenging terrain, then get your body and breathing under control to shoot steadily at distant targets." The new interest surprised her parents, who neither ski nor shoot, but they continued to be supportive of her athletic adventures. The training did interfere with high school competition, and she had to forego nordic ski competition for the 1999–2000 season.

Mission trips to Saint Vincent and the Grenadines promoting education for local health professionals and laser surgery for people in need became another interest dear to Carolyn's heart. The program, Sister Congregations Enjoying New Eyesight (SCENE), was founded by Kevin and received the full attention of the Treacy family beginning after Carolyn's graduation in 2000. "She has been on numerous ten-day trips and knows the benefits you can offer people. It may have led her to the medical field," says Kevin.

Deciding to defer full-time college, Carolyn developed a program for biathlete

CAROLYN TREACY COMPETING IN THE 2003 WORLD JR. CHAMPIONSHIP AT ZAKOPANE, POLAND
Photo credit: Kevin Treacy

training at the United States Olympic Training Center in Colorado Springs, Colorado, while attending Colorado College part-time. "I was a member of the world junior biathlon team from 1999 to 2003," Carolyn recalls. "I was racing quite well and very in tune with my body. I had a memorable race at the biathlon Junior World Championships in Austria in 2000. I placed sixteenth and was the first seventeen-year-old to finish." A photograph of Carolyn using a rifle with a fitted laser-tracking system appeared in a 2000 issue of *National Geographic*.

Preferring not to delay college for a third year, Carolyn opted to enroll at Dartmouth in Hanover, New Hampshire. "The location offered a skiing opportunity, it had a quarter system so that I could take off time, it's an Ivy League school, and shooting was available nearby," she summarizes her choice. The shooting range needed some cleaning and updating, and Carolyn showed her customary energy by re-starting the biathlon club on campus. Another person assisting with the shooting range clean-up was Anthony Bramante, her future husband.

The 2002 Olympic Trials were held in December 2001, and Carolyn—still under twenty years old—did not expect to make the team. Nevertheless, she had a strong showing and placed sixth overall, just shy of making the five-member team. Continuing to practice, Carolyn was a member on the 2002 relay team that won a silver medal at the biathlon Junior World Championship. She was the lead leg and had a clean (no

GRANDMA TREACY AND CAROLYN
Photo courtesy of Pete Treacy

missed shots) race on the targets. The Treacy grandparents both died shortly after her return, but there is a family picture of her grandfather looking at her medal.

Competing for the Dartmouth nordic team in 2003–04, Carolyn marvels, "It was an amazing training environment. The coaches, athletes, facilities, and trails are remarkable." Balancing her training and studies, she usually took a leave during the winter quarter to compete in biathlon and prepared for the 2006 Olympic Trials at Fort Kent, Maine. It is Kevin's most enduring memory of Carolyn's athletic career. "There were about twenty women vying for five spots. She skied well, cleaned all targets in the second stage, and finished third overall." Carolyn echoes the analysis, saying, "I had more shooting experience and had increased my skiing efficiency. It was very close going into the last race—and then I hit all my targets." Preceded only by Minnesotans Patrice Jankowski, Cloquet (1992); Joan Guetzkow, Minnetonka (1994); Kara (Hermanson) Salmela, Elk River (1998, 2002); and Andrea Nahrgang, Wayzata (2002), Carolyn Treacy was assured a place on the women's Olympic biathlon team going to Turin (Torino), Italy, the capital of the Piedmont region.

"The Olympics were an incredible experience. We were arranged in alphabetical order by country before entering the hockey arena. It felt like Chariots of Fire," Carolyn remembers. She was disappointed with the results of her individual race, eightieth of eighty-three competitors in the 7.5-kilometer sprint. The difficult course was at the Cesana San Sicario Arena in the Olympic Park. She and the 4 x 6 kilometer relay team of Rachel Steer and twins Tracy and Lanny Barnes were determined to bounce back and finish higher than their eighteenth-place ranking. Receiving the tag in seventeenth place for the anchor leg, Carolyn missed her first target shot in the prone position. She redeemed herself by hitting the next four and then hitting the missed target with her first extra bullet. On the second set of targets in the standing position, she repeated her earlier performance but then missed the first target with her first extra bullet. Fortunately, Carolyn hit it with her second extra bullet and skied on past racers from Japan and Canada to help the team to a fifteenth-place finish, the highest ever recorded for an American

MASON AGUIRRE, A 2006 OLYMPIAN IN SNOWBOARDING AND A DULUTH NEIGHBOR OF THE TREACY FAMILY, AND CAROLYN IN TORINO, ITALY
Photo credit: Kevin Treacy

**KEVIN, JOHN, CAROLYN, AND ANN TREACY, 2005
(JUST BEFORE THE 2006 OLYMPIC TRIALS)**
Photo credit: Molly Hottinger

women's biathlon relay team.

Sarah Konrad, an Olympian holding the unique distinction of qualifying for two events in the same Olympics, biathlon and nordic skiing, enjoyed having Carolyn as a teammate. "She differentiated herself from some other athletes and was very interested in the world. I enjoyed having discussions with her. She is very bright, likable, and driven, yet approachable. She was a great teammate."

In July of 2006, Carolyn and Anthony married; Carolyn would complete her education at Dartmouth by obtaining a degree in sociology with a minor in biology while Anthony would begin a four-year tour with the Marine Corps. Following graduation in December, Carolyn decided on attending medical school at the U of M but again deferred it—this time for eight months—to participate in the 2007 World Championships in biathlon. While studying at medical school, Carolyn continued her humanitarian efforts when she founded interprofessional Street Outreach Program (iSTOP), an organization that sought to bring healthcare to the underserved population in the Twin Cities. Still juggling a demanding load, Carolyn again competed in the 2009 biathlon World Championships although she did not make the 2010 Winter Olympic team.

Anthony and Carolyn Treacy Bramante now live in the Baltimore, Maryland, area where she is a pediatrics/internist resident at Johns Hopkins University. They have two children, Leo and Eleanor; she and Anthony hope to duplicate her positive family experiences. "I realize and appreciate that I had a loving, supportive home that allowed me to compete. It is such a joy."

Photo courtesy of University of Minnesota Athletics

LINDSAY WHALEN

Minnesota's Hometown Olympian

EMBRACED AND BELOVED BY THE POPULACE OF MIN-nesota, Olympian and professional basketball star Lindsay Whalen returns the warmth and affection. Lindsay steadily greets passersby near the Minnesota Lynx offices in Target Center and high-fives those whom she beckons to stop and visit. Lindsay was born (in 1982) and raised in Hutchinson, Minnesota, the largest city in McLeod County. The city of 14,000 people promotes itself as Minnesota's Hometown. With sentiment, Lindsay says, "Hutchinson is a hardworking community. I'm really proud to be from there, and I'm proud of my family."

Located sixty miles west of Minneapolis, Hutchinson is the corporate headquarters of Hutchinson Technology and has a large 3M facility particularly known for its tape manufacturing division, where Lindsay's parents, Neil and Kathy, are employed. Hutchinson High School has had tremendous success in its sports programs, with Cory Sauter (University of Minnesota), Mitch Erickson (South Dakota State), and Nate Swift and Lydon Murtha (University of Nebraska) shining in football at the collegiate level.

But the best-known athlete to graduate from Hutchinson High School is 5-feet-9 Lindsay Whalen, the oldest of five children, who admits all her extracurricular activities in school revolved around sports. "I played both singles and doubles tennis all four years [in high school], ran track until my junior year, then focused on basketball." Current football coach and former girls' head basketball coach Andy Rostberg saw her talent and leadership early. "I remember it well the first time I saw the little girl with the ponytail on top of her head. From the start, people, regardless of age, were drawn to her. What it was that brought people to the gym was her style of play and her style as a person. Lindsay has a genuine compassion and interest for the people around her. The attribute that I always think of—when I think back to the little girl with the ponytail—is her belief that nothing's impossible . . . along with her ability to, in the blink of an eye, make all around her believers too."

In the Missota Conference, Lindsay gained all-conference honors in tennis, where her speed, hand-eye coordination, and anticipation benefited her. But it was her spirited play and prolific scoring in basketball that enthralled crowds at games. Although she was named to four all-conference basketball teams, Lindsay was not named to an all-state team by the time she graduated in 2000. Still, Lindsay was recruited to play college basketball and made official visits to the Universities of Iowa, Wisconsin, and North Dakota, yet she was always leaning toward the University of Minnesota (U of M) Gophers, saying simply, "I wanted to play for my home state."

Cheryl Littlejohn was the women's basketball coach during Lindsay's first season at the U of M as the team struggled to a single conference victory and had an 8–20 overall record. Lindsay, though, had a solid first year starting as the team's point guard, leading the team in steals and averaging 17 points per game (ppg). Brenda Oldfield replaced Littlejohn after the dismal season, and the turnaround was immediate: the team was invited to the NCAA tournament with 22 victories and an 11–5 conference record. Lindsay was a primary force in the team's reversal: she averaged 22.2 ppg, led the team in steals and assists, and was named Big 10 Player of the Year for the 2001–02 season. It was a heady time for the team, and Lindsay rates it as one of her favorite collegiate athletic memories. "My sophomore year, we beat a ranked Wisconsin team in Madison in front of eighteen thousand screaming fans and then our first NCAA appearance in North Carolina, those are highlights," Lindsay confirms. The Gophers won their first-round game before falling to the host team, the University of North Carolina, 72–69.

To the surprise of the team, Oldfield resigned after a single year to accept the head coaching position at the University of Maryland, where she still coaches. Pam Borton, the women's basketball associate head coach at Boston College, was hired to take over the Gophers' rising program. The team improved to a 25–6 record during Lindsay's junior year, and her senior year, 2003–04, culminated with a trip to the NCAA Final Four after upsetting Duke in the regional finals before losing to eventual champion, the University of Connecticut. The team's winning ways and native roster (ten of the thirteen women on the 2003–04 team graduated from Minnesota high schools) boosted attendance at women's basketball games to 9,700 per game, a nine-fold increase during Lindsay's career at the U of M. Lindsay was named to the All–Big 10 and All-American teams both years. She ended her Gophers career with a record 2,285 points (20.2 ppg), a 79.8 free throw percentage, 235 steals, and 578 assists (second highest behind Debbie Hunter). About the numerous coaching changes, Lindsay muses, "I liked all my coaches. You had to learn new systems, but when you're a college kid, you can adapt pretty easily. It worked out really well."

Borton quickly realized she had inherited an athlete who contributed in multiple ways. "She is probably the most competitive person I know," declares her college coach. "Lindsay knows the game extremely well. She can see a play and the game unfolding. In a game, she can get to the rim. Lindsay was a great captain in every way— she was a great leader on and off the court." The most memorable performance by Lindsay that comes to mind for Borton was the first-round game in the NCAA tournament in 2004 played in Minneapolis against University of California–Los Angeles (UCLA). "It was her first game back after five weeks from a broken hand—she wore a plastic cast. She still scored thirty-one points and willed our team to win [92–81]."

LINDSAY WHALEN WAS THE STARTING POINT GUARD FOR THE GOPHERS FROM 2000–04
Photo courtesy of University of Minnesota Athletics

Following her emergence and recognition as a collegiate basketball player, Lindsay began to think about her future in the sport. "I thought pro after my sophomore year. I realized I could play at a high level, and that became what I wanted to do." Graduating in 2004 with a degree in sports management, Lindsay was eligible for the WNBA draft and was selected fourth overall by the Connecticut Sun. Minnesota fans were disappointed that the local Minnesota Lynx team had not been more aggressive in moving up the draft board to choose her. It turned out well for Lindsay and the Sun, however, as she took the role of starting point guard in the second game—and has started every WNBA game for the past decade—becoming instrumental to the Sun winning the Eastern Conference Championship before losing in the WNBA finals. Lindsay was named to USA Today's All-Rookie team and was fifth in the league in assists. Lindsay reflects, "Being away from home and going to Connecticut may have been a good experience. I matured and made lifelong friends." Lindsay and Ben Greve of Annandale, Minnesota, mar-

**LINDSAY WHALEN ON MEDIA DAY AS A MEMBER
OF THE MINNESOTA LYNX**
*Photo courtesy of the Minnesota Lynx and permission
of NBA Entertainment*

ried in 2007. Ben was on an athletic scholarship for golf at the U of M and had a stint as a club pro before transitioning into the insurance industry. In 2008, Lindsay was named to the WNBA first-team and was runner-up for the Most Valuable Player Award, averaging 14 ppg and leading the league in assists per game.

Lindsay played for the Sun from 2004–09, when a blockbuster trade landed her with the Lynx in her native state. Now twenty-eight years old, Lindsay found the first year challenging. "In 2010 we worked through the year, but stayed positive. We won only thirteen games [out of thirty-four], but that year really built our championship year." Yes, in another turnaround, the Lynx more than doubled their number of victories (twenty-seven) and won the WNBA Championship! Lindsay was once again named to the WNBA first-team and led the league in assists. The championship and Lindsay's awards would be repeated two years later in 2013. Minnesota citizens had been hungry for another world championship, and a native daughter was an integral part of bringing not only one, but two, home.

Besides playing professionally in the WNBA, Lindsay has spent many years playing in Europe. "I've played for four different teams. I loved Prague. It definitely takes a toll—more mentally because of being in a foreign country," she says summing up the experience. Lindsay also participated on the 2010 World Championship team that went undefeated, won the gold medal, and was a forerunner of the 2012 Olympic women's basketball team. "I earned my way onto that team," says Lindsay. She did become a proud member of the team heading to London, England, for the 2012 Summer Games.

The US women's basketball team powered over most of the competition. Geno Auriemma, the Olympic women's basketball head coach, assembled Seimone Augustus, Maya Moore, and Lindsay of the Lynx, Sue Bird, Diana Taurasi, Angel Mc-Coughtry, Tina Charles, and other WNBA stars to comprise a formidable team. In the semifinal game, the United States trailed Australia by four points at halftime when Lindsay sparked a second-half comeback by scoring six consecutive points for the American squad. "The Australian game was a highlight. The Olympics were a positive experience, and London is an amazing city. It was also fun getting to know some of the NBA guys," she says, citing her favorite Olympic memories. Lindsay was the sixth-leading scorer on the team, averaging eight points through their eight victories to a gold medal.

Auriemma, also the University of Connecticut women's basketball head coach, has this rousing tribute to Lindsay: "I've been a huge fan of Lindsay Whalen since she was at the University of Minnesota. I remember watching film of them leading up to that game [the 2004 NCAA semifinal] and thinking there would be no way we can guard this kid. It was an incredible performance and great to watch her and Diana [Taurasi] go at each other. Watching her play, you get one impression of her, but the chance to coach her for two World Championships and an Olympics, each and every time I'm around her, I walk away even more impressed. She gets better and better as a player every year, and she gets better in every area of the game: leadership, shooting, ball handling, defense, everything. There is only one thing she can't get better at and that's as a person. She is one of the best people I've ever met during the forty years I've been coaching."

While Lindsay has not had any knee surgeries, she has had ankle surgery twice. She works diligently at conditioning and making her body feel good through treatment to prevent sports injuries—her consecutive-game string in the WNBA is proof that she has been successful despite the exhausting travel schedule and demands of practice and treatments. Lindsay believes staying focused and rested have been essential to her achievements.

What's up next for Minnesota's truly Hometown Olympian? Lindsay was on the 2014 World Championship women's basketball team roster—a forerunner to the 2016 US Olympic team.

LINDSAY WHALEN HAS STARTED ALL BUT ONE GAME AS A WNBA PROFESSIONAL PLAYER ENTERING THE 2015 SEASON
Photo courtesy of the Minnesota Lynx and permission of NBA Entertainment

LINDSAY WILLIAMS AND HER DOG, ZENA
Photo courtesy of Lindsay Williams

LINDSAY WILLIAMS

Spicing Things Up

HASTINGS, MINNESOTA, A CITY WITH A POPULATION of approximately 22,000 at the confluence of the Mississippi, St. Croix, and Vermillion rivers, has the distinction of being the home to two winter Olympians whose paths seldom crossed despite being in similar events: biathlete Dan Campbell and nordic (cross country) skier Lindsay Williams.

As a young child, Lindsay did not participate in organized sports as her sister, Sarah, did. Lindsay was very content with the active general play most youths experience and doing some horseback riding at Windy Ridge Ranch in Woodbury, Minnesota. Lindsay's first experience in the sport that led to a berth on the 2006 winter Olympic team was making loops and trails on an old pair of cross country skis in her family backyard and at Cottage Grove Ravine Regional Park.

Lindsay joined the Hastings nordic team in eighth grade using old skis that had three-prong bindings, but she actually quit the team when she became disillusioned due to her lack of success with the equipment, which was considered ancient by racing standards. By now Lindsay was in other organized sports, cross country running and track, but she did not consider herself an outstanding runner.

In ninth grade, Lindsay returned to the high school nordic team with new Fisher "combies" (combination freestyle and classic skis). While enjoying the practices with teammates, she was content to not compete in races until the very end of the season. "Instead I tried to teach our white husky, Zena, to mush and pull me on my skis," she laughingly recalls.

As with many people who achieve elite status in a particular career, Lindsay can pinpoint the exact moment when she decided on what she would pursue for the next decade. "I was sitting in a snowbank watching the nordic racers in the section meet when I saw teammate Megan Lien leading," recounts Lindsay. "I saw the power and speed and grace of a skier all at the same time. It was then that I said, 'That's what I want to do!'" What most people do not do is put the thought into action, but Lind-

LINDSAY WILLIAMS PRACTICING AT WASHINGTON PARK IN COTTAGE GROVE, FEBRUARY 14, 2000
Photo credit: St. Paul Pioneer Press

say became focused and almost single-minded about a training plan. She joined the Wilson-Brochman Nordic Program and "trained like a maniac. I did rollerskiing, strength training, biking, and running throughout the summer. Sometimes I later spiced things up with a triathlon."

All of the nordic dryland training continued through the fall, when she persuaded teammates Katie Thurmes and Ashley Siebels to train with her instead of returning to cross country running. The constant training paid huge dividends during the nordic ski season as the team qualified for the Minnesota State High School Nordic Ski Meet in 2000. The girls' team placed second, and Lindsay's rapid rise must have been the talk of nordic skiing circles when she placed third in pursuit, a 5-kilometer (K) classical race, made a quick change of skis, and then skied a 5K freestyle race, at Giants Ridge near Biwabik. Her ascension from noncompetitor to a top-three place winner is nothing short of stunning. Lindsay finished less than four seconds behind runner-up and fellow tenth grader Lindsey Weier of Mahtomedi; senior Anna Mc-Loon of Roseville Area High School won the event. Lindsay and Weier, a high school superstar who made the Olympic nordic ski team two years later, pushed and challenged each other throughout high school and eventually became close friends and teammates at college.

Dedicated training led to continued success in Lindsay's junior and senior years in high school. She won both the pursuit with a time of 35 minutes, 46.7 seconds (35:46.7) and 5K classic (in 18:30.2) events at the state meet in 2001 and was runner-up in pursuit behind Weier in 2002. Lindsay was also named to the junior national nordic ski team, a spot she retained until she turned nineteen years old. During the three years Lindsay raced on this demanding team, she and Weier competed on the world stage in Germany, Sweden, and Norway. The first year she was limited to a single race, but each year her participation and success increased, once placing fourth in a sprint race (1.5 km).

Lindsay was determined to pursue nordic skiing at the collegiate level. A visit to Northern Michigan University (NMU) in Marquette, Michigan, cemented her choice. "I was impressed by the coaches, Sten Fjeldheim and Jenny Ryan. The local snow conditions lent itself to the sport. And I received a partial scholarship, which later became a full scholarship," she says, explaining her decision.

Years later Coach Ryan, a native of Burnsville, Minnesota, who competed in the biathlon and nordic skiing Olympic Trials, described the 5-feet-5 recruit as "lean but solid. Lindsay had great energy, is a great person, positive, and fun to work with. She always did the little extra things to improve herself. She built herself to be one of the strongest athletes in the program.

NORTHERN MICHIGAN UNIVERSITY ASSISTANT NORDIC SKI COACH JENNY RYAN AND LINDSAY WILLIAMS IN SLOVENIA AT THE UNDER-23 CHAMPIONSHIPS IN 2006
Photo courtesy of Jenny Ryan

I would also say that she is humble and a good sportswoman."

Lindsay's training consisted of sprint workouts in the morning and a run with an intense gym workout that included plyometrics (exercises using explosive movements) in the afternoon. On Sundays, the team would do a two- to four-hour slow distance skiing practice. Excluding the time required for waxing skis and watching video, Lindsay estimates that she trained twenty hours per week. She reaped many awards in 2005 and 2007 for her dedicated effort. Lindsay earned All-American honors twice each year at the NCAA Nordic Ski Championships: in the 5K classic race and 15K freestyle race in 2005 and then reversing the ski style in 2007 by placing second in the 15K classic race and claiming victory in the 5K freestyle race. In 2005 she was named NMU Female Athlete of the Year.

Squeezed between those outstanding performances were the 2006 Olympics. The selection of the Olympic nordic ski team is a lengthy and complicated process that takes nearly a full year, and Lindsay was proud to be chosen at the age of twenty-one to represent the United States. The team was comprised of six women and ten men,

NORTHERN MICHIGAN UNIVERSITY SWEPT THE PODIUM AT THE 2007 NCAA CHAMPIONSHIPS: (LEFT TO RIGHT) LINDSEY (WEIER) DEHLIN (THIRD), LINDSAY WILLIAMS (CHAMPION), AND MORGAN SMYTH (RUNNER-UP)
Photo courtesy of Jenny Ryan

with half of the women's contingent having roots in Minnesota and also having NMU connections: Lindsay from Hastings, Lindsey Weier of Mahtomedi (now a second-time Olympian), and Abby Larson of Elk River.

Along with the ski jumping and nordic combined events, the cross country skiing competition was actually held at Pragelato in the province of Torino (Turin, in Piedmontese) in northern Italy. Lindsay did not participate in the opening ceremonies because she had a race the next morning. One anxious experience at the Olympics was especially memorable. Lindsay explains, "We were supposed to take a taxi to Pragelato on race days, but the vehicle was not in the designated place. After waiting a while, we began to panic and cry when we were not understood. Finally an Italian police officer who comprehended the situation gave us a ride with lights flashing and the siren wailing!"

Lindsay tied for thirty-eighth out of sixty-five entrants in the women's sprint with a time of 2:20.28. She placed sixty-second on a very difficult course in the 15K pursuit race, split equally between the classic and freestyle techniques. "The Olympic Games were a fun, exhausting experience," reflects Lindsay. "And the closing ceremonies were a joy-filled celebration."

Kikkan Randall, a member of three US Olympic women's nordic ski teams, is the person Lindsay considers her favorite athlete. "She's a very dedicated and amazing athlete. I have trained with her, and she is the elite American female nordic skier," says Lindsay, taking pride in her former teammate, who has now won a World Cup race.

Lindsay was still a young competitor at age twenty-five when she attended the Olympic Trials in Utah in 2010. She had endured several injuries from training and

LINDSAY WILLIAMS COOKING AT THE JAMES BEARD HOUSE, 2014
Photo credit: Jeremy Gurwin

undergone three surgeries on her legs and another that resulted in having a "titanium thumb." She withdrew from the competition when the lack of circulation in her legs caused slow times. Lindsay returned to Hastings for another operation and to recuperate and reevaluate the next stage of her life. It was a painful and slow recovery, but many months later she declared herself healthy.

Two courses shy of a sports science major at NMU, Lindsay decided to follow another area of interest—cooking. She had enjoyed working at Casa Calabria, an Italian restaurant in Marquette, Michigan, in 2007 and wanted to explore a profession in food and cooking. In 2010, Lindsay enrolled in a two-year course in culinary arts at the Art Institute International Minnesota in downtown Minneapolis. She found it similar to cross country skiing, explaining, "It's fast paced, challenging, requires the right technique and good form."

A 2012 graduate of the culinary school, Lindsay entered the cooking profession, spicing things up as a line cook at the Bachelor Farmer restaurant in the Warehouse District of Minneapolis. The eatery, owned by Eric and Andrew Dayton, sons of Governor Mark Dayton, grows some of its own produce on its rooftop garden, which Lindsay also tends. Still active and athletic, Lindsay now runs and skis for fun.

GREG WINDSPERGER AT IRONWOOD, MICHIGAN
Photo courtesy of Greg Windsperger

GREG WINDSPERGER

Up on the Hill, It's Just You

GAZING OUT THE WINDOWS OF ST. MARGARET MARY School in Golden Valley, Minnesota, as a schoolboy, Greg Windsperger feasted his eyes on the ski jumps at nearby Theodore Wirth Park. When a boy named Jeff Wright joined Greg's sixth-grade class in the west Minneapolis suburb and told Greg that he had jumped from the "big one," Greg felt it was a challenge he could not refuse. It introduced Greg to taking flight, eventually leading to jumping off the world's largest ski jumps, including one in Innsbruck, Austria, at the 1976 Winter Olympics.

The third oldest of six children from an athletic, blue-collar family, Greg was born in 1951 to John and Gisela Windsperger. John had risen to the AAA level in the St. Louis Cardinals baseball organization and was mystified why his son was more interested in soccer and ski jumping. While Greg did play baseball, it was ski jumping that became his passion. Through a free Minneapolis Park and Recreation Board program hosted at Theodore Wirth Park, Greg and his brothers, Denny and Tom, and friend Jeff Wright met a postal clerk named Selmer Swanson who worked nights and donated his time and energy to coaching kids in ski jumping during the day. "He was a tremendously spirited man who was always out there," Greg says in tribute to

Swanson, who is credited with coaching sixteen thousand kids in a sport that intimidates most people. "That park and rec program developed a whole host of national jumpers—Jerry and Jay Martin and John Balfanz, for example."

Wright and Greg had "immediately bonded. We were such bosom buddies, and later we were room-

SKI JUMPING COMPETITION AT THEODORE WIRTH PARK
Photo courtesy of the Minneapolis Park and Recreation Board

GREG WINDSPERGER, MINNESOTA STATE HIGH SCHOOL LEAGUE SKI JUMPING CHAMPION, 1969
Photo courtesy of the Minnesota State High School League

mates." The two became part of a feeder program that advanced to higher jumps and stiffer competition, one site being the Bush Lake Ski Jump in Bloomington. Along the way they met another mentor, Ed Brisson. "He was a great coach, a great leader. He could take you places—he had his own stucco and plaster business. We worked for him too."

A member of a strong ski jumping team at Robbinsdale High School, Greg won the individual crown his senior year at the Minnesota State High School League Ski Jumping Championships in 1969 as the team won its first of three consecutive titles. Only seventeen years old when he graduated, Greg accepted an athletic scholarship in soccer and ski jumping at the University of Wyoming. Greg, now standing 5 feet 11 and weighing 165 pounds, placed sixth in the 1970 NCAA Ski Jumping Championships. He was also monitoring the scene across the country and knew the prominent position Minnesotans had achieved at the national level. From 1963–77, ski jumpers from Minnesota won all but two of the national championships—including Gene Kotlarek (1963, 1966, and 1967), Dave Hicks (1965), Adrian Watt (1969), Greg Swor (1972), and Jim Denney (1976 and 1977), all from the Duluth area; and former Theodore Wirth ski jumpers Balfanz (1964) and the Martin brothers, Jay (1968) and Jerry (1971, 1973, and 1975). Greg was determined to join them.

"I left school to chase my ski jumping dream," Greg says with a smile, explaining his decision to leave Wyoming after two years. Gaining experience traveling and competing internationally, Greg attempted to make the 1972 Olympic team. Although he placed fifth in the points standing, he was named as the second alternate on the four-man team and did not go to Sapporo, Japan. Minnesotans Jerry Martin and Swor did make the team and competed in both the normal hill (70-meter) and large hill (90-meter) jumps. Greg is in awe of one of the most incredible ski jumping feats of all time, which Martin pulled off at the Olympic Trials at Leavenworth, Washington; Westby, Wisconsin; and Iron Mountain, Michigan. In September of 1971, Martin was injured in a construction accident and lost sight in his right eye. Less than four months later, Martin overcame the staggering odds of lacking peripheral vision and depth perception to finish first in the trials, and then placed a respectable thirty-fourth at the Olympics in the normal hill competition, the top American.

Pursuing his Olympic hopes, Greg continued to train and compete around the world. He did strength training three times per week, endurance training twice per week, and plyometrics (bounding exercises) often. "The only real way to train for ski jumping is to ski jump," Greg concludes in discussing training. Very few lift lines existed at ski jumps—meaning skiers had to walk with their equipment to the top—so getting ten to fifteen jumps in a day was probably the maximum. The standard style at the time was to keep the skis parallel, have an extreme forward bend, and to keep your arms straight and behind your hips. Streaking down the track of the world's biggest ski jumps at a speed of 75 miles per hour (mph) at takeoff, the skier would then slice through the air and hit the extraordinary speed of 85 mph before landing. In 1974 Greg's efforts were rewarded by setting an American record of 479 feet (146 meters) on a jump in Planica, Yugoslavia (now Slovenia). He also placed seventh overall at Zakopane, Poland, his favorite ski jumping site, where "the people were remarkably friendly," enhancing the experience. It proved to be a banner year for Greg in his personal life too—he and Mary Reeves of Roseville married.

Unfortunately, the start of 1975 bore tragic and unsettling news. Jeff Wright, a member of the US national ski jumping team and Greg's longtime friend, died at age twenty-two as a result of a fall in a jump at Harris Hill in Brattleboro, Vermont. In 2008 Wright was inducted into the US Ski Jumping Hall of Fame in Red Wing, Minnesota. Speaking on Wright's behalf was his bosom buddy, Greg Windsperger.

Innsbruck, Austria, played host to the 1976 Winter Olympic Games that were originally awarded to Denver, Colorado. The citizens of Denver balked at the cost and the predicted environmental impact the Olympics would have on their city and overwhelmingly defeated a bond referendum to help finance the Games. With time of the essence, the Olympics returned to Innsbruck, the site of the 1964 Winter Games. This time Greg, now twenty-four years old, placed third in the point standings at the Olympic Trials, assuring him a spot on the US ski jump team. "It was grueling," comments Greg. "More mentally than anything else," he adds. Indomitable Jerry Martin and four other Minnesotans would be among the seven ski jumpers on the team: Jim Denney and Terry Kern (Duluth); Kip Sundgaard (North St. Paul); and Jim Maki (Grand Rapids). Sundgaard, the 1974 Minnesota state high school ski jump champion and also the 1973 state high school pole vault champion, appreciated having Greg on the team. "Greg was a strong jumper. He was like a big brother—someone I looked up to and respected. When I was seeking advice, he was more than willing to help me out." Sundgaard, a student athlete at the University of Utah, would become the 1976 NCAA ski jumping champion two months later.

Each Olympian jumped twice and was judged on style and measured distance of the jump. Participating only on the normal hill (70-meter) event, Greg jumped 76 meters and 75.5 meters, finishing thirty-fourth out of fifty-five competitors at the Olympics. "More times than not, I did not perform as well as I trained," Greg confesses about his results at the picturesque ski jump site in the Austrian Alps.

> *" A lot of guys' lives were changed because of Greg—because he did such a great job and was so passionate. His hard work made me a better person."*

Encouraged by Mary, his wife, Greg returned to college, transferring to Northern Michigan University (NMU) and obtaining a degree in business management. Part of the allure was that he was offered the ski jumping coaching position at NMU in 1978. The team won the 1980 NCAA ski jumping championship, the sport's final collegiate year. Liability concerns, the high percentage of non-American jumpers on athletic scholarships, and the costs associated with maintaining ski jumps spelled the demise of the thrilling sport. Jim Grahek of Ely, Minnesota, a member of the NMU team who earned third place in the individual competition, would make the 1980 Olympic ski jump team. Grahek observed Greg in dual roles. "He reminded me of a guy more willing to let it out when he jumped. I knew him more as a coach. A lot of guys' lives were changed because of Greg—because he did such a great job and was so passionate. His hard work made me a better person. He brought the US team to its peak from 1983–88."

National ski jumping coach Gene Kotlarek, a native of Duluth, resigned from the position after the 1980 Olympics, and Greg was recommended for the prestigious position. Greg attributes Grahek's success to helping him land the coaching job that he maintained with the able assistance of Erling Rimeslåtten from 1980–88. At the 1982 World Championships, Greg witnessed Swedish ski jump Jan Boklöv spread his skis in a V shape throughout his flight after leaving the ramp. "The oth-

1980 NCAA SKI JUMPING CHAMPIONSHIP TEAM FROM NORTHERN MICHIGAN UNIVERSITY (LEFT TO RIGHT): JOHN BENZIE, GEIR BERGVIN, JIM GRAHEK, JYRKI SAHLSTROM-PAIMIO, AND GREG WINDSPERGER (KNEELING)
Photo courtesy of Jim Grahek

er coaches and I looked at each other and asked, 'What the hell was that?'" Greg now laughs. Before the decade ended, Boklöv would be the overall World Cup champion, and many more skiers would be adopting the style that significantly increased a jumper's distance. "It's wonderful; it's slower and safer," he reports of the technique, which curbs the acceleration at take-off and dramatically decreases speed in flight as the skier prepares to land.

The 1984 Olympic Winter Games in Sarajevo, Yugoslavia (now Bosnia and Herzegovina), nearly produced the first Olympic medal for an American ski jumping team in sixty years when Jeff Hastings was edged out of a bronze medal by less than two points in the large hill event. An advocate of positive reinforcement, Greg's coaching philosophy was to "set realistic goals. Improve your performance, take baby steps. Think about personal performance goals."

In 1988, a father of two children and thirty-six years old, Greg decided to seek a job opportunity that didn't require the demanding travel schedule of skiing, which had him away from his family 230 days each year. Reconnecting with a business he had worked for ten years earlier, Airtex Industries, Greg secured a position and was able to enjoy more time with Mary and their children, Lee and Elizabeth. Greg now serves as sales manager for the company, which has evolved into Federal Foam Technologies. Lee is a math professor at Winona State University in Winona, Minnesota, and Elizabeth is in training to be a registered nurse.

Trim and physically fit, Greg is an avid golfer, enjoys time with Mary and three young grandchildren, exercises regularly, and plays soccer in an over-sixty league. He was inducted into the US Ski Jumping Hall of Fame in 2008.

Greg expresses his gratitude to Swanson, Brisson, and other coaches and people who promoted the enthralling sport that played a significant role in his life. "Up on the hill, it's just you. It's your toughness, your ability, your hard work. I have the utmost deep respect for ski jumpers."

ACKNOWLEDGMENTS

NATURALLY, THE PEOPLE WHO WILLINGLY PARTICI-pated in the interviewing and reviewing of the conversations shared in this book are to be thanked. The Minnesota athletes and their families were gracious, articulate, friendly, intelligent, and very modest. Always. I was surprised and delighted by their receptiveness to share their stories. It seemed to matter little whether the athlete was a serious gold medal contender or admitted they had only a remote chance of winning in their event; each person was honored to be competing on the world stage. They generously shared their stories, and I was moved by their trust in me to write about their lives, dreams, families, and achievements. I was moved by their stories and their trust in me to write about their lives, dreams, families, and achievements. Many thanks to all fifty-seven Minnesota athletes and their families, coaches, and teammates who contributed to this book. To me, you are truly Minnesota Gold.

Joel Rippel may never realize how vital his role was to the completion of this book. He listened to a children's book author's idea of writing a book about Minnesota athletes competing at the international level and encouraged me to pursue it. Then he offered his skills to edit the stories—one by one—with constant support, gentle corrections, and checking of facts. To me, Joel Rippel is an appreciated writer who has contributed significantly to Minnesota sports journalism.

Mark Cox and Tom Hyland, Minnesota sports fans and friends of our family, simulated Joel. They too offered encouragement, made significant improvements in drafts through thoughtful and insightful comments, and took a genuine interest in the project throughout its journey. To me, Mark and Tom are sportswriters successful in other professions.

Amy Quale, cofounder and project manager of Wise Ink Creative Publishing; Anitra Budd, an extraordinary editor and educator; and Emily Schaffer Rodvold, a creative book cover and interior layout designer, guided and nurtured this project to its final product. Hardworking, talented, patient, and thoughtful, each team member took a sincere interest in creating a high-grade book in quality, appearance, and design. To me, they are recommended book professionals.

Scores of sports information assistants and directors, photographers, historical society archivists, school athletic personnel, and researchers in a variety of departments contributed with timely information, photographs, and offers of assistance. To me, they make the world go round.

My siblings, Jim, Mary Jo, Stan, Greg, Barbara, and George, and their family members have always been like the "rock" Kara Goucher refers to in her story. We share, we laugh, we tease. To me, they are support.

Karl and Ellen, your growth and independence are wonderful to witness. To me, you are pride and inspiration.

Karen, you continue to enrich my life daily. To me, you are the greatest Minnesota Gold!

BIBLIOGRAPHY

Amateur Athletic Union. "AAU: The Official Home of the Amateur Athletic Union." 2015. http://www.aausports.org/

Anderson, Philip and Blanck, Dag. *Swedes in the Twin Cities: immigrant life and Minnesota's urban frontier.* St. Paul: Minnesota Historical Society, 2001.

"Basketball-Reference.com." *Sports Reference LLC.* 2015. http://www.basketball-reference.com/

Boston Athletic Association. 2015. http://www.baa.org/

Boucha, Henry Charles. *Henry Boucha, Ojibwa, Native American Olympian.* 2013.

"Boys' Hockey Hub: Star Tribune High School Sports." *Star Tribune.* 2013. http://www.mnhockeyhub.com.

BoxRec.com. Accessed July 7, 2015. http://boxrec.com.

Brain Injury Research Institute. "Protect the Brain." 2015. http://www.protectthebrain.org.

"City of Babbit, Minnesota." *City of Babbit.* 2015. http://www.babbitt-mn.com.

"City of Cold Spring, Minnesota." Accessed July 7, 2015. http://www.coldspring.govoffice.com.

"City of Eveleth." *City of Eveleth.* Accessed July 7, 2015. http://www.evelethmn.com.

"City of Hutchinson." *City of Hutchinson.* 2008. http://www.ci.hutchinson.mn.us.

"Collegiate Wrestling Statistics." *wrestlingstats.com.* Last updated May 9, 2013. http://www.wrestlingstats.com.

"College Basketball." *Sports-Reference LLC.* 2015. http://www.sports-reference.com/cbb.

Colorado College Athletics website. "The Official Site of the Colorado College Tigers." 2011. http://www.cctigers.com.

"County of Olmsted." *Olmsted County, Minnesota.* 2015. http://www.co.olmsted.mn.us/Pages/default.aspx.

"Dayton, Minnesota: Two Rivers, One Story." *City of Dayton.* 2013. http://cityofdaytonmn.com.

Encyclopedia Britannica. 2015. http://www.britannica.com.

Imdb.com. 2015. http://www.imdb.com.

International Falls Journal. 2015 http://www.ifallsjournal.com.

Julien, Connie. "Copper Country Hockey History: The Birthplace of Organized Professional Hockey." 2011. http://www.cchockeyhistory.org.

Gustavus Adolphus College. Accessed July 7, 2015. https://gustavus.edu.

"Hockeydb." *Hockeydb.com.* 2012. http://www.hockeydb.com.

History Colorado website. Accessed July 7, 2015. http://www.historycolorado.org.

"HometownFocus.us." *Hometown Media Partners LLC.* 2015. http://www.hometownfocus.us.

Hymans, Richard. "The History of the United States Olympic Trials." *USA Track and Field. 2008.* PDF. http://www.usatf.org/usatf/files/69/695a8112-b7a0-4b9d-9dbb-8b4bca22677c.pdf.

Iron Range Tourism Bureau. "Visit the Range." 2014. http://www.ironrange.org.

Life in Norway. Accessed July 7, 2015. http://www.lifeinnorway.net.

"Lilydale, Minnesota." *City of Lilydale.* http://www.lilydale.govoffice.com.

Mayo Clinic. 2015. http://www.mayoclinic.org.

MGoBlue.com. *CBS Interactive.* 2015. http://www.mgoblue.com.

"Minnesota.gov." *Minnesota.gov.* Accessed July 7, 2015. http://mn.gov/portal.

Minnesota Hockey Heritage. 2015. http://www.vintagemnhockey.com.

Minnesota State High School League website. "Minnesota State High School League." 2015. http://www.mshsl.org/mshsl/index.asp.

Minnesota State Legislature. July 7, 2015. http://www.leg.state.mn.us.

"Minnesota Storm Wrestling Club." *mn-storm.org.* 2015. http://mn-storm.org/wp.

Midway Speed Skating Club. Accessed July 7, 2015. http://midwayspeedskating.org.

MLS. "Major League Soccer." 2015. http://www.mlssoccer.com.

MNThunder.com. 2014. http://www.mnthunder.com.

National Association of Intercollegiate Athletics website. Accessed July 7, 2015. http://www.naia.org.

National Collegiate Athletic Association website. 2015. http://www.ncaa.com.

"New Ulm, Minnesota." *City of New Ulm.* Accessed July 7, 2015. http://www.ci.new-ulm.mn.us.

"Northern Michigan University Wildcats." *NMU Board of Trustees.* 2012. http://www.nmuwildcats.com/landing/index.

"Olympic Athlete Directory." *Sports Reference LLC.* 2015. http://www.sports-reference.com/olympics/athletes.

Radke, Katrina. *Be Your Best Without the Stress: it's not about the medal.* Henderson: Motivational Press, 2012.

Rippel, Joel A. *Minnesota Sports Almanac: 125 Glorious Years.* St. Paul: Minnesota Historical Society, 2006.

Smith, David C. *Minneapolis Park History.* 2015. http://minneapolisparkhistory.com.

SoccerTimes.com. Accessed July 7, 2015. http://www.soccertimes.com.

Skijumpeast.com. Accessed July 7, 2015. http://www.skijumpeast.com.

St. Cloud State. "St. Cloud State Huskies." 2015. http://www.scsuhuskies.com.

St. Paul Figure Skating Club. "St. Paul Figure Skating Club." 2014. http://www.stpaulfsc.org.

Saint Paul Public Schools. "Johnson Aerospace and Engineering School." 2012. http://johnsonsr.spps.org.

Team USA Olympics and Paralympics Home. Accessed July 20, 2015. olympics.usahockey.com.

"The City of Edina." *City of Edina, Minnesota.* 2015. http://edinamn.gov.

"The City of Roseau, Minnesota." *City of Roseau.* Accessed July 7, 2015. http://www.city.roseau.mn.us.

The Extra Alarm Association of the Twin Cities. 2015. http://www.extraalarm.org.

The Guillotine. "The Guillotine: Website for Minnesota's Amateur Wrestling Community." 2015. http://theguillotine.com/wp.

"Track and Field News." *Track & Field News*. Accessed July 7, 2015. http://www.trackandfieldnews.com.

Twin Cities in Motion. 2015. https://www.tcmevents.org.

United States Olympic Committee. "Team USA." 2015. http://www.teamusa.org.

USA Diving. 2015. http://www.usadiving.org.

USA Fencing. 2015. http://www.usfencing.org.

USA Basketball. 2015. http://www.usab.com.

USA Swimming. 2010. http://www.usaswimming.org.

USHockey.com. Accessed July 7, 2015. https://www.ushockey.com.

US Ski and Snowboard Association. "US Ski Team." 2011. http://usskiteam.com.

"US Rowing." *USRowing.org*. Accessed July 7, 2015. http://www.usrowing.org.

United States Olympic Committee. "U.S. Biathalon." 2015. http://www.teamusa.org/US-Biathlon.

University of Colorado Athletics. "Colorado Buffalos." Accessed July 7, 2015. http://www.cubuffs.com.

University of Minnesota Athletics. "Golden Gophers." Accessed July 7, 2015. http://www.gophersports.com.

University of Minnesota Duluth. 2015. http://www.d.umn.edu.

University of North Dakota. 2015. http://www.undsports.com.

Vancouver 2010 Olympic Winter Games. Accessed July 21, 2015. http://www.isuresults.com/results/owg2010.

VisitBemidji.com. "Visit Bemidji." 2015. http://www.visitbemidji.com.

Wayzata Cross Country. "Minnesota Prep Track and Field and Cross Country." 2013. http://www.mnpreptrack.com.

World Figure Skating Museum and Hall of Fame. "World Figure Skating Museum and Hall of Fame." 2015. http://www.worldskatingmuseum.org.

MINNESOTA CITY INDEX

O

P

R

S

CARRIE TOLLEFSON ON TRACK WAVING TO CROWD
Photo credit: Villanova University Athletics Communication

NAME INDEX

*Page numbers in *italics* indicate the person is in a photograph

A

B

Y-Z

JENNY POTTER
Photo courtesy of UMD Sports Information Department:
Photo credit Brett Groehler